D1466223

Taste of Home

more
GRANDMA'S
FAVORITES

TASTE OF HOME BOOKS • RDA ENTHUSIAST BRANDS, LLC • MILWAUKEE, WI

Visit us at **tasteofhome.com** for other
Taste of Home books and products.

International Standard Book Number:
978-1-62145-926-2

Component Number:
117600114H

Chief Content Officer, Home & Garden:
Jeanne Sidner
Content Director: Mark Hagen
Creative Director: Raeann Thompson
Senior Editor: Christine Rukavena
Senior Art Director: Courtney Lovetere
Designer: Carrie Peterson
Deputy Editor, Copy Desk:
Dulcie Shoener
Copy Editor: Kara Dennison
Contributing Editor:
Michelle Rozumalski

Photographer: Mark Derse
Set Stylist: Melissa Franco
Food Stylist: Josh Rink

Pictured on front cover:
Vertical Carrot Cake, p. 266

Pattern: MarinaMays/Getty Images

Pictured on back cover:
Savory Stuffing Bread, p. 76; Smoky
& Spicy Vegetable Bisque, p. 192;
Braciole, p. 102

Printed in China
1 3 5 7 9 10 8 6 4 2

CONTENTS

Welcome back to Grandma's kitchen, a place where memories are made, celebrations are had and delicious surprises abound. At *Taste of Home* we cherish those iconic moments, gatherings and flavors, which is why we're so excited about this all-new edition of comforting classics.

From special Sunday dinners to in-a-hurry standbys, this keepsake collection features 297 of the heartwarming specialties Grandma was known for. Best of all, the dishes found here are made easy for today's home cooks!

Surprise your family with:

- **Grandma's Favorite Breakfasts.** Spending the night at Grandma's was always special. Relive those times with more than 2 dozen eye-opening recipes.

- **Grandma's Favorite Breads.** Take your baking to new heights with golden loaves and scrumptious rolls, biscuits, coffee cakes and other oven-fresh delights.

- **Grandma's Favorite Entrees.** Roasted chicken, beef Stroganoff and herbed turkey—these are just a few of the main courses you'll find inside.

- **Grandma's Favorite Cookies.** You'll always have time for a snack with these sweet treats loaded with flavor, convenience and remember-when charm.

Whether starting the day with a hearty bite or capping off dinner with an unforgettable dessert, the sensational recipes in this delightful cookbook are sure to satisfy taste buds and rekindle memories of times gone by. After all, treating your family to a time-honored dish is the next best thing to pulling up a chair and sitting at Grandma's very own kitchen table.

EVERYTHING
BREAKFAST
SLIDERS, PAGE 13

SUNDAY DINNER MENUS

Whether you're new to meal planning or a longtime pro, consider this handy guide
that relies on recipes from this book to create complete meals.

Mom's Oven-Barbecued
Ribs, p. 106 • Dad's Baked
Beans, p. 152 • Corn Bread
With A Kick, p. 81 • Peach
Melba Trifle, p. 278

Slow-Cooked Turkey with
Herbed Stuffing, p. 107 •
Aunt Margaret's Sweet
Potato Casserole, p. 153 •
Scalloped Sweet Corn
Casserole, p. 146 • Apple
Dumplings, p. 283

Pressure-Cooker Wine-
Braised Beef Shanks,
p. 115 • Colcannon Irish
Potatoes, p. 143 •
Grandma's Yeast Rolls,
p. 75 • Old-Fashioned Rice
Pudding, p. 284

Sassy Southwest Stuffed
Shells, p. 100 • Apple &
Gorgonzola Salad, p.145 •
Bacon-Cheese Biscuit
Bites p. 50 • Chocolate
Hazelnut Pudding Torte,
p. 296

Grandma's Pressure-
Cooker Chicken Noodle
Soup, p. 182 • Freezer
Crescent Rolls, p. 71 •
Quick Fried Green
Tomatoes, p. 54 • Date
Swirl Cookies, p. 225

Ham Loaf, p. 113 • Green
Bean & Potato Salad,
p. 140 • Smoky Macaroni &
Cheese p. 170 • Audrey's
Lemon Meringue Bars,
p. 223

Garlic Beef Stroganoff,
p. 118 • Grandma's Yeast
Rolls, p. 75 • Creamy
Blueberry Gelatin Salad,
p. 152 • Icebox Cookies,
p. 210

Mom's Celery Seed
Brisket, p. 129 • Glazed
Julienned Carrots, p. 170 •
Creamed Potatoes & Peas,
p. 154 • Easy Apple
Strudel, p. 288

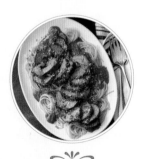

Braciole, p. 102 • Focaccia
Barese, p. 65 • Tangy Bean
Soup, p. 178 • Italian
Pineapple Trifle, p. 289

Crescent Turkey
Casserole, p.110 • A Bit
Nutty Boston Brown
Bread, p. 86 • Air-Fryer
Candied Acorn Squash
Slices, p. 141 • Gimlet
Bars, p. 218

Air-Fryer Salmon Patties,
p. 132 • Hearty Quinoa &
Corn Chowder, p. 184 •
Golden Beet Curry Risotto
with Crispy Beet Greens,
p. 165 • Champagne
Blondies, p. 233

Greek Sausage & Peppers,
p.134 • Wild Rice Bread
with Sunflower Seeds,
p. 74 • Onion Potato
Pancakes, p. 29 • Frozen
Chocolate Mint Dessert,
p. 284

CREAMY STRAWBERRY
FRENCH TOAST BAKE,
PAGE 30

GRANDMA'S FAVORITE

BREAKFAST

When Grandma calls everyone to the breakfast table,
late sleepers and early risers alike come running.
These memorable morning treats will remind you why!

CARNITAS HUEVOS RANCHEROS

I spent one of my summers during college in Colorado, where I discovered Mexican food. When I was back living in the Midwest, authentic Mexican fare was scarce. Then I met some Texas natives and learned to make so many amazing dishes. This versatile slow-cooked pork is delicious served for dinner with eggs. You may have extra meat left over—and that's always a plus!

—*Lonnie Hartstack, Clarinda, IA*

PREP: 35 MIN. • **COOK:** 7 HOURS • **MAKES:** 12 SERVINGS

1 **boneless pork shoulder butt roast (3 lbs.), halved**
2 **tsp. olive oil**
3 **garlic cloves, thinly sliced**
½ **tsp. salt**
½ **tsp. pepper**
1 **medium onion, chopped**
2 **cans (4 oz. each) chopped green chiles**
1 **cup salsa**
½ **cup minced fresh cilantro**
½ **cup chicken broth**
½ **cup tequila or additional chicken broth**
1 **can (15 oz.) black beans, rinsed and drained**

ASSEMBLY

12 **large eggs**
1 **jar (16 oz.) salsa**
4 **medium ripe avocados, peeled and sliced**
12 **flour tortillas (6 in.), warmed and quartered**

1. Rub roast with oil, garlic, salt and pepper. Place in a 4- or 5-qt. slow cooker. Top with onion, green chiles, salsa, cilantro, broth and tequila. Cook, covered, on low 7-8 hours or until meat is tender.

2. Remove roast; shred with 2 forks. Discard cooking juices, reserving 1 cup. Return cooking juices and meat to slow cooker. Stir in beans; heat through.

3. Meanwhile, coat a large skillet with cooking spray; place over medium-high heat. Working in batches, break eggs, 1 at a time, into pan; reduce heat to low. Cook until whites are set and yolks begin to thicken, turning once if desired. Divide pork mixture among 12 serving bowls. Top with salsa, eggs, avocados and additional cilantro. Serve with tortillas.

FREEZE OPTION: Freeze cooled meat mixture and juices in freezer containers. To use, partially thaw in the refrigerator overnight. Heat through in a saucepan, stirring occasionally; add water if necessary.

1 SERVING: 509 cal., 27g fat (8g sat. fat), 254mg chol., 858mg sod., 32g carb. (3g sugars, 7g fiber), 31g pro.

FROM GRANDMA'S KITCHEN: To mince cilantro or parsley without dirtying a cutting board, place sprigs in a small glass container and snip with kitchen shears until chopped to desired fineness.

ORANGE-GLAZED BACON

What's better than plain bacon? Those savory strips drizzled with a sweetly simple glaze of orange juice, honey and Dijon mustard, plus a little ginger and pepper. Yum!
—Taste of Home *Test Kitchen*

PREP: 20 MIN. • **BAKE:** 25 MIN. • **MAKES:** 8 SERVINGS

¾ **cup orange juice**	¼ **tsp. ground ginger**
¼ **cup honey**	⅛ **tsp. pepper**
1 **Tbsp. Dijon mustard**	1 **lb. bacon strips**

1. Preheat oven to 350°. In a small saucepan, combine the first 5 ingredients. Bring to a boil; cook until liquid is reduced to ⅓ cup.

2. Place bacon on a rack in an ungreased 15x10x1-in. baking pan. Bake for 10 minutes; drain.

3. Drizzle half of the glaze over bacon. Bake for 10 minutes. Turn bacon and drizzle with the remaining glaze. Bake until golden brown, 5-10 minutes longer. Place bacon on waxed paper until set. Serve warm.

3 GLAZED BACON STRIPS: 146 cal., 8g fat (3g sat. fat), 21mg chol., 407mg sod., 12g carb. (11g sugars, 0 fiber), 7g pro.

ASPARAGUS HAM STRATA

I serve my cheesy egg strata year-round for large groups, such as my card and garden clubs. Everything goes in the pan ahead of time, then in the fridge. All that's left to do is bake and eat!
—Ethel Pressel, New Oxford, PA

PREP: 20 MIN. + CHILLING • **BAKE:** 55 MIN. + STANDING • **MAKES:** 8 SERVINGS

12 **slices white bread**
12 **oz. Velveeta, diced**
1½ **lbs. fresh asparagus, trimmed**
2 **cups diced cooked ham**
6 **large eggs**
3 **cups 2% milk**
2 **Tbsp. finely chopped onion**
½ **tsp. salt**
¼ **tsp. ground mustard**

1. Using a doughnut cutter, cut 12 circles and holes from bread; set aside. Tear remaining bread in pieces and place in a greased 13x9-in. baking dish.

2. Layer with cheese, asparagus and ham; arrange bread circles and holes on top. Lightly beat eggs with milk. Add onion, salt and mustard; mix well. Pour egg mixture over bread circles and holes. Cover and refrigerate at least 6 hours or overnight.

3. Bake, uncovered, at 325° until the top is light golden brown, 55 minutes. Let stand for 10 minutes before serving.

1 PIECE: 420 cal., 21g fat (10g sat. fat), 211mg chol., 1427mg sod., 32g carb. (10g sugars, 2g fiber), 27g pro.

DUTCH BABY PANCAKE WITH STRAWBERRY-ALMOND COMPOTE

Pannekoeken, or Dutch baked pancakes, are a favorite treat in my husband's family. For a change, use lemon zest, vanilla extract and blueberries to flavor the pancake. Or try the apple-honey variation at the end of the recipe.

—Jennifer Beckman, Falls Church, VA

PREP: 15 MIN. • BAKE: 20 MIN. • MAKES: 6 SERVINGS (3 CUPS TOPPING)

- 2 Tbsp. butter
- 4 large eggs, room temperature
- ⅔ cup 2% milk
- 2 Tbsp. grated orange zest
- ½ tsp. almond extract
- ⅔ cup all-purpose flour
- 2 Tbsp. sugar
- ½ tsp. kosher salt

TOPPING

- 1 lb. fresh strawberries, hulled and quartered
- ½ cup slivered almonds, toasted
- 2 Tbsp. orange juice
- 1 Tbsp. sugar

1. Preheat oven to 400°. Place butter in a 9-in. pie plate. Place in oven for 4-5 minutes or until butter is melted; carefully swirl to coat evenly.

2. Meanwhile, in a large bowl, whisk eggs, milk, orange zest and extract until blended. Whisk in flour, sugar and salt. Pour into hot pie plate. Bake 20-25 minutes or until puffed and sides are golden brown and crisp.

3. In a small bowl, combine topping ingredients. Remove pancake from oven; serve immediately with topping.

1 SLICE WITH ½ CUP TOPPING: 252 cal., 13g fat (4g sat. fat), 153mg chol., 245mg sod., 27g carb. (13g sugars, 3g fiber), 9g pro. DIABETIC EXCHANGES: 1 starch, 1 fruit, 1 medium-fat meat, 1½ fat.

APPLE-HONEY DUTCH BABY: Omit topping. Saute 2 large sliced apples in 1 Tbsp. butter until lightly browned. Stir in ½ cup honey, 2 tsp. lemon juice and ½ tsp. cardamom. Mix 1 tsp. cornstarch and 2 tsp. cold water until smooth; add to apple mixture. Bring to a boil; cook and stir 2 minutes or until thickened. Spoon into pancake.

"Dutch babies are a favorite around our house. They are so fun for the kids because they puff up. This compote is just wonderful. It is a little tangy and it doesn't overpower the delicate flavor of the pancake."

—RANDCBRUNS, TASTEOFHOME.COM

BACON POTATO
WAFFLES WITH
APPLESAUCE

BACON POTATO WAFFLES WITH APPLESAUCE

My mother liked adding bacon to recipes for extra flavor. I took a cue from her and did the same with these waffles. They're terrific for using up yesterday's mashed potatoes.
—*Laura Fall-Sutton, Buhl, ID*

PREP: 15 MIN. • BAKE: 5 MIN./BATCH • MAKES: 12 WAFFLES

1 cup all-purpose flour
2 Tbsp. sugar
2 tsp. baking powder
1 tsp. salt
2 large eggs,
    room temperature
1½ cups mashed potatoes
1 cup 2% milk
5 Tbsp. bacon drippings or
    canola oil
4 bacon strips, cooked
    and crumbled
¼ cup finely chopped onion
    Chunky applesauce

1. In a large bowl, combine flour, sugar, baking powder and salt. In another bowl, whisk eggs, mashed potatoes, milk and bacon drippings. Stir into dry ingredients just until moistened. Fold in bacon and onion.

2. Bake in a preheated waffle iron according to manufacturer's directions until golden brown. Serve with applesauce.

2 WAFFLES: 316 cal., 17g fat (6g sat. fat), 81mg chol., 895mg sod., 32g carb. (7g sugars, 1g fiber), 9g pro.

EVERYTHING BREAKFAST SLIDERS

Love lots of different breakfast foods? Pile mini bagel sandwiches high with eggs, cheese, two kinds of meat and more. I brush on a maple syrup glaze for good measure!
—*Rashanda Cobbins, Milwaukee, WI*

PREP: 30 MIN. • BAKE: 15 MIN. • MAKES: 8 SERVINGS

8 large eggs
¼ cup 2% milk
2 green onions,
    thinly sliced
¼ tsp. pepper
8 Tbsp. spreadable chive
    and onion cream cheese
8 miniature bagels, split
8 slices cheddar cheese,
    halved
8 slices Canadian bacon
8 cooked bacon strips,
    halved

GLAZE
2 Tbsp. butter, melted
1½ tsp. maple syrup
⅛ tsp. garlic powder
2 Tbsp. everything
    seasoning blend

1. Preheat oven to 375°. Heat a large nonstick skillet over medium heat. In a large bowl, whisk eggs, milk, green onions and pepper until blended; pour into skillet. Cook and stir until eggs are thickened and no liquid egg remains; remove from heat.

2. Spread cream cheese over bagel bottoms; place in a greased 13x9-in. baking dish. Layer each with half a slice of cheese and a slice of Canadian bacon. Spoon scrambled eggs over top. Layer with remaining halved cheese slices, cooked bacon and bagel tops. Stir together butter, maple syrup and garlic powder; brush over bagel tops. Sprinkle with everything seasoning blend.

3. Bake until the tops are golden brown and the cheese is melted, 12-15 minutes.

1 SLIDER: 415 cal., 26g fat (13g sat. fat), 253mg chol., 1070mg sod., 18g carb. (4g sugars, 1g fiber), 24g pro.

DAD'S BLUEBERRY BUTTERMILK PANCAKES

Saturdays just wouldn't be the same without Dad's signature flapjacks. The mix of oats, cornmeal and buttermilk in the batter gives them a heartiness we can't resist.
—*Gabrielle Short, Pleasant Hill, IA*

PREP: 15 MIN. + STANDING • **COOK:** 10 MIN./BATCH • **MAKES:** 12 PANCAKES

1 cup all-purpose flour
3 Tbsp. cornmeal
3 Tbsp. quick-cooking oats
3 Tbsp. sugar
1 tsp. baking powder
½ tsp. baking soda
½ tsp. salt
Dash ground nutmeg
1 large egg
1½ cups buttermilk
2 Tbsp. canola oil
1 tsp. vanilla extract
1 cup fresh or frozen blueberries

1. In a large bowl, whisk the first 8 ingredients. In another bowl, whisk egg, buttermilk, oil and vanilla until blended. Add to flour mixture; stir just until moistened (batter will be lumpy). Let stand 15 minutes.

2. Lightly grease a griddle or large nonstick skillet; heat over medium heat. Stir blueberries into the batter. Pour batter by ¼ cupfuls onto griddle or skillet. Cook until bubbles on top begin to pop and bottoms are golden brown. Turn; cook until second side is brown.

3 PANCAKES: 332 cal., 10g fat (2g sat. fat), 50mg chol., 746mg sod., 52g carb. (18g sugars, 2g fiber), 9g pro.

AUNT LILLIAN'S CRUMB CAKE

My Aunt Lillian treated us to her fabulous crumb cake every weekend when we came to visit. She shared the recipe with my mother, who passed it on to me. I've served it as a coffee cake for Sunday brunch and even as a dessert.
—*Rose Gearheard, Phoenix, OR*

PREP: 15 MIN. • **BAKE:** 35 MIN. + COOLING • **MAKES:** 9 SERVINGS

½ cup butter, softened
1 cup sugar
2 large eggs, room temperature
1 cup sour cream
1 tsp. vanilla extract
1½ cups all-purpose flour
1 tsp. baking soda
¼ tsp. salt

TOPPING
½ cup sugar
¼ cup chopped walnuts
2 Tbsp. sweetened shredded coconut
2 tsp. ground cinnamon

1. In a large bowl, cream the butter and sugar until light and fluffy, 5-7 minutes. Add eggs, 1 at a time, beating well after each addition.

2. Beat in sour cream and vanilla. Combine the flour, baking soda and salt; add to the creamed mixture and mix well. Spread half into a greased 9-in. square baking pan.

3. Combine the topping ingredients; sprinkle half over the batter. Carefully spread remaining batter on top; sprinkle with remaining topping. Gently swirl topping through batter with a knife.

4. Bake at 350° for 35-40 minutes or until a toothpick inserted in the center comes out clean. Cool for 15 minutes on a wire rack. Serve warm.

1 PIECE: 394 cal., 18g fat (10g sat. fat), 92mg chol., 340mg sod., 52g carb. (34g sugars, 1g fiber), 5g pro.

RAISIN BREAD & SAUSAGE MORNING CASSEROLE

When we had Sunday breakfasts with my grandparents, Mom baked this for Grandpa because he enjoyed it so much. The pork sausage and cinnamon bread make a surprisingly tasty combination.

—*Carolyn Levan, Dixon, IL*

PREP: 25 MIN. + CHILLING • BAKE: 35 MIN. • MAKES: 12 SERVINGS

½ lb. bulk pork sausage
1 loaf (1 lb.) cinnamon-raisin bread, cubed
6 large eggs
1½ cups 2% milk
1½ cups half-and-half cream
1 tsp. vanilla extract
¼ tsp. ground cinnamon
¼ tsp. ground nutmeg

TOPPING
1 cup chopped pecans
1 cup packed brown sugar
½ cup butter, softened
2 Tbsp. maple syrup

1. In a large skillet, cook the pork sausage over medium heat 4-6 minutes or until no longer pink, breaking it into crumbles; drain. In a greased 13x9-in. baking dish, combine the bread and sausage.

2. In a large bowl, whisk the eggs, milk, cream, vanilla, cinnamon and nutmeg until blended; pour over bread. Refrigerate, covered, several hours or overnight.

3. Preheat oven to 350°. Remove casserole from refrigerator while oven heats. In a small bowl, beat topping ingredients until blended. Drop by tablespoonfuls over casserole.

4. Bake, uncovered, 35-45 minutes or until golden brown and a knife inserted in center comes out clean. Let stand 5-10 minutes before serving.

1 PIECE: 425 cal., 25g fat (10g sat. fat), 141mg chol., 324mg sod., 41g carb. (26g sugars, 3g fiber), 11g pro.

"Great potluck recipe! A little sweet, a little salty and great for company. I think this would make a great Christmas morning dish. The topping is wonderful, so don't skip it!"
—LPHJKITCHEN, TASTEOFHOME.COM

BLUEBERRIES & CREAM COFFEE CAKE

This berry-filled treat is a must for our holiday get-togethers. It's not only easy to prepare and beautiful on the table, but it's also the most delicious coffee cake I've ever tasted.
—*Susan Ober, Franconia, NH*

PREP: 20 MIN. • BAKE: 55 MIN. + COOLING • MAKES: 12 SERVINGS

1 cup butter, softened
2 cups sugar
2 large eggs, room temperature
1 tsp. vanilla extract
1¾ cups all-purpose flour
1 tsp. baking powder
¼ tsp. salt
1 cup sour cream
1 cup fresh or frozen unsweetened blueberries
½ cup packed brown sugar
½ cup chopped pecans, optional
1 tsp. ground cinnamon
1 Tbsp. confectioners' sugar

1. In a large bowl, cream butter and sugar until light and fluffy, 5-7 minutes. Add the eggs, 1 at a time, beating well after each addition. Beat in vanilla. Combine the flour, baking powder and salt; add to the creamed mixture alternately with sour cream, beating well after each addition. Fold in blueberries.

2. Spoon half of batter into a greased and floured 10-in. fluted tube pan. In a small bowl, combine the brown sugar, pecans if desired, and cinnamon. Sprinkle half over the batter. Top with remaining batter; sprinkle with remaining brown sugar mixture. Cut through batter with a knife to swirl the brown sugar mixture.

3. Bake at 350° until a toothpick inserted near the center comes out clean, 55-60 minutes. Cool for 10 minutes before removing from pan to a wire rack to cool completely. Just before serving, dust with confectioners' sugar.

1 PIECE: 428 cal., 20g fat (12g sat. fat), 76mg chol., 233mg sod., 60g carb. (45g sugars, 1g fiber), 4g pro.

GRIDDLE CORN CAKES

I've been making these golden cakes ever since my husband and I got married. The recipe is a downsized version of one that came from his mother and has been in their family for more than 80 years.
—*Myrna Gerson, Staten Island, NY*

TAKES: 20 MIN. • MAKES: 2 SERVINGS

¾ cup all-purpose flour
2 Tbsp. sugar
½ tsp. baking powder
¼ tsp. salt
1 egg
1 can (8¼ oz.) cream-style corn
3 Tbsp. 2% milk
½ tsp. vanilla extract

1. In a small bowl, combine the flour, sugar, baking powder and salt. Combine the egg, corn, milk and vanilla; stir into dry ingredients just until moistened.

2. Drop batter by ¼ cupfuls onto a hot nonstick griddle. Cook for 4-5 minutes on each side or until golden brown.

4 CORN CAKES: 359 cal., 4g fat (1g sat. fat), 108mg chol., 792mg sod., 72g carb. (18g sugars, 3g fiber), 11g pro.

BLUEBERRIES &
CREAM COFFEE CAKE

GRANDMA'S
SECRET

The hole in a Bundt pan puts more
surface area of the cake in contact
with the oven's heat. This lets a rich,
sugary batter fully cook in the
center before browning too
much on the outside.

MUFFULETTA FRITTATA

Two of my favorite foods are Italian sub sandwiches and olives. To bring those flavors together in a low-carb dish, I created this frittata. I add arugula because I like its peppery taste, but feel free to substitute fresh spinach.
—*Donna Gribbins, Shelbyville, KY*

PREP: 25 MIN. • **COOK:** 25 MIN. • **MAKES:** 8 SERVINGS

1 Tbsp. vegetable oil
12 large eggs
1 cup half-and-half cream
3 Tbsp. grated Parmesan cheese
½ tsp. pepper
8 oz. fresh arugula, roughly chopped
2 oz. sliced capicola, chopped
2 oz. hard salami, chopped
2 oz. mortadella, chopped
1 cup shredded mozzarella and provolone cheese blend

OLIVE SALAD TOPPING
1 cup chopped assorted olives
1 cup chopped giardiniera (7 oz.)
¼ cup olive oil
2 Tbsp. red wine vinegar
2 Tbsp. minced fresh parsley
1 garlic clove, minced

1. Preheat oven to 375°. In a 12-in. cast-iron or ovenproof skillet, heat oil over medium heat.

2. In a large bowl, whisk eggs, half-and-half, Parmesan and pepper. Pour into skillet; layer arugula, capicola, salami and mortadella. Top with cheese blend. Cook for 3-5 minutes or until eggs start to set on sides.

3. Transfer to oven; bake for 20-25 minutes or until eggs are set and top is browned.

4. In a small bowl, combine all olive salad topping ingredients.

5. Cut into wedges; serve with olive topping.

1 PIECE WITH ¼ CUP OLIVE SALAD: 384 cal., 31g fat (10g sat. fat), 323mg chol., 1391mg sod., 6g carb. (2g sugars, 1g fiber), 20g pro.

PEACHY DUTCH PANCAKE

After my daughter attended a slumber party, she raved about the Dutch pancake they had for breakfast. She asked her friend's mother for the recipe so we could try it at home. Here's my version!
—Carol Rogers, Tipton, IA

TAKES: 30 MIN. • MAKES: 8 SERVINGS

¼ cup butter, cubed
2 cups fresh or frozen thinly sliced peaches, thawed and drained
4 large eggs, room temperature
1¼ cups fat-free milk
½ tsp. almond extract
1¼ cups all-purpose flour
½ cup sugar
¾ tsp. salt
Warm peach preserves and maple syrup

1. Preheat oven to 425°. Place butter in a 13x9-in. baking dish. Place in oven 3-4 minutes or until butter is melted; carefully swirl to coat bottom and sides of dish. Carefully add peaches; return to oven for 3-4 minutes or until bubbly.

2. Meanwhile, in a large bowl, whisk the eggs until frothy. Add milk and extract. Whisk in flour, sugar and salt. Pour into hot baking dish. Bake 10-12 minutes or until puffed and sides are golden brown.

3. Remove from oven; serve immediately with preserves and maple syrup.

TO MAKE AHEAD: Prepare pancake batter as directed. Refrigerate, covered, several hours or overnight. Remove from refrigerator 30 minutes before baking. Preheat oven to 425°. Prepare baking dish as directed. Whisk batter until blended; pour into hot baking dish. Bake, as directed, until puffed and sides are golden brown.

1 PIECE: 235 cal., 8g fat (4g sat. fat), 109mg chol., 319mg sod., 33g carb. (18g sugars, 1g fiber), 7g pro.

CHERRY SYRUP

My mom and grandma have been serving this fruity syrup with fluffy waffles and pancakes ever since I was a little girl. Now I make it for my sons, who love it as much as I do.
—Sandra Harrington, Nipomo, CA

TAKES: 30 MIN. • MAKES: 3 CUPS

1 pkg. (12 oz.) frozen pitted dark sweet cherries, thawed
1 cup water
2½ cups sugar
2 Tbsp. butter
½ tsp. almond extract
Dash ground cinnamon

1. Bring cherries and water to a boil in a small saucepan. Reduce heat; simmer, uncovered, for 20 minutes.

2. Add sugar and butter; cook and stir until sugar is dissolved. Remove from the heat; stir in extract and cinnamon.

3. Cool leftovers; transfer to airtight containers. Store in the refrigerator for up to 2 weeks.

2 TBSP.: 100 cal., 1g fat (1g sat. fat), 3mg chol., 7mg sod., 23g carb. (23g sugars, 0 fiber), 0 pro.

BACON POTPIE

The combination of bacon and cheese is hard to beat. Add some veggies and a homemade flaky pie crust, and you have a filling breakfast or cozy Sunday dinner.
—*Ashley Hudd, Holton, MI*

PREP: 30 MIN. • COOK: 50 MIN. • MAKES: 8 SERVINGS

2 cups all-purpose flour
⅓ cup shortening
¼ cup cold butter
5 to 7 Tbsp. ice water

FILLING
2 medium red potatoes, chopped
1 Tbsp. water
2 Tbsp. butter
3 Tbsp. all-purpose flour
2 cups 2% milk
¼ tsp. garlic powder
¼ tsp. pepper
1 lb. bacon strips, cooked and crumbled
1 medium onion, chopped
1 cup chopped fresh or frozen broccoli, thawed
1 cup shredded cheddar cheese

1. Place flour in a large bowl; cut in shortening and butter until crumbly. Gradually add ice water 1 tablespoonful at a time, tossing with a fork until dough holds together when pressed. Divide dough in half. Shape each into a disk; wrap and refrigerate 1 hour or overnight.

2. Preheat oven to 375°. In a microwave-safe bowl, combine potatoes and water; microwave, covered, on high until tender, 4-5 minutes. Cool; drain. In a small saucepan, melt butter over medium heat. Stir in flour until smooth; gradually whisk in milk, garlic powder and pepper. Bring to a boil, stirring constantly; cook and stir 2-3 minutes or until thickened. Cool.

3. On a lightly floured surface, roll half of dough to a ⅛-in.-thick circle; transfer to a 9-in. deep-dish pie plate. Trim even with rim. Place the potatoes in the crust. Top with bacon, onion, broccoli and cheese. Pour the sauce over the top. Roll remaining dough to a ⅛-in.-thick circle. Place over filling. Trim, seal and flute edge. Cut slits in top. Place on a baking sheet.

4. Bake until the crust is golden brown and the filling is bubbly, 50-60 minutes. Let stand 10 minutes before serving.

1 SERVING: 493 cal., 31g fat (14g sat. fat), 62mg chol., 558mg sod., 36g carb. (4g sugars, 2g fiber), 17g pro.

DAD'S ULTIMATE BREAKFAST BURRITOS

If your family craves burritos in the morning, look no further! Packed with scrambled eggs, shredded cheese, cubed potatoes and more, this recipe truly is the ultimate. Fresh pico de gallo pairs well on the side. Round out the menu with a fruit salad for a complete meal.

—*Stacey Nerness, Spencer, IA*

PREP: 45 MIN. • **BROIL:** 5 MIN. • **MAKES:** 10 SERVINGS

10 **medium red potatoes, cubed**
3 **bay leaves**
1½ **tsp. kosher salt, divided**
1 **medium green pepper, chopped**
1 **medium sweet red pepper, chopped**
1 **medium onion, chopped**
4 **Tbsp. olive oil, divided**
1 **can (15 oz.) black beans, rinsed and drained**
1 **cup frozen corn**
1 **jalapeno pepper, seeded and chopped**
2 **tsp. ground cumin**
1½ **tsp. garlic powder**
1½ **tsp. paprika**
½ **tsp. pepper**
10 **large eggs, beaten**
10 **flour tortillas (10 in.), warmed**
4 **cups shredded cheddar-Monterey Jack cheese**

1. Place the potatoes, bay leaves and ½ tsp. salt in a Dutch oven and cover with water. Bring to a boil. Reduce heat; cover and simmer for 5-6 minutes or until almost tender. Drain and discard bay leaves.

2. In a large skillet, cook the green and red peppers, onion and potatoes in 3 Tbsp. oil over medium heat for 10-15 minutes or until potatoes are tender. Add the beans, corn, jalapeno, cumin, garlic powder, paprika, pepper and remaining salt; heat through.

3. In a large skillet, heat remaining oil over medium-high heat. Add eggs. Cook and stir until almost set. Add to potato mixture.

4. Spoon 1 cup filling off-center on each tortilla. Sprinkle with ¼ cup cheese. Fold sides and ends over filling and roll up. Place on a greased baking sheet; sprinkle with remaining cheese. Broil 4 in. from the heat for 2-3 minutes or until cheese is melted.

NOTE: Wear disposable gloves when cutting hot peppers; the oils can burn skin. Avoid touching your face.

1 BURRITO: 798 cal., 35g fat (16g sat. fat), 314mg chol., 1384mg sod., 80g carb. (5g sugars, 14g fiber), 34g pro.

PEANUT BUTTER BANANA OVERNIGHT OATS

Mix just a few simple ingredients together tonight for a ready-made breakfast waiting in the fridge tomorrow. The easy, creamy oats are sure to satisfy you right up until lunchtime.
—Taste of Home *Test Kitchen*

PREP: 10 MIN. + CHILLING • **MAKES:** 1 SERVING

1 Tbsp. creamy peanut butter, warmed
1 Tbsp. honey
3 Tbsp. fat-free milk
⅓ cup old-fashioned oats
¼ cup mashed ripe banana
Optional: Sliced ripe banana and honey

In a small container, combine peanut butter, honey, milk, oats and banana until smooth. Seal; refrigerate overnight. If desired, top with sliced bananas and drizzle with honey.

1 SERVING: 325 cal., 10g fat (2g sat. fat), 1mg chol., 89mg sod., 54g carb. (29g sugars, 5g fiber), 9g pro.

POLISH APPLE PANCAKES

When I was a girl, my mom made these yummy cakes for me as a treat after school. All they needed on top was a sprinkle of confectioners' sugar.
—Jane Zielinski, Rotterdam Junction, NY

TAKES: 25 MIN. • **MAKES:** 5 SERVINGS (15 PANCAKES)

1 cup all-purpose flour
1 Tbsp. sugar, optional
½ tsp. salt
1 large egg, room temperature
1 cup fat-free milk
1 Tbsp. canola oil
5 medium apples, peeled and thinly sliced
Confectioners' sugar, optional

1. In a bowl, combine flour, sugar if desired and salt. In another bowl, lightly beat egg; add milk and oil. Add to dry ingredients and stir until smooth. Fold in apples.

2. Pour batter by ½ cupfuls onto a lightly greased hot griddle and spread to form a 5-in. circle. Turn when bubbles form. Cook the second side until golden brown and apples are tender. Sprinkle with confectioners' sugar if desired.

3 PANCAKES: 209 cal., 4g fat (1g sat. fat), 43mg chol., 275mg sod., 38g carb. (16g sugars, 3g fiber), 6g pro.

GREEN SHAKSHUKA

An egg dish that originated in North Africa, shakshuka comes together here with feta cheese and lots of flavorful green vegetables. What a nutritious way to start the day! Try using Italian parsley and a lemon-infused olive oil if you can find them in your store.
—*Carrie Dault, Baxter, TN*

PREP: 20 MIN. • COOK: 20 MIN. • MAKES: 4 SERVINGS

1 Tbsp. olive oil
½ lb. fresh Brussels sprouts, quartered
1 medium green pepper, chopped
1 tsp. kosher salt, divided
¼ cup reduced-sodium chicken broth or vegetable broth, divided
3 garlic cloves, minced
1 small bunch kale, trimmed and chopped (about 8 cups)
9 oz. fresh baby spinach, chopped (about 7 cups)
¼ cup fresh parsley leaves, minced
4 large eggs
¼ cup crumbled feta cheese
1 tsp. grated lemon zest

1. In a large skillet, heat the oil over medium-high heat. Add the Brussels sprouts, green pepper and ½ tsp. salt; cook and stir until lightly browned, 10-12 minutes. Add 2 Tbsp. broth and garlic; cook 1 minute longer. In batches if needed, add the kale, spinach and parsley; cook and stir until wilted, 3-4 minutes. Stir in remaining 2 Tbsp. broth and ½ tsp. salt.

2. With back of spoon, make 4 wells in vegetable mixture; break an egg into each well. Sprinkle with feta and lemon zest. Cook, covered, until egg whites are completely set and yolks begin to thicken but are not hard, 4-6 minutes.

1 EGG WITH 1 CUP VEGETABLE MIXTURE: 209 cal., 10g fat (3g sat. fat), 190mg chol., 756mg sod., 18g carb. (2g sugars, 6g fiber), 15g pro. DIABETIC EXCHANGES: 1 starch, 1 medium-fat meat, ½ fat.

CORNY BEEF BRUNCH

My mother passed on her passion for cooking to me, my daughters and my grandchildren. One of my daughters shared this simple but satisfying brunch bake with me after she made it as a newlywed for her first overnight guests.
—*Kathleen Lutz, Steward, IL*

PREP: 10 MIN. • BAKE: 35 MIN. • MAKES: 8-10 SERVINGS

3 cans (14 oz. each) corned beef hash
12 slices (1 oz. each) American cheese
12 large eggs
½ tsp. pepper

Spread hash in the bottom of a greased 13x9-in. baking dish. Layer cheese slices over hash. Beat eggs and pepper; pour over top. Bake at 350° for 35-40 minutes or until a knife inserted in the center comes out clean.

1 PIECE: 164 cal., 11g fat (4g sat. fat), 270mg chol., 282mg sod., 5g carb. (1g sugars, 0 fiber), 12g pro.

GREEN
SHAKSHUKA

TRUE BELGIAN WAFFLES

During a trip to see my husband's relatives in Europe, I received
this recipe for Belgian waffles. They're absolutely delectable
withany kind of topping, from berries and whipped cream
to fried apples and powdered sugar.
—*Rose Delemeester, St. Charles, MI*

TAKES: 30 MIN. • MAKES: 10 WAFFLES (ABOUT 4½ IN.)

2 cups all-purpose flour	1½ cups whole milk
¾ cup sugar	1 cup butter, melted
3½ tsp. baking powder	1 tsp. vanilla extract
2 large eggs, room temperature, separated	Sliced fresh strawberries or syrup

1. In a bowl, combine flour, sugar and baking powder. In another
bowl, lightly beat egg yolks. Add milk, butter and vanilla; mix well.
Stir into dry ingredients just until combined. Beat egg whites until
stiff peaks form; fold into batter.

2. Bake in a preheated waffle iron according to manufacturer's
directions until golden brown. Serve with strawberries or syrup.

2 WAFFLES: 696 cal., 41g fat (25g sat. fat), 193mg chol., 712mg sod.,
72g carb. (34g sugars, 1g fiber), 10g pro.

FROM GRANDMA'S KITCHEN: A Belgian waffle is thicker and
has fewer, but deeper, indentations than a standard waffle—
hello, big, beautiful pools of syrup. But this batter works in
whatever type of waffle iron you have.

AUNT BETTY'S JELLY CREPES

When I was a boy, my Aunt Betty would treat me to her homemade jelly-filled crepes.
They're so simple to make and taste so good that I've been eating them ever since.
—*Richard Ward, Three Rivers, MI*

TAKES: 20 MIN. • MAKES: 3 CREPES

2 large eggs, room
  temperature
¾ cup 2% milk
⅛ tsp. salt
½ cup all-purpose flour
  Butter, softened
  Strawberry or grape jelly
  Confectioners' sugar

In a small bowl, whisk eggs, milk and salt. Add flour; beat until
smooth. Melt 1 tsp. butter in a 10-in. nonstick skillet. Pour ¼ cup
batter into center of skillet; lift and turn pan to cover bottom. Cook
until lightly browned; turn and brown the other side. Remove and
keep warm. Repeat with remaining batter, adding butter to skillet
as needed. Spread crepes with butter and jelly; roll up. Dust with
confectioners' sugar. Serve immediately.

1 CREPE: 161 cal., 5g fat (2g sat. fat), 130mg chol., 172mg sod.,
19g carb. (3g sugars, 1g fiber), 8g pro.

QUICHE PASTRY CUPS

My grandmother served miniature quiches for our family brunches on special occasions. She liked to change up the ingredients in the filling, so it was always a surprise. As kids, we had fun turning it into a game— trying to guess whatwe'd find inside the little cups before taking a bite.
—*Denalee Standart, Rancho Mureta, CA*

PREP: 30 MIN. • BAKE: 15 MIN. • MAKES: 1½ DOZEN

1 pkg. (17.3 oz.) frozen puff pastry, thawed
4 large eggs, divided use
1 cup plus 2 Tbsp. half-and-half cream, divided
1 Tbsp. minced fresh thyme
½ tsp. salt
½ tsp. pepper
¼ tsp. ground nutmeg
1½ cups shredded Gruyere cheese
1½ cups chopped fresh spinach
1 medium sweet red pepper, chopped
8 bacon strips, cooked and crumbled

1. Preheat oven to 400°. On a lightly floured surface, unfold puff pastry. Roll each sheet into a 12-in. square; cut each into 9 squares. Place squares in ungreased muffin cups, pressing gently onto bottoms and up sides, allowing corners to point up.

2. In a small bowl, whisk 3 eggs, 1 cup cream, thyme and seasonings. In another bowl, combine cheese, spinach, red pepper and bacon; divide among pastry cups. Pour egg mixture over cheese mixture.

3. In a small bowl, whisk remaining egg with remaining 2 Tbsp. cream; brush over pastry edges. Bake 15-18 minutes or until golden brown. Remove to wire racks. Serve warm.

FREEZE OPTION: Cover and freeze baked pastries on greased baking sheets until firm. Transfer to resealable freezer containers; return to freezer. To use, reheat frozen pastries on ungreased baking sheets in a preheated 375° oven 17-20 minutes or until heated through.

1 PASTRY CUP: 229 cal., 14g fat (5g sat. fat), 63mg chol., 313mg sod., 17g carb. (1g sugars, 2g fiber), 8g pro.

CAPPUCCINO SMOOTHIES

Sprinkled with mini marshmallows, this icy cappuccino beverage is a twist on traditional fruit smoothies. My mom and I thought of it while trying to create a snack as an afternoon pick-me-up.
—*Michelle Cluney, Lake Mary, FL*

TAKES: 5 MIN. • MAKES: 3 SERVINGS

1 cup cappuccino or coffee yogurt
⅓ cup whole milk
3 Tbsp. confectioners' sugar, optional
1 Tbsp. chocolate syrup
1½ cups ice cubes
½ cup miniature marshmallows, divided

In a blender, combine the yogurt, milk, sugar if desired and chocolate syrup. Add ice cubes and ¼ cup marshmallows; cover and process until blended. Pour into chilled glasses; top with the remaining marshmallows. Serve immediately.

1 CUP: 166 cal., 3g fat (2g sat. fat), 11mg chol., 69mg sod., 30g carb. (27g sugars, 0 fiber), 5g pro.

SAUSAGE & APPLE CORNBREAD BAKE

For a hearty breakfast, I bake a cornbread-style casserole with sausage and tart apples.
A drizzle of sweet maple syrup is the perfect finishing touch.
—*Stevie Wilson, Fremont, IA*

PREP: 15 MIN. + CHILLING • **BAKE:** 30 MIN. + STANDING • **MAKES:** 4 SERVINGS

1 lb. bulk pork sausage
4 medium tart apples,
   peeled and sliced
   (about 4 cups)
1 pkg. (8½ oz.) cornbread/
   muffin mix
⅓ cup 2% milk
1 large egg
   Maple syrup

1. Preheat oven to 400°. In a large skillet, cook sausage over medium heat until no longer pink, 6-8 minutes, breaking into crumbles; drain. Transfer to a greased 8-in. square baking dish. Top with apples.

2. In a small bowl, combine muffin mix, milk and egg just until moistened. Pour over apples. Bake, uncovered, until edges are golden brown and a toothpick inserted in center comes out clean, 30-40 minutes. Let stand 10 minutes before serving. Serve with maple syrup.

TO MAKE AHEAD: Refrigerate the unbaked casserole, covered, several hours or overnight. To use, preheat oven to 400°. Remove casserole from refrigerator while oven heats. Bake as directed, increasing time as necessary until edges are golden brown and a toothpick inserted in center comes out clean. Serve with syrup.

1 SERVING: 618 cal., 34g fat (10g sat. fat), 111mg chol., 1209mg sod., 61g carb. (27g sugars, 6g fiber), 19g pro.

ONION POTATO PANCAKES

When Grandma made these cakes, she used an old-fashioned grater—great for potatoes but not for knuckles! I use my blender or food processor to mix cubed spuds into the batter.
In 20 minutes, I have a tasty side dish or even a light main course for dinner.
—*Joan Hutter, Warwick, RI*

TAKES: 20 MIN. • **MAKES:** 6 SERVINGS

2 large eggs
1 medium onion, quartered
2 tablespoons
   all-purpose flour
¾ teaspoon salt
¼ teaspoon pepper
¼ teaspoon baking powder
4 medium potatoes,
   peeled and cubed
   (about 1½ pounds)
2 tablespoons chopped
   fresh parsley
3 to 4 tablespoons
   vegetable oil

1. In a blender or food processor, place the eggs, onion, flour, salt, pepper, baking powder and ½ cup of potatoes. Cover and process on high until smooth. Add parsley and remaining potatoes; cover and pulse 2-4 times until potatoes are chopped.

2. Pour 1-2 tablespoons oil onto a hot griddle or skillet. Pour the batter by ⅓ cupfuls onto griddle; flatten slightly to a 4-in. to 5-in. diameter. Cook over medium heat until golden, 2-3 minutes on each side. Add oil to griddle as needed.

2 PANCAKES: 159 cal., 6g fat (1g sat. fat), 47mg chol., 262mg sod., 22g carb. (2g sugars, 3g fiber), 4g pro. **DIABETIC EXCHANGES:** 1½ starch, 1 fat.

HOMEMADE BREAKFAST SAUSAGE PATTIES

What's the secret to these pork patties? Buttermilk! It keeps them nice and moist.
A great blend of seasonings provides the zippy flavor.
—*Harvey Keeney, Mandan, ND*

PREP: 30 MIN. • **COOK:** 10 MIN./BATCH • **MAKES:** 20 PATTIES

¾ **cup buttermilk**
2¼ **tsp. kosher salt**
1½ **tsp. rubbed sage**
1½ **tsp. brown sugar**
1½ **tsp. pepper**
¾ **tsp. dried marjoram**
¾ **tsp. dried savory**
¾ **tsp. cayenne pepper**
¼ **tsp. ground nutmeg**
2½ **lbs. ground pork**

1. In a large bowl, combine the first 9 ingredients. Add the pork; mix lightly but thoroughly. Shape into twenty 3-in. patties.

2. In a large skillet coated with cooking spray, cook the patties in batches over medium heat until a thermometer reads 160°, 5-6 minutes on each side. Remove to paper towels to drain.

FREEZE OPTION: Wrap each cooked, cooled sausage patty; transfer to an airtight container. Freeze for up to 3 months. To use, unwrap patties and place on a baking sheet coated with cooking spray. Bake at 350° until heated through, about 15 minutes on each side.

1 SAUSAGE PATTY: 126 cal., 8g fat (3g sat. fat), 38mg chol., 251mg sod., 1g carb. (1g sugars, 0 fiber), 11g pro.

CREAMY STRAWBERRY FRENCH TOAST BAKE

PICTURED ON PAGE 6

On Sunday mornings I like to take it easy, but I also want my family to have a special breakfast.
Make-ahead French toast allows me to sleep in and still hear raves at the table. Win!
—*Alynn Hansen, Mona, UT*

PREP: 30 MIN. + CHILLING • **BAKE:** 40 MIN. • **MAKES:** 8 SERVINGS

3 **cups sliced fresh strawberries, divided**
2 **Tbsp. sugar**
1 **pkg. (8 oz.) cream cheese, softened**
½ **cup confectioners' sugar**
1 **Tbsp. grated orange zest**
1 **Tbsp. orange juice**
1 **tsp. vanilla extract**
1 **loaf (1 lb.) cinnamon bread, cut into 1-in. pieces**
5 **large eggs**
1 **cup half-and-half cream**
Sweetened whipped cream

1. Toss 2 cups strawberries with sugar. In another bowl, beat the next 5 ingredients until smooth. Place half the bread in a greased 13x9-in. baking dish. Spoon cream cheese mixture over bread. Layer with strawberry mixture and remaining bread. Whisk eggs and cream until blended; pour over top. Refrigerate, covered, overnight.

2. Preheat oven to 350°. Remove casserole from refrigerator while oven heats. Bake, uncovered, until a knife inserted in the center comes out clean, 40-45 minutes. Let stand 5 minutes before serving. Top with sweetened whipped cream and remaining 1 cup strawberries.

1 PIECE: 431 cal., 21g fat (10g sat. fat), 160mg chol., 382mg sod., 47g carb. (24g sugars, 5g fiber), 13g pro.

OMELET WAFFLES WITH SAUSAGE CHEESE SAUCE

This omelet-waffle mashup is smothered with sausage, onions, sweet peppers and a chunky cheesy sauce. It's a delicious combination any time of day.

—Ronna Farley, Rockville, MD

PREP: 30 MIN. • COOK: 5 MIN./BATCH • MAKES: 4 SERVINGS

- 1 lb. bulk pork sausage
- ½ lb. whole fresh mushrooms, chopped
- ½ cup chopped onion
- ½ cup chopped sweet red pepper
- 2 Tbsp. all-purpose flour
- 2 cups half-and-half cream, divided
- 1 tsp. seasoned salt, divided
- 1 cup shredded sharp cheddar cheese
- 8 large eggs, room temperature
- 1 Tbsp. minced fresh parsley

1. Preheat waffle maker. In a large skillet, cook sausage, mushrooms, onion and red pepper over medium heat until sausage is no longer pink and vegetables are tender, 8-10 minutes, breaking sausage into crumbles; drain. Remove from heat and keep warm.

2. Meanwhile, in a large saucepan, whisk flour, 1¾ cups cream and ½ tsp. seasoned salt until smooth. Bring to a boil, stirring constantly; cook and stir until thickened, 2-3 minutes. Stir in cheese and 1 cup sausage mixture until cheese is melted. Remove from heat and keep warm.

3. In a large bowl, whisk eggs and the remaining ¼ cup cream and ½ tsp. seasoned salt until blended. Bake in a well-greased waffle maker until golden brown, 2-3 minutes. Serve with sausage mixture and cheese sauce; sprinkle with parsley.

2 WAFFLES: 734 cal., 56g fat (24g sat. fat), 521mg chol., 1461mg sod., 15g carb. (7g sugars, 1g fiber), 38g pro.

"Halved this recipe and made it for my husband and me this morning as a special brunch. We liked it very much, and it was just enough for 1 hearty serving each. I plan to make it again."

—HOLLYEATON-BRADFIELD, TASTEOFHOME.COM

CHORIZO & GRITS BREAKFAST BOWLS

Growing up, I bonded with my dad over breakfasts of chorizo and eggs.
To give that dish a twist, I incorporated grits and black beans.
—*Jenn Tidwell, Fair Oaks, CA*

TAKES: 30 MIN. • MAKES: 6 SERVINGS

2 tsp. olive oil
1 pkg. (12 oz.) fully cooked
  chorizo chicken sausages
  or flavor of choice, sliced
1 large zucchini, chopped
3 cups water
¾ cup quick-cooking grits
1 can (15 oz.) black beans,
  rinsed and drained
½ cup shredded
  cheddar cheese
6 large eggs
  Optional: Pico de
  gallo and chopped
  fresh cilantro

1. In a large skillet, heat oil over medium heat. Add the sausage; cook and stir until lightly browned, 2-3 minutes. Add zucchini; cook and stir until tender, 4-5 minutes longer. Remove from pan; keep warm.

2. Meanwhile, in a large saucepan, bring water to a boil. Slowly stir in grits. Reduce heat to medium-low; cook, covered, until thickened, stirring occasionally, about 5 minutes. Stir in beans and cheese until blended. Remove from heat.

3. Wipe skillet clean; coat with cooking spray and place over medium heat. In batches, break 1 egg at a time into the pan. Immediately reduce heat to low; cook until whites are completely set and yolks begin to thicken but are not hard, about 5 minutes.

4. To serve, divide grits mixture among 6 bowls. Top with chorizo mixture, eggs and, if desired, pico de gallo and cilantro.

1 SERVING: 344 cal., 14g fat (5g sat. fat), 239mg chol., 636mg sod., 30g carb. (4g sugars, 4g fiber), 24g pro. DIABETIC EXCHANGES: 3 medium-fat meat, 2 starch.

HERB & CHEESE SCRAMBLED EGGS

I was raised on a farm where fresh eggs and herbs were plentiful in summer.
My mother made this tasty scramble, and now I make it for my own family. Just add toast!
—*Patricia Nieh, Portola Valley, CA*

TAKES: 15 MIN. • MAKES: 4 SERVINGS

8 large eggs
½ cup 2% milk or
  half-and-half cream
4 oz. cream cheese,
  softened
1 Tbsp. minced
  fresh parsley
1 Tbsp. minced chives
½ tsp. minced fresh thyme
⅛ to ¼ tsp. salt
⅛ tsp. white pepper
1 Tbsp. butter
  Additional minced
  fresh herbs

Whisk together the first 8 ingredients. In a large nonstick skillet, heat butter over medium heat. Pour in egg mixture; cook and stir until eggs are thickened and no liquid egg remains. Sprinkle with additional minced herbs.

1 SERVING: 284 cal., 23g fat (11g sat. fat), 411mg chol., 343mg sod., 4g carb. (3g sugars, 0 fiber), 15g pro.

CHORIZO & GRITS
BREAKFAST BOWLS

PIZZA PUFFS,
PAGE 57

GRANDMA'S FAVORITE

SNACKS

Grandma's recipes are so scrumptious, it's hard to wait
for mealtime—unless you have her amazing finger
foods, appetizers and munchies to tide you over!

AUNT KAREN'S SHRIMP SALAD

Serving guests at a bridal shower or luncheon is easy with this crowd-size recipe. Most of it goes together the night before. The next day, just stir in a few more ingredients and spoon the salad into lettuce leaves.
—*Karen Moore, Jacksonville, FL*

PREP: 10 MIN. • COOK: 10 MIN. + CHILLING • MAKES: 24 SERVINGS

2 lbs. uncooked shrimp (26-30 per lb.), peeled and deveined and halved
1 Tbsp. white vinegar
1 Tbsp. lemon juice
⅓ cup plus 1 Tbsp. mayonnaise, divided
½ tsp. garlic salt
2 celery ribs, chopped
5 hard-boiled large eggs, chopped
¼ cup chopped sweet red pepper
24 Bibb lettuce leaves or Boston lettuce leaves Sliced green onions, optional

1. In a Dutch oven or large saucepan, bring 6 cups water to a boil. Add shrimp; cook, uncovered, until shrimp turn pink, 3-5 minutes. Drain. Transfer to a large bowl. Add vinegar, lemon juice, 1 Tbsp. mayonnaise and garlic salt; toss to coat. Refrigerate, covered, at least 4 hours or overnight.

2. To serve, stir in the remaining ⅓ cup mayonnaise, celery, eggs and red pepper. Serve in lettuce leaves. If desired, top with sliced green onions.

¼ CUP: 74 cal., 4g fat (1g sat. fat), 85mg chol., 120mg sod., 1g carb. (0 sugars, 0 fiber), 8g pro. DIABETIC EXCHANGES: 1 lean meat, 1 fat.

"Since I am on a KETO diet, this was perfect for me. I followed the recipe exactly, except I cut it in half and did not add red pepper since I didn't have one. Nice lightly dressed shrimp salad. A pleasant change from some of the heavier versions. I give it 5 stars for sure!"
—BICKTASW, TASTEOFHOME.COM

SWEET & SAVORY PINEAPPLE CHEESE BALL

When I was a kid, my mom made cheese balls dotted with pineapple and green peppers. Now I prepare my own for get-togethers and always hear raves.
—*Susan Harrison, Laurel, MD*

PREP: 15 MIN. + CHILLING • MAKES: 2 CHEESE BALLS (2 CUPS EACH)

2 pkg. (8 oz. each) reduced-fat cream cheese
1 can (20 oz.) crushed pineapple, well drained
3 cups finely chopped pecans, divided
¼ cup finely chopped green pepper
1 Tbsp. finely chopped onion
1 tsp. seasoned salt Assorted crackers

1. In a large bowl, beat the cream cheese until smooth. Stir in the pineapple, 1½ cups pecans, green pepper, onion and seasoned salt. Shape into 2 balls. Wrap in plastic; refrigerate at least 30 minutes.

2. Place remaining pecans in a small shallow bowl; roll cheese balls in pecans to coat evenly. Serve with crackers.

2 TBSP.: 117 cal., 10g fat (3g sat. fat), 10mg chol., 108mg sod., 5g carb. (3g sugars, 1g fiber), 3g pro.

AUNT KAREN'S
SHRIMP SALAD

TOSTONES

I grew up eating many dishes from Puerto Rico, but tostones have always been a favorite. I still make these fried plantain snacks when I'm missing my family.
—*Leah Martin, Gilbertsville, PA*

PREP: 15 MIN. + SOAKING • **COOK:** 5 MIN./BATCH • **MAKES:** 3 DOZEN

3 garlic cloves, minced
1 Tbsp. garlic salt
½ tsp. onion powder
6 green plantains, peeled and cut into 1-in. slices
   Oil for deep-fat frying

SEASONING MIX
1 Tbsp. garlic powder
1½ tsp. garlic salt
½ tsp. onion powder
½ tsp. kosher salt
   Optional: Guacamole and pico de gallo

1. In a large bowl, combine the garlic, garlic salt and onion powder. Add the plantains; cover with cold water. Soak for 30 minutes.

2. Drain plantains; place on paper towels and pat dry. In a deep cast-iron or electric skillet, heat oil to 375°. Add plantains, a few at a time, and cook until lightly browned, 30-60 seconds. Remove with a slotted spoon; drain on paper towels.

3. Place plantain pieces between 2 sheets of aluminum foil. With the bottom of a glass, flatten to ½-in. thickness. Fry until golden brown, 2-3 minutes longer.

4. Combine seasoning mix ingredients; sprinkle over tostones. If desired, serve with guacamole and pico de gallo.

1 TOSTONE: 63 cal., 3g fat (0 sat. fat), 0 chol., 103mg sod., 10g carb. (2g sugars, 1g fiber), 0 pro.

PHYLLO-WRAPPED BRIE WITH SUN-DRIED TOMATOES

Wrapping Brie cheese in flaky phyllo dough is an elegant yet easy serving idea. My mom and I would often prepare this special appetizer together.
—Katie Klee, Noblesville, IN

PREP: 10 MIN. • BAKE: 20 MIN. + STANDING • MAKES: 8 SERVINGS

2 Tbsp. butter, melted
1 Tbsp. oil from oil-packed sun-dried tomatoes
4 sheets phyllo dough
1 Tbsp. chopped oil-packed sun-dried tomatoes
1 round (8 oz.) Brie cheese, rind removed
Assorted crackers

1. In a small bowl, combine butter and oil. Lightly brush 1 sheet of phyllo with some of the butter mixture; place another sheet of phyllo on top and brush with butter mixture. Repeat twice.

2. Cut the layered phyllo into a 9-in. square; discard trimmings. Spread chopped tomatoes in the center of the square. Place Brie over tomatoes.

3. Brush corners of phyllo with 1 tsp. butter mixture. Fold pastry over the cheese and pinch edges to seal. Place seam side down on a greased baking sheet. Brush with remaining butter mixture.

4. Bake at 350° for 18-22 minutes or until golden brown. Let stand for 10 minutes before serving with crackers.

1 SERVING: 167 cal., 13g fat (7g sat. fat), 36mg chol., 246mg sod., 7g carb. (1g sugars, 0 fiber), 7g pro.

FESTIVE APPLE DIP

When my dad surprised me with a big bag of apples, I came up with my own layered peanut butter treat for dipping. It's yummy with graham crackers, vanilla wafers, banana chunks and animal crackers, too.
—Theresa Tometich, Coralville, IA

TAKES: 20 MIN. • MAKES: 8 SERVINGS

1 pkg. (8 oz.) cream cheese, softened
½ cup creamy peanut butter
⅓ cup packed brown sugar
1 tsp. vanilla extract
½ cup miniature marshmallows
1 jar (11¾ oz.) hot fudge ice cream topping
2 Tbsp. chopped mixed nuts or peanuts
3 each medium red and green apples, cut into thin wedges
2 Tbsp. lemon juice

1. For dip, beat first 4 ingredients until smooth; stir in miniature marshmallows. Spoon half the mixture into a 3-cup bowl; top with half the fudge topping. Repeat layers. Sprinkle with nuts.

2. To serve, toss apples with lemon juice. Serve with dip.

¼ CUP DIP WITH ¾ APPLE: 403 cal., 22g fat (9g sat. fat), 29mg chol., 218mg sod., 49g carb. (38g sugars, 3g fiber), 8g pro.

CRANBERRY &
BACON SWISS
CHEESE DIP

CRANBERRY & BACON SWISS CHEESE DIP

Paired with toasted French bread, this creamy warm dip makes a wonderful appetizer for holiday gatherings. I love that I can do the prep in advance, pop the dish in the fridge and then bake just before serving time.
—*Jeanne Holt, St. Paul, MN*

PREP: 20 MIN. • BAKE: 25 MIN. • MAKES: 3 CUPS

⅔ cup mayonnaise
⅓ cup spreadable chive and onion cream cheese
1 Tbsp. stone-ground mustard
¼ tsp. garlic pepper blend
3 cups shredded Swiss cheese
1 pkg. (10 oz.) frozen chopped onions, thawed and patted dry
8 pieces ready-to-serve fully cooked bacon, chopped
½ cup sliced almonds, divided
⅓ cup dried cranberries, chopped
Slices French bread baguette (¼ in. thick), toasted

1. Preheat oven to 325°. In a large bowl, combine mayonnaise, cream cheese, mustard and garlic pepper blend. Add Swiss cheese; mix well. Stir in the onions, bacon, ¼ cup almonds and dried cranberries. Spread into a greased 1- or 2-qt. baking dish. Sprinkle with remaining ¼ cup almonds. Place on a baking sheet.

2. Bake, uncovered, until bubbly, 25-30 minutes. Serve warm with baguette slices.

¼ CUP: 266 cal., 22g fat (8g sat. fat), 30mg chol., 222mg sod., 8g carb. (5g sugars, 1g fiber), 10g pro.

"This was delicious. Great with crusty French bread and sliced carrots. I bet I could even eat this on pieces of cardboard—it's that good!"
—EJSHELLABARGER, TASTEOFHOME.COM

MARINATED SHRIMP

My husband's aunt shared her delicious shrimp recipe with me ages ago. It became a Christmas Eve tradition not only in my home, but in the homes of our grown children as well.
—*Delores Hill, Helena, MT*

PREP: 10 MIN. + MARINATING • COOK: 10 MIN. • MAKES: ABOUT 3 DOZEN

2 lbs. uncooked jumbo shrimp, peeled and deveined
1 cup olive oil
2 garlic cloves, minced
4 tsp. dried rosemary, crushed
2 tsp. dried oregano
2 bay leaves
1 cup dry white wine or chicken broth
¾ tsp. salt
⅛ tsp. pepper

1. In a bowl, combine the shrimp, oil, garlic, rosemary, oregano and bay leaves. Cover and refrigerate for 2-4 hours.

2. Pour the shrimp and marinade into a large deep skillet. Add wine or broth, salt and pepper. Cover and cook over medium-low heat for 10-15 minutes or until the shrimp turn pink, stirring occasionally. Discard bay leaves. Transfer with a slotted spoon to a serving dish.

1 PIECE: 40 cal., 2g fat (0 sat. fat), 31mg chol., 42mg sod., 0 carb. (0 sugars, 0 fiber), 4g pro.

BOURBON HAM BALLS

Grandma Nette was the queen of ham ball recipes. I like mine salty-sweet
with a bourbon and vinegar kick. Enjoy them alone, in a sandwich or over pasta or rice.
—*Kimla Carsten, Grand Junction, CO*

PREP: 70 MIN. + FREEZING • **BAKE:** 15 MIN. • **MAKES:** ABOUT 3½ DOZEN

2 **lbs. fully cooked boneless ham**
1 **thick boneless pork loin chop (8 oz.)**
½ **lb. bacon strips**
1 **cup panko bread crumbs**
1 **cup 2% milk**
2 **large eggs, lightly beaten**
 Oil for frying

SAUCE
1½ **cups packed brown sugar**
½ **cup white vinegar**
½ **cup bourbon**
2 **tsp. spicy brown mustard**

1. Cut the ham, pork chop and bacon into 1-in. pieces; arrange in a single layer in a foil-lined 15x10x1-in. pan. Freeze 30 minutes or until partially frozen.

2. Preheat oven to 350°. Transfer the meat to a food processor in batches; pulse until coarsely ground, 20-24 pulses. In a large bowl, combine bread crumbs, milk and eggs. Add meat mixture; mix lightly but thoroughly. Shape into 1½-in. balls.

3. In a large skillet, heat ¼ in. oil over medium heat. Add ham balls in batches; cook 3-4 minutes or until cooked through, turning occasionally. Remove from pan; drain on paper towels.

4. In a large bowl, whisk the sauce ingredients; reserve 1 cup for serving. Add the ham balls to the sauce, a few at a time, allowing them to soak 1-2 minutes. Transfer ham balls to a foil-lined 15x10x1-in. baking pan. Bake 15-20 minutes or until heated through, brushing occasionally with remaining sauce from soaking. Serve with reserved sauce.

1 HAM BALL WITH 1 TSP. SAUCE: 138 cal., 8g fat (2g sat. fat), 27mg chol., 276mg sod., 9g carb. (8g sugars, 0 fiber), 6g pro.

PEPPER JELLY HOGS IN A BLANKET

These grown-up pigs in a blanket are addictive!
So much flavor is wrapped up in each little bite.
—*Becky Hardin, St. Peters, MO*

PREP: 20 MIN. • BAKE: 15 MIN. • MAKES: 2 DOZEN

1 tube (8 oz.) refrigerated
crescent rolls
1 pkg. (12 oz.) fully cooked
spicy chicken sausage
links, cut into 1-in. slices

¼ cup pepper jelly
Stone-ground mustard

1. Preheat oven to 375°. Coat 24 mini muffin cups with cooking spray.

2. Unroll the crescent dough and separate into 2 rectangles; press perforations to seal. Cut dough lengthwise into ¾-in. strips. Wrap a strip of dough around a sausage slice, gently stretching dough as you roll. Place cut side up in a muffin cup; repeat with remaining dough and sausage. Spoon pepper jelly over each slice.

3. Bake until golden brown, 12-15 minutes. Let stand 5 minutes before removing to a serving plate. Serve warm with mustard.

1 APPETIZER: 65 cal., 3g fat (0 sat. fat), 11mg chol., 152mg sod., 7g carb. (3g sugars, 0 fiber), 3g pro.

HONEY-ORANGE CHICKEN WINGS

I love my mom's tangy recipe for chicken wings. She served them hot
as a main dish, but I often make them as an appetizer—hot or cold.
—*Marie Schnerch, Winnipeg, MB*

PREP: 15 MIN. • BAKE: 35 MIN. • MAKES: 2 SERVINGS

6 whole chicken wings
⅓ cup ketchup
½ cup all-purpose flour
3 Tbsp. orange juice
4½ tsp. honey
¾ tsp. lemon juice
¾ tsp. Worcestershire
sauce
⅛ tsp. ground ginger
Dash garlic powder

1. Cut chicken wings into 3 sections; discard wing tip sections. Brush wings with ketchup; coat with flour. Place in a shallow baking pan coated with cooking spray. Bake, uncovered, at 350° for 20 minutes.

2. In a small bowl, combine remaining ingredients. Brush some of the mixture over wings. Bake 15-20 minutes longer or until chicken juices run clear, basting frequently with remaining orange juice mixture.

6 EACH: 533 cal., 22g fat (6g sat. fat), 92mg chol., 586mg sod., 51g carb. (20g sugars, 1g fiber), 33g pro.

CAULIFLOWER CEVICHE

My mom showed me how to make this delicious vegetarian appetizer that tastes
so much like seafood ceviche. Serve tortilla chips or crackers on the side.
—*Beatriz Barranco, El Paso, TX*

PREP: 20 MIN. + CHILLING • MAKES: 8 CUPS

1 medium head cauliflower,
  finely chopped
1 cup ketchup
1 cup orange juice
3 medium tomatoes,
  chopped
1 medium onion,
  finely chopped
½ cup minced fresh cilantro
¼ tsp. salt
¼ tsp. pepper
3 medium ripe avocados,
  peeled and cubed
  Optional: Lemon wedges,
  tortilla chip scoops and
  hot pepper sauce

1. In a large skillet, bring 1 cup water to a boil. Add cauliflower; cook, uncovered, just until crisp-tender, 5-8 minutes. Remove with a slotted spoon; drain and pat dry. Meanwhile, stir together ketchup and orange juice.

2. In a large bowl, combine cauliflower with tomatoes and onion. Add ketchup mixture, cilantro, salt and pepper; toss to coat. Refrigerate, covered, at least 1 hour.

3. Stir in avocado cubes. If desired, serve with lemon wedges, tortilla chip scoops and hot pepper sauce.

¾ CUP: 129 cal., 7g fat (1g sat. fat), 0 chol., 387mg sod., 18g carb. (11g sugars, 5g fiber), 3g pro.

ZESTY PEPPERONI DIP

Here's a holiday snack our whole family looks forward to. I combined my mother's cheese ball
recipe with a favorite dip from my husband's aunt. Feel free to use reduced-fat
cream cheese and either reduced-fat pepperoni or turkey pepperoni.
—*Heather Church, Gaffney, SC*

TAKES: 15 MIN. • MAKES: 2 CUPS

6 oz. sliced pepperoni,
  chopped (1½ cups)
1 pkg. (8 oz.) cream cheese,
  softened
6 Tbsp. 2% milk
1½ pkg. Italian salad
  dressing mix
1 Tbsp. olive oil
  Dash hot pepper sauce
  Dash Worcestershire
  sauce
½ cup shredded Italian
  cheese blend
2 Tbsp. chopped
  green pepper
2 Tbsp. finely chopped
  onion
  Assorted crackers

1. Place the pepperoni on a paper towel-lined microwave-safe plate; microwave, covered, on high for 1-2 minutes or until fat is rendered.

2. In a large bowl, beat the cream cheese, milk, salad dressing mix, oil, pepper sauce and Worcestershire sauce until blended. Stir in pepperoni, cheese, green pepper and onion. Serve at room temperature with crackers.

¼ CUP: 259 cal., 23g fat (11g sat. fat), 55mg chol., 964mg sod., 4g carb. (3g sugars, 0 fiber), 8g pro.

CAULIFLOWER
CEVICHE

SLOW-COOKER CRAB & GREEN ONION DIP

This warm and creamy dip reminds me of my dad, who took us crabbing as kids. Our fingers were always tired after those excursions, but eating the fresh catch was worth it!
—*Nancy Zimmerman, Cape May Court House, NJ*

PREP: 10 MIN. • **COOK:** 3 HOURS • **MAKES:** 16 SERVINGS (4 CUPS)

- **3** pkg. (8 oz. each) cream cheese, cubed
- **2** cans (6 oz. each) lump crabmeat, drained
- **4** green onions, chopped
- **¼** cup 2% milk
- **2** tsp. prepared horseradish
- **2** tsp. Worcestershire sauce
- **¼** tsp. salt
  Baked pita chips and assorted fresh vegetables

In a greased 3-qt. slow cooker, combine the first 7 ingredients. Cook, covered, on low 3-4 hours or until heated through, stirring occasionally. Serve with chips and fresh vegetables.

¼ CUP: 167 cal., 15g fat (8g sat. fat), 68mg chol., 324mg sod., 2g carb. (2g sugars, 0 fiber), 7g pro.

BETTER THAN FRIED SHRIMP

Want an alternative to shrimp that's battered or deep-fried? Coat it with panko bread crumbs, spray with cooking spray and then bake for a wonderful crunch without all the saturated fat and calories.
—*Cher Schwartz, Ellisville, MO*

TAKES: 30 MIN. • **MAKES:** 2½ DOZEN

- **1½** cups panko bread crumbs
- **2** large egg whites
- **1** Tbsp. fat-free milk
- **3** Tbsp. all-purpose flour
- **3** tsp. seafood seasoning
- **¼** tsp. salt
- **¼** tsp. pepper
- **30** uncooked large shrimp, peeled and deveined
  Olive oil-flavored cooking spray

1. Place bread crumbs in a shallow bowl. In another shallow bowl, combine egg whites and milk. In a third shallow bowl, combine flour, seafood seasoning, salt and pepper. Dip the shrimp in flour mixture, egg mixture, then bread crumbs.

2. Place prepared shrimp on a baking sheet coated with olive oil–flavored cooking spray; spritz shrimp with cooking spray. Bake at 400°for 8-12 minutes or until shrimp turn pink and coating is golden brown, turning once.

1 SERVING: 28 cal., 1g fat (0 sat. fat), 20mg chol., 86mg sod., 2g carb. (0 sugars, 0 fiber), 3g pro.

BEEF WELLINGTON AIR-FRIED WONTONS

I scale down classic beef Wellington into party-size wontons using
my air fryer. They're fancy, fun and delicious!
—*Dianne Phillips, Tallapoosa, GA*

PREP: 35 MIN. • **COOK:** 10 MIN./BATCH • **MAKES:** 3½ DOZEN

½ lb. lean ground beef
(90% lean)
1 Tbsp. butter
1 Tbsp. olive oil
2 garlic cloves, minced
1½ tsp. chopped shallot
1 cup each chopped fresh
shiitake, baby portobello
and white mushrooms
¼ cup dry red wine
1 Tbsp. minced
fresh parsley
½ tsp. salt
¼ tsp. pepper
1 pkg. (12 oz.)
wonton wrappers
1 large egg
1 Tbsp. water
Cooking spray

1. Preheat air fryer to 325°. In a small skillet, cook and crumble ground beef over medium heat until no longer pink, 4-5 minutes. Transfer to a large bowl. In the same skillet, heat butter and olive oil over medium-high heat. Add garlic and shallot; cook 1 minute. Stir in mushrooms and wine. Cook until mushrooms are tender, 8-10 minutes; add to beef. Stir in parsley, salt and pepper.

2. Place about 2 tsp. filling in the center of each wonton wrapper. Combine egg and water. Moisten wonton edges with egg mixture; fold opposite corners over filling and press to seal.

3. In batches, arrange wontons in a single layer on greased tray in air-fryer basket; spritz with cooking spray. Cook until lightly browned, 4-5 minutes. Turn; spritz with cooking spray. Cook until golden brown and crisp, 4-5 minutes longer. Serve warm.

FREEZE OPTION: Cover and freeze the unbaked wontons on parchment-lined baking sheets until firm. Transfer to freezer containers; return to freezer. To use, cook wontons as directed.

NOTE: If you don't have an air fryer, you can make this recipe in a deep fryer, in an electric skillet or on the stovetop.

1 WONTON: 42 cal., 1g fat (0 sat. fat), 9mg chol., 82mg sod., 5g carb. (0 sugars, 0 fiber), 2g pro.

PEACHY-KEEN
HALLOUMI
FRITTERS

PEACHY-KEEN HALLOUMI FRITTERS

A golden corn fritter filled with gooey Halloumi cheese and served with juicy peaches—what a treat! These decadent bites have extra heartiness when you add prosciutto. Enjoy them as a special party snack, or as a topper for mixed greens to jazz up your salads.
—*Chainey Kuykendall, Richmond, VA*

PREP: 25 MIN. + STANDING • **COOK:** 5 MIN./BATCH • **MAKES:** 2½ DOZEN

1¼ cups cornmeal
2 Tbsp. minced fresh basil
1 tsp. baking powder
1 tsp. salt
½ tsp. pepper
1 large egg plus 1 large egg white, room temperature
¾ cup 2% milk
2 Tbsp. honey
1 cup finely chopped sweet onion
½ cup diced Halloumi cheese
Oil for deep-fat frying
1 medium peach, chopped
4 thin slices prosciutto, cut into thin strips

1. In a large bowl, whisk the first 5 ingredients. In another bowl, whisk egg, egg white, milk and honey until blended. Add to the dry ingredients, stirring just until moistened. Fold in onion and cheese; let stand 10 minutes.

2. In an electric skillet or deep fryer, heat oil to 375°. Stir batter. Drop batter by tablespoonfuls, a few at a time, into the hot oil. Fry until golden brown, 2-3 minutes on each side. Drain on paper towels. Keep cooked fritters warm on a baking sheet in a 200° oven until all fritters are made.

3. Serve fritters with chopped peach and prosciutto; sprinkle with additional pepper.

1 FRITTER: 71 cal., 4g fat (1g sat. fat), 10mg chol., 159mg sod., 8g carb. (2g sugars, 0 fiber), 2g pro.

CRUNCHY PEANUT BUTTER APPLE DIP

A neighbor gave this yummy recipe to my mom years ago. She always made it for us in fall when apples were in season. Now I carry on the tradition with my own kids.
—*Juli Meyers, Hinesville, GA*

TAKES: 10 MIN. • **MAKES:** 2½ CUPS

1 carton (8 oz.) reduced-fat spreadable cream cheese
1 cup creamy peanut butter
¼ cup fat-free milk
1 Tbsp. brown sugar
1 tsp. vanilla extract
½ cup chopped unsalted peanuts
Apple slices

In a small bowl, beat the first 5 ingredients until blended. Stir in peanuts. Serve with apple slices. Refrigerate leftovers.

2 TBSP.: 126 cal., 10g fat (3g sat. fat), 5mg chol., 115mg sod., 5g carb. (3g sugars, 1g fiber), 5g pro.

"I made this for a retirement gathering at work. Needed something tasty and gluten-free, as two of my co-workers are gluten-intolerant. This was a hit! I was asked by several of my co-workers for the recipe."
—GK33061, TASTEOFHOME.COM

GAME DAY MINIATURE PEPPERS

My mom's recipe for stuffed peppers inspired this mini version perfect for munching.
I make them healthier by using ground turkey and brown rice, but feel free to stuff
them with pork, beans or goat cheese—let your imagination go wild!
—Rose Muccio, Methuen, MA

PREP: 55 MIN. • BAKE: 20 MIN. • MAKES: 2 DOZEN

8 each miniature
   sweet red, orange
   and yellow peppers
4 oz. ground turkey
½ cup finely chopped
   fresh mushrooms
¼ cup chopped sweet onion
1 garlic clove, minced
1 can (15 oz.) tomato sauce,
   divided
¼ cup cooked brown rice
1 Tbsp. grated
   Parmesan cheese
1 Tbsp. shredded part-
   skim mozzarella cheese
½ tsp. dried basil
¼ tsp. salt
¼ tsp. cayenne pepper
¼ tsp. pepper

1. Cut tops off peppers and reserve; remove seeds. Cut thin slices from pepper bottoms to level; set aside peppers.

2. In a large skillet, cook the turkey, mushrooms, onion and garlic over medium heat until meat is no longer pink, breaking turkey into crumbles. Remove from the heat; let stand for 5 minutes.

3. Stir in ¼ cup tomato sauce, rice, cheeses and seasonings; spoon into peppers. Place upright in a greased 11x7-in. baking dish. Spoon the remaining tomato sauce over peppers; replace pepper tops. Cover and bake at 400° for 18-22 minutes or until heated through and peppers are crisp-tender.

1 APPETIZER: 23 cal., 1g fat (0 sat. fat), 4mg chol., 116mg sod., 3g carb. (1g sugars, 1g fiber), 1g pro.

BACON-CHEESE BISCUIT BITES

As a busy mom, I look for quick recipes that please everyone and are easy enough
for the kids to help with. These savory snacks check all the boxes!
—Margo Lewis, Lake City, MI

PREP: 20 MIN. • BAKE: 15 MIN. • MAKES: 20 APPETIZERS

4 oz. cream cheese,
   softened
1 large egg
1 Tbsp. 2% milk
⅓ cup real bacon bits
¼ cup shredded
   Swiss cheese
1 Tbsp. dried minced onion
1 large plum tomato,
   seeded and finely
   chopped, divided
1 tube (10.2 oz.)
   large refrigerated
   flaky biscuits

1. In a small bowl, beat cream cheese, egg and milk until smooth. Stir in the bacon, cheese, onion and half of the tomato; set aside.

2. Cut each refrigerated biscuit into 4 pieces; press each piece into a greased miniature muffin cup. Fill with the cream cheese mixture; top with remaining tomato.

3. Bake at 375° for 14-16 minutes or until a knife inserted in the center comes out clean.

1 APPETIZER: 80 cal., 5g fat (2g sat. fat), 18mg chol., 174mg sod., 7g carb. (1g sugars, 0 fiber), 3g pro.

BABA GANOUSH

Baba ganoush (also spelled baba ghanoush or baba ghanouj)
is a Lebanese dip made with roasted eggplant and is typically
served as a starter. Just add pita bread or fresh veggies.
—*Nithya Narasimhan, Chennai, India*

PREP/COOK: 35 MIN. • MAKES: 8 SERVINGS (1 CUP)

1 **medium eggplant**	2 **Tbsp. tahini**
3 **Tbsp. olive oil, divided**	1 **garlic clove, minced**
1 **tsp. salt, divided**	1 **tsp. lemon juice**
½ **tsp. paprika**	**Chopped fresh parsley**

1. Preheat oven to 450°. Cut the eggplant in half lengthwise. Place cut side up on an ungreased baking sheet. Brush 1 Tbsp. olive oil over the cut sides. Sprinkle with ½ tsp. salt and paprika. Bake until dark golden brown, 20-25 minutes. Remove eggplant from pan to a wire rack to cool.

2. Peel the skin from eggplant; discard. Put the flesh into a food processor and pulse to mash; transfer to bowl. Stir in the tahini, garlic, lemon juice and remaining ½ tsp. salt. Spoon into serving dish. Drizzle with additional olive oil. Sprinkle with parsley and additional paprika.

2 TBSP.: 89 cal., 8g fat (1g sat. fat), 0 chol., 297mg sod., 5g carb. (2g sugars, 2g fiber), 1g pro.

FROM GRANDMA'S KITCHEN: Store baba ganoush in an airtight container in the refrigerator for up to 4 days. You might find it tastes even better after the flavors meld for a day or 2!

JAMAICAN BEEF PATTIES

My mom was born in Jamaica and lived there until she moved to the United States during her university years. I've loved this Jamaican beef patty recipe for most of my life. The savory flavor and spices are just right, and the pastry is flaky and delicious.

—*Natasha Watson, Douglasville, GA*

PREP: 35 MIN. • BAKE: 25 MIN. • MAKES: 8 SERVINGS

1 **lb. ground beef**
1 **medium onion, chopped**
1 **tsp. curry powder**
1 **tsp. dried thyme**
1 **tsp. pepper**
¾ **tsp. salt**

CRUST
2 **cups all-purpose flour**
1½ **tsp. curry powder**
  Dash salt
½ **cup cold butter**
⅓ **cup ice water**
1 **large egg, lightly beaten**

1. Preheat oven to 350°. In a large skillet, cook beef and onion over medium heat until beef is no longer pink and onion is tender, 6-8 minutes, breaking up beef into crumbles; drain. Stir in curry powder, thyme, pepper and salt; set aside. For crust, in a large bowl, whisk together flour, curry powder and salt. Cut in butter until mixture resembles coarse crumbs. Add ice water; stir just until moistened. Divide dough into 8 portions. On a lightly floured surface, roll each portion into a 6-in. circle. Place about ¼ cup filling on half of each circle. Fold crust over filling. Press edges with a fork to seal.

2. Transfer to parchment-lined baking sheets; brush with beaten egg. Bake until light brown, 22-25 minutes. Remove to wire racks. Serve warm.

FREEZE OPTION: Cover and freeze the unbaked pastries on a parchment-lined baking sheet until firm. Transfer to freezer containers; return to freezer. To use, bake pastries on a parchment-lined baking sheet in a preheated 350° oven until heated through, 25-30 minutes.

1 SERVING: 336 cal., 19g fat (10g sat. fat), 89mg chol., 373mg sod., 26g carb. (1g sugars, 2g fiber), 14g pro.

QUICK FRIED GREEN TOMATOES

My grandmother came up with her own version of fried green tomatoes years ago. Our family loves them! It's a traditional taste of the South that anyone anywhere can enjoy.

—*Melanie Chism, Coker, AL*

PREP: 10 MIN. + STANDING • **COOK:** 10 MIN. • **MAKES:** 8 SERVINGS

- **4 medium green tomatoes**
- **1 tsp. salt**
- **¼ tsp. lemon-pepper seasoning**
- **¾ cup cornmeal**
- **½ cup vegetable oil**

Slice the tomatoes ¼ in. thick. Sprinkle both sides with salt and lemon-pepper. Let stand 20-25 minutes. Coat with cornmeal. In a large skillet, heat the oil over medium heat. Fry the tomatoes until tender and golden brown, 3-4 minutes on each side. Drain on paper towels. Serve immediately.

2 PIECES: 166 cal., 11g fat (1g sat. fat), 0 chol., 317mg sod., 16g carb. (4g sugars, 2g fiber), 2g pro.

FROM GRANDMA'S KITCHEN: Make sure to blot the tomato slices with paper towels before salting and breading to get rid of excess moisture. This will help the cornmeal stick. You can also use panko bread crumbs if you don't have cornmeal. Just dip the tomato slices in buttermilk before coating them in the panko bread crumbs to help the crumbs adhere.

AUNT SHIRLEY'S LIVER PATE

While living in San Francisco, I created my liver pate to serve at get-togethers with friends.
Now my nieces and nephews request it for family gatherings, too.
—Shirley Brownell, Amsterdam, NY

PREP: 20 MIN. + CHILLING • MAKES: 18 SERVINGS (2¼ CUPS)

¾ cup butter, divided
1¼ lbs. chicken livers, halved
¼ cup chopped onion
2 tsp. Worcestershire sauce
1 Tbsp. minced fresh parsley
¼ cup sliced pimiento-stuffed olives
Additional parsley, optional
Crackers

1. In a large skillet, melt ½ cup butter. Add the chicken livers, onion, Worcestershire sauce and parsley. Saute over medium heat for 6-8 minutes or until chicken is no longer pink. Remove from the heat; cool for 10 minutes.

2. Transfer to a blender; process until smooth. Melt remaining butter; cool to lukewarm. Add to blender and process until blended.

3. Pour into a 2½-cup mold lined with plastic wrap. Cover and chill for 8 hours or overnight.

4. Before serving, unmold the pate onto a chilled plate. Press the olives into top of pate; garnish with parsley if desired. Serve with crackers.

2 TBSP.: 110 cal., 10g fat (5g sat. fat), 129mg chol., 130mg sod., 1g carb. (0 sugars, 0 fiber), 5g pro.

CRISPY CHICKEN WINGS APPETIZER

I'm a beginner at cooking, so if I can prepare these chicken wings, anybody can!
The recipe came from a co-worker at the hospital where I am a nurse's aide.
I make them for Christmas, picnics, parties—you name it.
—Nancy Lesky, La Crosse, WI

PREP: 15 MIN. • BAKE: 50 MIN. • MAKES: 20 APPETIZERS

2 lbs. chicken wings
½ cup butter, melted
¼ tsp. garlic powder
1 cup dry bread crumbs
½ cup grated Parmesan cheese
2 Tbsp. minced fresh parsley
½ tsp. salt
¼ tsp. pepper

1. Cut chicken wings into 3 sections; discard wing tip sections.

2. In a small shallow bowl, combine the butter and garlic powder. In another bowl, combine the remaining ingredients. Dip chicken into butter mixture, then into crumb mixture.

3. Place on greased baking sheet; bake at 350° for 50-60 minutes or until chicken juices run clear.

2 CHICKEN WINGS: 243 cal., 18g fat (8g sat. fat), 57mg chol., 407mg sod., 8g carb. (0 sugars, 0 fiber), 13g pro.

CHIPPED BEEF
CHEESE BALL

CHIPPED BEEF CHEESE BALL

A tradition at our Christmas and New Year's celebrations, this recipe is near and dear to our family. My mom made the delicious appetizer for more than 30 years.
—*Molly Sumner, Creve Coeur, MO*

PREP: 10 MIN. + CHILLING • **MAKES:** 2 CUPS

5 pkg. (2 oz. each) thinly sliced dried beef
12 oz. cream cheese, softened
⅓ cup finely chopped sweet onion
4 drops Worcestershire sauce
Ritz crackers and assorted fresh vegetables

1. Place the beef in a food processor; pulse until finely chopped. In a large bowl, beat cream cheese until smooth. Stir in ⅔ cup beef and the onion and Worcestershire sauce. Refrigerate, covered, at least 1 hour.

2. Place remaining beef in a small shallow bowl. Shape cheese mixture into a ball; roll in beef to coat evenly. Wrap; refrigerate at least 1 hour. Serve with crackers and vegetables.

1 TBSP.: 47 cal., 4g fat (2g sat. fat), 16mg chol., 136mg sod., 1g carb. (0 sugars, 0 fiber), 2g pro.

PIZZA PUFFS

PICTURED ON PAGE 34

What's more fun than a pizza puff? Skip the frozen kind sold in the store and try a homemade version. Feel free to substitute any meat or vegetable for the pepperoni and any cheese for the mozzarella.
—*Vivi Taylor, Middleburg, FL*

TAKES: 30 MIN. • **MAKES:** 20 SERVINGS

1 loaf (1 lb.) frozen pizza dough, thawed
20 slices pepperoni
8 oz. part-skim mozzarella cheese, cut into 20 cubes
¼ cup butter
2 small garlic cloves, minced
Dash salt
Marinara sauce, warmed
Optional: Crushed red pepper flakes and grated Parmesan cheese

1. Preheat oven to 400°. Shape dough into 1½-in. balls; flatten into ⅛-in.-thick circles. Place 1 pepperoni slice and 1 cheese cube in center of each circle; wrap dough around pepperoni and cheese. Pinch edges to seal; shape into a ball. Repeat with the remaining dough, cheese and pepperoni. Place seam side down on greased baking sheets; bake until light golden brown, 10-15 minutes. Cool slightly.

2. Meanwhile, in a small saucepan, melt the butter over low heat. Add the garlic and salt, taking care not to brown butter or garlic; brush over puffs. Serve with marinara sauce; if desired, sprinkle with red pepper flakes and Parmesan.

FREEZE OPTION: Cover and freeze the unbaked pizza puffs on waxed paper-lined baking sheets until firm. Transfer to an airtight freezer container; seal and return to freezer. To use, preheat oven to 400°; bake pizza puffs on greased baking sheets as directed, increasing time as necessary until golden brown.

1 PIZZA PUFF: 120 cal., 6g fat (3g sat. fat), 15mg chol., 189mg sod., 11g carb. (1g sugars, 0 fiber), 5g pro.

CREOLE SHRIMP & CRAB CHEESECAKE

We live on the beach and love to eat seafood. A stay-at-home mom, I also enjoy experimenting in the kitchen. I came up with this savory spread as a special appetizer.
—*Christy Hughes, Sunset Beach, NC*

PREP: 30 MIN. • **BAKE:** 1 HOUR + CHILLING • **MAKES:** 24 SERVINGS

¾ **cup dry bread crumbs**
¼ **cup grated**
 Parmesan cheese
½ **tsp. dill weed**
2 **Tbsp. butter, melted**

CHEESECAKE
2 **Tbsp. butter**
1 **medium sweet red**
 pepper, finely chopped
1 **small onion,**
 finely chopped
1 **medium carrot,**
 finely chopped
½ **tsp. dill weed**
½ **tsp. Creole seasoning**
¼ **tsp. salt**
¼ **tsp. pepper**
3 **pkg. (8 oz. each) cream**
 cheese, softened
½ **cup heavy whipping**
 cream
1 **Tbsp. sherry or**
 additional cream
4 **large eggs, lightly beaten**
1 **lb. peeled and deveined**
 cooked shrimp, chopped
2 **cans (6 oz. each) lump**
 crabmeat, drained
1 **cup shredded Gouda**
 cheese

SAUCE
1 **cup mayonnaise**
2 **Tbsp. Dijon mustard**
½ **tsp. Creole seasoning**
 Assorted crackers

1. Preheat oven to 350°. In a small bowl, mix the bread crumbs, Parmesan cheese and dill; stir in butter. Press onto the bottom of a greased 9-in. springform pan. Place pan on a baking sheet.

2. For the cheesecake, in a large skillet, heat the butter over medium-high heat. Add red pepper, onion and carrot; cook and stir until tender. Stir in seasonings. Cool slightly.

3. In a large bowl, beat cream cheese, cream and sherry until smooth. Add eggs; beat on low just until combined. Fold in the vegetable mixture, shrimp, crab and Gouda cheese. Pour over the crust.

4. Bake 60-65 minutes or until center is almost set. Cool on a wire rack 10 minutes. Loosen sides from pan with a knife. Cool 1 hour longer. Refrigerate overnight, covering when completely cooled.

5. In a small bowl, mix the mayonnaise, Dijon mustard and Creole seasoning. Remove rim from springform pan. Serve cheesecake with sauce and crackers.

1 SLICE: 283 cal., 24g fat (11g sat. fat), 137mg chol., 411mg sod., 5g carb. (1g sugars, 0 fiber), 12g pro.

FROM GRANDMA'S KITCHEN: To make your own Creole seasoning, combine 7½ tsp. paprika, 2 tsp. garlic powder, and 1 tsp. each of salt, pepper, onion powder, dried oregano, dried thyme and cayenne pepper. Store in an airtight container.

FIVE CHEESE BAKED FONDUTA

If melted cheese isn't one of the most mouth-watering foods ever, I don't know what is! This Italian fondue blends five different kinds for extra indulgence.
—*Cheri Gilmore, Festus, MO*

TAKES: 30 MIN. • MAKES: 3 CUPS

- 3 Tbsp. melted butter, divided
- 1 pkg. (8 oz.) cream cheese, softened
- 2 cups shredded part-skim mozzarella cheese
- 1 cup shredded fontina cheese
- 1 cup shredded cheddar cheese
- ½ cup grated Parmesan cheese
- 4 garlic cloves, thinly sliced
- 1 tsp. dried rosemary, crushed
- 1 tsp. dried thyme
- ½ tsp. pepper
  Optional: Toasted French bread baguette slices, baked pita chips or assorted fresh vegetables

Preheat oven to 450°. Brush an 8-in. cast-iron or other ovenproof skillet with 1 Tbsp. butter; set aside. In a large bowl, beat cream cheese and mozzarella, fontina, cheddar and Parmesan cheeses with garlic, rosemary, thyme, pepper and remaining 2 Tbsp. butter until combined. Spread into prepared skillet. Bake until bubbly and golden brown, 15-20 minutes. Serve with baguette slices, pita chips or vegetables.

¼ CUP: 237 cal., 20g fat (12g sat. fat), 61mg chol., 402mg sod., 4g carb. (1g sugars, 0 fiber), 11g pro.

SECRET-INGREDIENT STUFFED EGGS

My take on Mom's deviled egg recipe is full of surprises. I add an instant twist with mango chutney, goat cheese and chopped pecans.
—*Beth Satterfield, Dover, DE*

TAKES: 15 MIN. • MAKES: 1 DOZEN

- 6 hard-boiled large eggs
- 4 Tbsp. crumbled goat cheese, divided
- 3 Tbsp. finely chopped pecans, divided
- 3 Tbsp. mayonnaise
- 2 Tbsp. finely chopped celery
- 2 Tbsp. mango chutney
- ¼ tsp. salt
- ⅛ tsp. pepper

1. Cut eggs in half lengthwise. Remove yolks; set whites aside. In a small bowl, mash yolks. Add 3 Tbsp. goat cheese, 2 Tbsp. pecans, mayonnaise, celery, chutney, salt and pepper; mix well. Stuff into egg whites. Refrigerate until serving.

2. Just before serving, sprinkle with the remaining goat cheese and pecans.

1 STUFFED EGG HALF: 94 cal., 7g fat (2g sat. fat), 110mg chol., 140mg sod., 3g carb. (2g sugars, 0 fiber), 4g pro.

AIR-FRYER EGG ROLLS

My mom taught me how to prepare amazing egg rolls, and I think of her every time I make them. This air-fryer version tastes so good, you'll never want the fast-food kind again.
—*Jenniffer Love, South Waltham, MA*

PREP: 20 MIN. • COOK: 15 MIN./BATCH • MAKES: 18 SERVINGS

2 cups hot water
3 cups fresh bean sprouts
1 lb. ground chicken
6 green onions, chopped
1 Tbsp. minced fresh gingerroot
3 garlic cloves, minced
1 jar (11 oz.) Chinese-style barbecue sauce
1 Tbsp. fish sauce or soy sauce
1 tsp. soy sauce
1 pkg. (14 oz.) coleslaw mix
1 pkg. (10 oz.) frozen chopped spinach, thawed and squeezed dry
18 egg roll wrappers
   Cooking spray

1. Pour the hot water over bean sprouts in a small bowl; let stand 5 minutes. Drain.

2. Meanwhile, in a Dutch oven, cook chicken over medium heat until no longer pink, 6-8 minutes, breaking into crumbles. Add the green onions, ginger and garlic. Cook 1 minute longer; drain. Stir in ½ cup Chinese-style sauce, fish sauce and soy sauce; transfer to a large bowl. Wipe pan clean.

3. In the same pan, cook and stir the coleslaw mix, spinach and drained bean sprouts until crisp-tender, 4-5 minutes. Stir into chicken mixture. Cool slightly.

4. Preheat air fryer to 400°. With a corner of an egg roll wrapper facing you, place ⅓ cup filling just below center of wrapper. (Cover remaining wrappers with a damp paper towel until ready to use.) Fold the bottom corner over filling; moisten remaining wrapper edges with water. Fold the side corners toward center over filling. Roll egg roll up tightly, pressing at tip to seal. Repeat.

5. In batches, arrange the egg rolls in a single layer in greased air-fryer basket; spritz with cooking spray. Cook until golden brown, 8-12 minutes. Turn; spritz with additional cooking spray. Cook until golden brown, 4-6 minutes longer. Serve with the remaining Chinese-style sauce.

NOTE: This recipe was tested with Ah-So brand Chinese-style barbecue sauce.

1 EGG ROLL: 187 cal., 3g fat (1g sat. fat), 20mg chol., 388mg sod., 33g carb. (7g sugars, 2g fiber), 9g pro.

GRANDMA'S SECRET
Swap in ground pork for the chicken, and get creative with your vegetables. Mushrooms, bok choy, carrots or water chestnuts are all fantastic additions.

LAYERED MEDITERRANEAN DIP WITH PITA CHIPS

Looking for a change of pace from your usual layered dip? The bold combination of hummus and Greek yogurt is guaranteed to please at your next party or gathering.

—Elizabeth Dumont, Madison, MS

PREP: 15 MIN. + CHILLING • BAKE: 10 MIN. • MAKES: 5 CUPS (120 CHIPS)

- 1 cup plain Greek yogurt
- 1 medium seedless cucumber, chopped
- 1 tsp. white wine vinegar
- 2 tsp. minced fresh mint or 1 tsp. dried mint
- 1 carton (10 oz.) hummus
- 1 medium red onion, chopped
- 1 cup chopped roasted sweet red peppers, drained
- 2 pkg. (4 oz. each) crumbled feta cheese
- ½ cup pitted Greek olives, sliced
- 2 plum tomatoes, chopped
  Optional: Minced fresh parsley and additional minced fresh mint

PITA CHIPS

- 20 pita pocket halves
- ¼ cup olive oil
- ½ tsp. salt
- ¼ tsp. pepper

1. Line a strainer with 4 layers of cheesecloth or 1 coffee filter and place over a bowl. Place yogurt in prepared strainer and cover with the edges of cheesecloth. Refrigerate for 8 hours or overnight. In a small bowl, combine the strained yogurt, cucumber, vinegar and mint.

2. Spread hummus in the bottom of a 9-in. deep dish pie plate. Layer with onion, peppers, feta cheese, olives, tomatoes and yogurt mixture. Top with parsley and additional mint if desired. Chill until serving.

3. Cut each pita half into 3 wedges; separate each wedge into 2 pieces. Place in a single layer on ungreased baking sheets. Brush both sides with olive oil; sprinkle with salt and pepper.

4. Bake at 400° for 8-10 minutes or until crisp, turning once. Serve with dip.

¼ CUP DIP WITH 6 CHIPS: 178 cal., 8g fat (2g sat. fat), 8mg chol., 478mg sod., 20g carb. (2g sugars, 2g fiber), 6g pro.

TOMATO FRITTERS

Eating these golden brown bites right after they've been fried, when they're still hot and crispy, is one of our favorite summertime treats. I received the basic recipe from a friend, then tweaked it to suit my family.
—*Pam Halter, Bridgeton, NJ*

PREP: 15 MIN. • **COOK:** 5 MIN./BATCH • **MAKES:** ABOUT 2½ DOZEN

1 cup all-purpose flour
1 tsp. baking powder
½ tsp. salt
   Dash dried basil
   Dash dried oregano
   Dash pepper
1 large tomato,
   finely chopped
½ cup chopped onion
½ cup shredded
   Parmesan cheese
1 jalapeno pepper, seeded
   and finely chopped
1 garlic clove, minced
1 to 6 Tbsp. water, optional
   Oil for deep-fat frying

1. In a large bowl, whisk the flour, baking powder, salt, basil, oregano and pepper. Gently stir in the tomato, onion, cheese, jalapeno and garlic just until moistened. If the batter seems thick, add water 1 Tbsp. at a time to thin it slightly until it loosens up and mixes easily.

2. In a cast-iron or other heavy skillet, heat oil to 375°. Drop batter by rounded tablespoonfuls, a few at a time, into hot oil. Fry until golden brown, about 1½ minutes per side. Drain on paper towels.

1 FRITTER: 40 cal., 2g fat (0 sat. fat), 1mg chol., 79mg sod., 4g carb. (0 sugars, 0 fiber), 1g pro.

"Made these to accompany low country boil for our July 4th cookout. They were simple and quick to make. I actually followed the recipe (something I rarely do), and they turned out great. We had 20 people and everyone loved them. They were gone before the meal. I look forward to making them again."
—TRACEYCRIGGER, TASTEOFHOME.COM

HAM PICKLE PINWHEELS

My mom introduced me to these tasty little pinwheels, and I've been making them ever since. They're so easy to prepare and always go over well with guests.
—*Gloria Jarrett, Loveland, OH*

PREP: 15 MIN. + CHILLING • **MAKES:** 3½ DOZEN

1 pkg. (8 oz.) cream cheese,
   cubed
¼ lb. sliced Genoa salami
1 Tbsp. prepared
   horseradish
7 slices deli ham
14 to 21 okra pickles or
   7 dill pickle spears

1. In a food processor, add the cream cheese, salami and horseradish; cover and process until blended. Spread over ham slices.

2. Remove stems and ends of okra pickles. Place 2 or 3 okra pickles or 1 dill pickle down the center of each ham slice. Roll up tightly and cover. Refrigerate for at least 2 hours. Cut into 1-in. pieces.

1 PIECE: 34 cal., 3g fat (1g sat. fat), 9mg chol., 105mg sod., 1g carb. (0 sugars, 0 fiber), 2g pro.

FOCACCIA
BARESE

FOCACCIA BARESE

My mom's family has passed down this homemade focaccia recipe for generations. It's an appetizer I've become known for at parties. In fact, I'm not allowed to attend unless I bring it!
—Dora Travaglio, Mount Prospect, IL

PREP: 30 MIN. + RISING • BAKE: 30 MIN. • MAKES: 8 SERVINGS

1⅛ tsp. active dry yeast
¾ cup warm water (110° to 115°), divided
½ tsp. sugar
⅓ cup mashed potato flakes
1½ tsp. plus 2 Tbsp. olive oil, divided
¼ tsp. salt
1¾ cups bread flour

TOPPING
2 medium tomatoes, thinly sliced
¼ cup pitted Greek olives, halved
1½ tsp. minced fresh or dried oregano
½ tsp. coarse salt

1. In a large bowl, dissolve yeast in ½ cup warm water. Add sugar; let stand for 5 minutes. Add potato flakes, 1½ tsp. oil, salt, 1 cup flour and remaining ¼ cup water. Beat until smooth. Stir in enough remaining flour to form a soft dough.

2. Turn onto a floured surface; knead until smooth and elastic, 6-8 minutes. Place in a greased bowl, turning once to grease the top. Cover and let rise in a warm place until doubled, about 1 hour. Punch dough down. Cover and let rest for 10 minutes.

3. Place 1 Tbsp. olive oil in a 10-in. cast-iron or other ovenproof skillet; tilt pan to evenly coat. Add dough; shape to fit pan. Cover and let rise until doubled, about 30 minutes.

4. With fingertips, make several dimples over the top of dough. Brush with remaining 1 Tbsp. oil. Blot tomato slices with paper towels. Arrange tomato slices and olives over dough; sprinkle with oregano and salt.

5. Bake at 375° for 30-35 minutes or until golden brown.

1 PIECE: 142 cal., 4g fat (1g sat. fat), 0 chol., 269mg sod., 24g carb. (1g sugars, 1g fiber), 4g pro.

PICKLED EGGS WITH BEETS & HOT CHERRY PEPPERS

I wanted to duplicate my grandmother's pickled eggs, but she never measured when she cooked. So, I had to guess. These were the result! The longer they marinate, the more intense the color becomes.
—Judie Thurstenson, Colcord, OK

PREP: 15 MIN. + CHILLING • MAKES: 12 SERVINGS

1 can (15 oz.) whole beets, undrained
4 cups cider vinegar
12 hard-boiled large eggs
8 pickled hot cherry peppers
6 pearl onions
2 garlic cloves, sliced
½ tsp. salt

Drain beets, reserving ½ cup juice. Place in a large glass bowl; add the remaining ingredients. Cover and refrigerate overnight.

1 SERVING: 100 cal., 6g fat (2g sat. fat), 212mg chol., 297mg sod., 5g carb. (3g sugars, 1g fiber), 7g pro.

SOUR CREAM CUT-OUT
BISCUITS, PAGE 97

GRANDMA'S FAVORITE

BREADS, BISCUITS & MORE

Golden brown rolls, melt-in-your-mouth muffins,
braided loaves—the fresh-baked goods that came from
Grandma's oven were simply the best. See for yourself!

BRAIDED ROUND CHALLAH

On a Jewish holiday, I surprised one of my friends with a fresh-baked loaf
of traditional challah. She was thrilled at how it turned out!

—*Angela Mathews, Fayetteville, NY*

PREP: 45 MIN. + RISING • **BAKE:** 25 MIN. • **MAKES:** 1 LOAF (20 PIECES)

1 **pkg. (¼ oz.) active
dry yeast**
1 **cup warm 2% milk
(110° to 115°)**
¼ **cup honey**
¼ **cup butter, melted**
2 **large eggs, room
temperature**
1½ **tsp. salt**
3¾ **to 4¼ cups all-purpose
flour**

EGG WASH
1 **large egg**
1 **tsp. cold water**

1. In a small bowl, dissolve yeast in warm milk. In a large bowl,
combine honey, butter, eggs, salt, yeast mixture and 2 cups flour;
beat on medium speed until smooth. Stir in enough remaining
flour to form a soft dough (dough will be sticky).

2. Turn the dough onto a floured surface; knead until smooth
and elastic, 6-8 minutes. Place in a greased bowl, turning once
to grease the top. Cover and let rise in a warm place until doubled,
about 1 hour.

3. Punch down dough. Turn onto a lightly floured surface; divide
into thirds. Roll each portion into an 18-in. rope. Place the ropes
on a greased baking sheet and braid. Starting at 1 end of braid,
loosely wrap dough around itself to form a coil. Tuck ends under;
pinch to seal. Cover with a kitchen towel and let rise in a warm
place until doubled, about 45 minutes. Meanwhile, preheat oven
to 350°.

4. For egg wash, whisk the egg with cold water; brush over loaf.
Bake until golden brown, 25-30 minutes. Remove from the pan
to a wire rack to cool.

1 PIECE: 135 cal., 3g fat (2g sat. fat), 30mg chol., 211mg sod.,
22g carb. (4g sugars, 1g fiber), 4g pro.

CARROT HONEY LOAF

As a busy mom and health-care professional, I love finding time
in the kitchen to make special gifts. Here's one I often share
for events like a housewarming or welcoming a new baby.
—*Krystal Horudko, Charlottetown, PE*

PREP: 20 MIN. • **BAKE:** 1 HOUR • **MAKES:** 1 LOAF (16 PIECES)

2 **large eggs, room**
  temperature
¾ **cup canola oil**
¾ **cup honey**
2 **tsp. vanilla extract**
1 **cup all-purpose flour**
1 **cup whole wheat flour**

2 **tsp. baking powder**
2 **tsp. ground cinnamon**
1 **tsp. ground nutmeg**
½ **tsp. salt**
¼ **tsp. baking soda**
2 **cups grated carrots**
  (about 3 large carrots)

1. Preheat oven to 350°. Combine the eggs, oil, honey and vanilla;
beat until smooth. In another bowl, whisk the next 7 ingredients
for 30 seconds. Stir flour mixture into egg mixture just until
combined. Add carrots; mix well.

2. Pour batter into a lightly greased 9x5-in. loaf pan; bake until
a toothpick inserted in center of loaf comes out clean, about
1 hour. Cool 10 minutes before removing to a wire rack.

1 PIECE: 212 cal., 11g fat (1g sat. fat), 23mg chol., 173mg sod.,
26g carb. (14g sugars, 2g fiber), 3g pro.

SPICED PEAR BREAD

My mother and I put up our own pears, so I always have plenty on hand when I find
myself craving these mini loaves. They're incredibly moist and delicious!
—*Rachel Barefoot, Linden, MI*

PREP: 15 MIN. • **BAKE:** 50 MIN. + COOLING • **MAKES:** 4 MINI LOAVES (6 PIECES EACH)

3¼ **cups all-purpose flour**
1 **cup sugar**
3 **tsp. ground cinnamon**
1 **tsp. baking soda**
1 **tsp. baking powder**
1 **tsp. ground cloves**
½ **tsp. salt**
3 **large eggs, room**
  temperature
3 **cans (15¼ oz. each)**
  sliced pears, drained
  and mashed
¼ **cup unsweetened**
  applesauce
¼ **cup canola oil**

1. In a large bowl, combine the first 7 ingredients. In a small
bowl, whisk eggs, pears, applesauce and oil. Stir into the dry
ingredients just until moistened.

2. Pour into four 5¾x3x2-in. loaf pans coated with cooking spray.
Bake at 350° for 50-60 minutes or until a toothpick inserted in the
center comes out clean. Cool for 10 minutes before removing
from pans to wire racks.

1 PIECE: 160 cal., 3g fat (0 sat. fat), 27mg chol., 131mg sod.,
30g carb. (17g sugars, 1g fiber), 3g pro. **DIABETIC EXCHANGES:**
2 starch, ½ fat.

FREEZER CRESCENT ROLLS

I'm so glad my aunt gave me the recipe for this freezer-friendly dough. It's really convenient to have homemade rolls ready to bake any time I want, especially during the holidays.
—*Kristine Buck, Payson, UT*

PREP: 30 MIN. + FREEZING • **BAKE:** 15 MIN. • **MAKES:** 32 ROLLS

2 pkg. (¼ oz. each)
active dry yeast
2 cups warm water
(110° to 115°)
½ cup butter, softened
⅔ cup nonfat dry
milk powder
½ cup sugar
½ cup mashed potato flakes
2 large eggs, room
temperature
1½ tsp. salt
6 to 6½ cups all-purpose
flour

1. In a large bowl, dissolve yeast in warm water. Add butter, milk powder, sugar, potato flakes, eggs, salt and 3 cups flour; beat until smooth. Stir in enough remaining flour to form a soft dough.

2. Turn the dough onto a well-floured surface; knead until smooth and elastic, 6-8 minutes. Place in a greased bowl, turning once to grease the top. Cover; let rise in a warm place until doubled, about 1 hour.

3. Punch down the dough. Turn onto a lightly floured surface; divide in half. Roll each portion into a 12-in. circle; cut each into 16 wedges. Roll up wedges from the wide ends. Place on waxed paper-lined baking sheets, point side down; curve to form crescents. Freeze until firm. Transfer to airtight freezer containers; freeze up to 4 weeks.

4. To use frozen rolls: Arrange frozen rolls 2 in. apart on greased baking sheets. Cover with lightly greased waxed paper; thaw in the refrigerator overnight. To bake, preheat oven to 350°. Let rolls rise in a warm place until doubled, about 1 hour. Bake until golden brown, 15-17 minutes. Serve warm.

1 ROLL: 137 cal., 3g fat (2g sat. fat), 20mg chol., 147mg sod., 23g carb. (4g sugars, 1g fiber), 4g pro.

TO BAKE ROLLS WITHOUT FREEZING: Prepare and shape rolls as directed; arrange 2 in. apart on greased baking sheets. Cover and let rise in a warm place until doubled, about 45 minutes. Preheat oven to 350°. Bake until golden brown, 15-17 minutes.

STRAWBERRY MUFFINS

STRAWBERRY MUFFINS

I stir plenty of strawberry jam into the batter for these sweet, luscious bites before popping them into the oven. They have a feathery texture and are wonderful warm or cold.
—Marion Kirst, Troy, MI

TAKES: 30 MIN. • **MAKES:** 1½ DOZEN

- 2 cups all-purpose flour
- 1 cup sugar
- 1 tsp. baking soda
- 1 tsp. ground cinnamon
- 1 tsp. ground nutmeg
- ½ tsp. salt
- 2 large eggs, room temperature
- ½ cup canola oil
- ½ cup buttermilk
- ½ cup strawberry jam

1. Preheat oven to 375°. In a large bowl, whisk flour, sugar, baking soda, cinnamon, nutmeg and salt. In another bowl, whisk eggs, oil and buttermilk until blended. Add to flour mixture; stir just until moistened. Gently fold in jam.

2. Fill well-greased or paper-lined muffin cups three-fourths full. Bake until a toothpick inserted in the center of a muffin comes out clean, 18-20 minutes. Cool 5 minutes before removing from pans to wire racks.

1 MUFFIN: 181 cal., 7g fat (1g sat. fat), 24mg chol., 150mg sod., 28g carb. (17g sugars, 0 fiber), 2g pro.

LOUISIANA PECAN BACON BREAD

One Christmas, the babysitter arrived at our house with holiday gifts and a basket of goodies, including a scrumptious pecan bread. Whenever I make that recipe now, I remember her kindness.
—Marina Castle-Kelley, Canyon Country, CA

PREP: 20 MIN. • **BAKE:** 50 MIN. + COOLING • **MAKES:** 1 LOAF (16 PIECES)

- 6 bacon strips, chopped
- 6 oz. cream cheese, softened
- ⅓ cup sugar
- 1 large egg, room temperature
- 2 cups all-purpose flour
- 2½ tsp. baking powder
- ½ tsp. salt
- ¾ cup 2% milk
- 1 cup chopped pecans
- ¼ cup finely chopped onion
- ¼ cup chopped green pepper

1. Preheat oven to 350°. In a large skillet, cook the bacon over medium-low heat until crisp, stirring occasionally. Remove with a slotted spoon; drain on paper towels. Reserve 2 Tbsp. drippings; cool slightly.

2. In a large bowl, beat the cream cheese, sugar and reserved drippings until smooth. Beat in egg. In another bowl, whisk flour, baking powder and salt; add to cream cheese mixture alternately with milk, beating well after each addition. Fold in pecans, onion, pepper and bacon. Transfer to a greased 9x5-in. loaf pan.

3. Bake until a toothpick inserted in the center comes out clean, 50-60 minutes. Cool in pan 10 minutes before removing to a wire rack to cool.

FREEZE OPTION: Securely wrap cooled loaves and freeze. To use, thaw in the refrigerator.

1 PIECE: 198 cal., 12g fat (4g sat. fat), 29mg chol., 242mg sod., 18g carb. (6g sugars, 1g fiber), 5g pro.

WILD RICE BREAD WITH SUNFLOWER SEEDS

Every chance I got when I was a kid, I skipped eating in our school cafeteria and went to my grandma's house for lunch. The ingredients in this hearty loaf reflect northeastern Minnesota, where she spent most of her life.

—Crystal Schlueter, Northglenn, CO

PREP: 35 MIN. + RISING • **BAKE:** 35 MIN. • **MAKES:** 2 LOAVES (16 PIECES EACH)

2 pkg. (¼ oz. each) active dry yeast
1 cup warm water (110° to 115°)
1 pkg. (8.8 oz.) ready-to-serve long grain and wild rice
1 cup plus 1 Tbsp. unsalted sunflower kernels, divided
1 cup warm fat-free milk (110° to 115°)
⅓ cup honey or molasses
¼ cup butter, softened
2 Tbsp. ground flaxseed
2 tsp. salt
3 cups whole wheat flour
2¾ to 3¼ cups all-purpose flour
1 large egg white, lightly beaten
1 Tbsp. toasted wheat germ, optional

1. In a small bowl, dissolve the yeast in the warm water. In a large bowl, combine the rice, 1 cup sunflower kernels, milk, honey, butter, flaxseed, salt, yeast mixture, whole wheat flour and 1 cup all-purpose flour; beat on medium speed until combined. Stir in enough remaining flour to form a stiff dough (the dough will be sticky).

2. Turn the dough onto a floured surface; knead until elastic, 6-8 minutes. Place in a greased bowl, turning once to grease the top. Cover and let rise in a warm place until doubled, about 1¼ hours.

3. Punch down dough. Turn onto a lightly floured surface; divide in half. Roll each half into a 12x8-in. rectangle. Roll up jelly-roll style, starting with a short side; pinch the seam and ends to seal. Place each in a 9x5-in. loaf pan coated with cooking spray, seam side down.

4. Cover with kitchen towels; let rise in a warm place until almost doubled, about 45 minutes. Preheat oven to 375°.

5. Brush the loaves with egg white; sprinkle with the remaining sunflower kernels and, if desired, toasted wheat germ. Bake 35-45 minutes or until dark golden brown. Cool in pans 5 minutes. Remove to a wire rack to cool.

1 PIECE: 142 cal., 4g fat (1g sat. fat), 4mg chol., 205mg sod., 23g carb. (4g sugars, 2g fiber), 4g pro. **DIABETIC EXCHANGES:** 1½ starch, ½ fat.

"Loved this earthy, crunchy bread! I cut the recipe in half to make 1 loaf. Came out fine. Rose nicely in a warm oven. Delicious with butter."
—GUEST682, TASTEOFHOME.COM

GRANDMA'S YEAST ROLLS

My grandmother used to bake her homemade rolls for family get-togethers and holidays. The applesauce may be unexpected, but it adds so much flavor.
—Nancy Spoth, Festus, MO

PREP: 20 MIN. + RISING • BAKE: 15 MIN. • MAKES: 2 DOZEN

- 1 pkg. (¼ oz.) active dry yeast
- 1 cup 2% milk (110° to 115°)
- ¼ cup sugar
- ¼ cup unsweetened applesauce
- 2 large egg whites, room temperature, beaten
- 1 tsp. salt
- 3½ to 4 cups all-purpose flour

1. In a large bowl, dissolve the yeast in warm milk. Add the sugar, applesauce, egg whites, salt and 2 cups flour; beat until smooth. Stir in enough remaining flour to form a soft dough.

2. Turn onto a lightly floured surface; knead until smooth and elastic, 6-8 minutes (dough will be slightly sticky). Place in a bowl coated with cooking spray, turning once to coat top. Cover and let rise in a warm place until doubled, about 1 hour.

3. Turn dough onto a lightly floured surface; divide into 24 pieces. Shape each portion into an 8-in. rope; tie into a knot. Place on 2 baking sheets coated with cooking spray.

4. Cover and let rise until doubled, about 30 minutes. Bake at 375° until golden brown, 12-16 minutes. Remove from the pans to wire racks to cool.

1 ROLL: 83 cal., 1g fat (1g sat. fat), 1mg chol., 109mg sod., 17g carb. (0 sugars, 1g fiber), 3g pro. **DIABETIC EXCHANGES:** 1 starch.

SAVORY STUFFING BREAD

Poultry seasoning and celery salt make this hearty loaf taste like stuffing. Serve slices with your holiday turkey, then make sandwiches the next day with the leftovers.

—Elizabeth King, Duluth, MN

PREP: 30 MIN. + RISING • **BAKE:** 20 MIN. + COOLING • **MAKES:** 2 LOAVES (16 PIECES EACH)

2 Tbsp. sugar
2 pkg. (¼ oz. each)
    active dry yeast
1½ tsp. poultry seasoning
½ tsp. salt
½ tsp. celery salt
½ tsp. pepper
5½ to 6 cups all-purpose
    flour
¼ cup butter, cubed
1 small onion,
    finely chopped
1 can (14½ oz.) chicken
    broth
2 large eggs, room
    temperature

1. In a large bowl, mix sugar, yeast, seasonings and 2 cups flour. In a small saucepan, heat butter over medium-high heat. Add onion; cook and stir 2-3 minutes or until tender. Stir in chicken broth; heat to 120°-130°. Add to dry ingredients; beat on medium speed 2 minutes. Add eggs; beat on high 2 minutes. Stir in enough remaining flour to form a soft dough (dough will be sticky).

2. Turn the dough onto a well-floured surface; knead until smooth and elastic, 6-8 minutes. Place in a greased bowl, turning once to grease the top. Cover and let rise in a warm place until doubled, about 1 hour.

3. Punch down dough. Turn onto a lightly floured surface; divide in half. Shape into 2 loaves. Place in 2 greased 9x5-in. loaf pans, seam side down.

4. Cover with kitchen towels; let rise in a warm place until doubled, about 30 minutes.

5. Preheat oven to 375°. Bake 18-22 minutes or until golden brown. Remove from pans to wire racks to cool completely.

1 PIECE: 102 cal., 2g fat (1g sat. fat), 16mg chol., 127mg sod., 18g carb. (1g sugars, 1g fiber), 3g pro.

GRANDMA'S SECRET

Steam can help produce standout breads. Place a cast iron skillet in the oven on a lower rack and fill with boiling water; preheat the oven and bake the bread according to directions.

EASY CAST-IRON PEACH BISCUIT ROLLS

I used to stop at the local coffee shop to enjoy one of their fresh peach cinnamon rolls. Now I'm a busy mom and don't have the time, so I re-create them at home with my own easy version.
—*Heather Karow, Burnett, WI*

PREP: 25 MIN. • **BAKE:** 25 MIN. + COOLING • **MAKES:** 1 DOZEN

1 cup packed brown sugar
¼ cup butter, softened
3 tsp. ground cinnamon

DOUGH
2 cups all-purpose flour
2 Tbsp. sugar
1 Tbsp. baking powder
1 tsp. salt
3 Tbsp. butter
¾ cup 2% milk
1 can (15 oz.) sliced peaches in juice, undrained
1 cup confectioners' sugar

1. Preheat oven to 350°. In a small bowl, mix brown sugar, butter and cinnamon until crumbly. Reserve half for topping. Sprinkle the remaining crumb mixture onto bottom of a 10-in. cast-iron or other ovenproof skillet.

2. For dough, in a large bowl, mix flour, sugar, baking powder and salt. Cut in butter until crumbly. Add milk; stir to form a soft dough (dough will be sticky). Roll into an 18x12-in. rectangle. Sprinkle reserved topping to within ½ in. of edges.

3. Drain peaches, reserving 2 Tbsp. juice for glaze. Chop peaches; place over the topping. Roll up jelly-roll style, starting with a long side; pinch the seam to seal. Cut into 12 slices. Place in prepared skillet, cut side down.

4. Bake until lightly browned, 25-30 minutes. Cool on a wire rack 10 minutes. For the glaze, combine the confectioners' sugar and 1-2 Tbsp. reserved peach juice to reach desired consistency. Drizzle over warm rolls.

1 ROLL: 279 cal., 7g fat (4g sat. fat), 19mg chol., 746mg sod., 52g carb. (35g sugars, 1g fiber), 3g pro.

SWEDISH CARDAMOM BRAIDS

Swedish people love their coffee—especially with a traditional coffee cake like this one!
The recipe came from my father's aunt, and I remember my mom crushing cardamom
seeds to make it. Back then, you couldn't buy cardamom already ground.
—*Harriet Meola, Mauldin, SC*

PREP: 45 MIN. + RISING • BAKE: 20 MIN. + COOLING • MAKES: 2 LOAVES (12 PIECES EACH)

1 pkg. (¼ oz.) active
  dry yeast
¼ cup warm water
  (110° to 115°)
1¼ cups warm 2% milk
  (110° to 115°)
½ cup butter, softened
⅓ cup sugar
3 large egg yolks
2½ tsp. ground cardamom
⅛ tsp. salt
5 to 5½ cups all-purpose
  flour

TOPPING
2 Tbsp. butter, melted
¼ cup chopped pecans
2 Tbsp. sugar
2 tsp. ground cinnamon

1. In a large bowl, dissolve yeast in warm water. Add the milk, butter, sugar, egg yolks, cardamom, salt and 3 cups flour. Beat until smooth. Stir in enough remaining flour to form a soft dough.

2. Turn dough onto a floured surface; knead until smooth and elastic, 6-8 minutes. Place in a greased bowl, turning once to grease top. Cover and let rise in a warm place until doubled, about 1 hour.

3. Punch dough down; divide in half. Divide each half into 3 portions. On a lightly floured surface, shape each portion into a 16-in.-long rope. Place 3 ropes on a greased baking sheet and braid; pinch ends to seal and tuck under. Repeat with remaining dough. Cover and let rise until doubled, about 45 minutes.

4. Bake at 375° for 20-25 minutes or until golden brown. Remove from pans to wire racks. Brush warm loaves with butter. Combine the pecans, sugar and cinnamon; sprinkle over loaves.

1 PIECE: 175 cal., 7g fat (3g sat. fat), 39mg chol., 54mg sod., 25g carb. (5g sugars, 1g fiber), 4g pro.

"I made this for my husband's Swedish grandmother and she loved it. It is not supposed to be overly sweet (that's the American expectation). The topping adds enough sweetness for me. Spicy, fluffy, light and fabulous! I would make this every week if I could."
—BEKAHGRRL1, TASTEOFHOME.COM

CORN BREAD
WITH A KICK

CORN BREAD WITH A KICK

To me, nothing says down-home southern cooking like crisp corn bread made
in a cast-iron skillet. I use a very old one that belonged to my great-aunt.
—*Geordyth Sullivan, Cutler Bay, FL*

PREP: 20 MIN. • BAKE: 20 MIN. • MAKES: 8 SERVINGS

⅔ cup all-purpose flour
⅔ cup cornmeal
1 Tbsp. sugar
½ tsp. baking powder
½ tsp. salt
¼ tsp. baking soda
1 large egg, room temperature
1 cup buttermilk
3 Tbsp. butter
3 chipotle peppers in adobo sauce, drained and chopped
6 bacon strips, cooked and crumbled

1. In a large bowl, combine the first 6 ingredients. In another bowl, whisk egg and buttermilk.

2. Place the butter in an 8-in. cast-iron or other ovenproof skillet; heat skillet in a 425° oven until the butter is melted, 3-5 minutes. Meanwhile, stir the egg mixture into the dry ingredients just until moistened. Fold in peppers and bacon.

3. Carefully swirl the butter in the skillet to coat the sides and bottom of pan; add batter. Bake at 425° until a toothpick inserted in the center comes out clean, 18-22 minutes. Cut into wedges; serve warm.

1 PIECE: 174 cal., 8g fat (4g sat. fat), 44mg chol., 431mg sod., 21g carb. (4g sugars, 1g fiber), 6g pro.

GLUTEN-FREE BANANA NUT MUFFINS

I baked these gluten-free muffins to take along on our trip to see Grandma. We liked them
so much that I whipped up another batch when we returned home so we could have
a grab-and-go breakfast during the week. Packed with banana-walnut
flavor, they're a satisfying treat for the whole family.
—*Gingerlemongirl, tasteofhome.com*

PREP: 20 MIN. • BAKE: 20 MIN. • MAKES: 1 DOZEN

1½ cups mashed ripe bananas (2 to 3 medium)
⅔ cup sugar
2 large eggs, room temperature
¼ cup fat-free plain yogurt
2 Tbsp. plus 1½ tsp. canola oil
1 tsp. vanilla extract
½ cup millet flour
½ cup sorghum flour
½ cup tapioca flour
1 Tbsp. ground flaxseed
2 tsp. baking powder
½ tsp. baking soda
¼ tsp. xanthan gum
⅓ cup chopped walnuts

1. In a large bowl, beat the first 6 ingredients until well blended. In a large bowl, combine the flours, flax, baking powder, baking soda and xanthan gum; gradually beat into banana mixture until blended. Stir in walnuts.

2. Coat muffin cups with cooking spray or use paper liners; fill three-fourths full with batter. Bake at 350° for 18-22 minutes or until a toothpick inserted in the center comes out clean.

3. Cool for 5 minutes before removing from pan to a wire rack.

1 MUFFIN: 191 cal., 6g fat (1g sat. fat), 35mg chol., 135mg sod., 32g carb. (15g sugars, 2g fiber), 4g pro.

BLUE-RIBBON DOUGHNUTS

I prepared these goodies so many times for our eight children. Now they're grown and no longer living at home, but I'm still making doughnuts—they've become a favorite with my 16 grandchildren! The kids love to help by cutting the shapes in the dough.

—Kay McEwen, Sussex, NB

PREP: 30 MIN. + CHILLING • **COOK:** 5 MIN./BATCH • **MAKES:** 3 DOZEN

3 **large eggs, room temperature**
2 **cups sugar**
1 **cup heavy whipping cream**
1 **cup whole milk**
1 **tsp. vanilla extract**
6 **to 7 cups all-purpose flour**
4 **tsp. cream of tartar**
2 **tsp. baking soda**
1 **tsp. salt**
1 **tsp. ground nutmeg**
   Oil for deep-fat frying

1. In a large bowl, beat eggs for 5 minutes. Gradually add sugar; beat 1-2 minutes longer (mixture will be thick and light in color). Add the cream, milk, vanilla, 2 cups flour, cream of tartar, baking soda, salt and nutmeg; beat until smooth. Add enough remaining flour to form a soft dough.

2. Turn onto a floured surface; knead until smooth, 8-10 minutes. Place in a greased bowl, turning once to grease top. Cover and refrigerate for 2-3 hours.

3. On a floured surface, roll dough to ½-in. thickness. Cut with a lightly floured 2½-in. doughnut cutter.

4. In an electric skillet or deep-fat fryer, heat oil to 375°. Fry doughnuts, a few at a time, until browned, about 2 minutes on each side. Drain on paper towels.

1 DOUGHNUT: 197 cal., 8g fat (2g sat. fat), 27mg chol., 147mg sod., 28g carb. (12g sugars, 1g fiber), 3g pro.

GLAZED DOUGHNUTS: Combine 2 cups sifted confectioners' sugar and 3-4 Tbsp. milk, lemon juice or orange juice. Dip cooled doughnuts in glaze.

SUGARED DOUGHNUTS: Roll warm doughnuts in sugar or cinnamon-sugar.

ALMOND TEA BREAD

My aunt brought her tea bread recipe with her from Scotland.
Enjoying a fresh-baked, cherry-filled loaf has become
a family tradition during the holiday season.
—*Kathleen Showers, Briggsdale, CO*

PREP: 15 MIN. • BAKE: 1¼ HOURS + COOLING
MAKES: 2 LOAVES (16 PIECES EACH)

1 can (8 oz.) almond paste
¼ cup butter, softened
1 cup sugar
3 large eggs,
    room temperature
1½ cups fresh pitted cherries
    or blueberries

3 cups all-purpose flour,
    divided
4 tsp. baking powder
½ tsp. salt
¾ cup whole milk

1. In a large bowl, combine almond paste and butter; beat until
well blended. Gradually add sugar, beating until light and fluffy,
5-7 minutes. Add the eggs, 1 at a time, beating well after each
addition. In a small bowl, gently toss cherries and 1 Tbsp. flour.
Set aside.

2. Combine the baking powder, salt and remaining flour; add to
the creamed mixture alternately with the milk, beating well after
each addition.

3. Spoon a sixth of the batter into each of 2 greased and floured
8x4-in. loaf pans; sprinkle layers with half of the fruit. Cover with
another layer of batter and sprinkle with remaining fruit. Top with
remaining batter; smooth with spatula.

4. Bake at 350° until a toothpick inserted in the center comes out
clean, about 1¼ hours. Cool for 10 minutes before removing from
pans to wire racks to cool.

1 PIECE: 130 cal., 4g fat (1g sat. fat), 25mg chol., 111mg sod.,
21g carb. (10g sugars, 1g fiber), 3g pro.

GRANDMA NARDI'S ITALIAN EASTER BREAD

With dyed eggs nestled inside, my grandma's bread is a special part of our Easter celebration.
I fondly remember her teaching me the recipe when I was a little girl.

—Pat Merkovich, Milwaukee, WI

PREP: 35 MIN. + RISING • BAKE: 30 MIN. + COOLING • MAKES: 1 LOAF (16 PIECES)

3 large eggs
Assorted food coloring

BREAD
⅔ cup warm 2% milk (70° to 80°)
2 large eggs, room temperature
2 Tbsp. butter, melted
2 Tbsp. sugar
1½ tsp. salt
3 cups bread flour
1 pkg. (¼ oz.) quick-rise yeast
1 Tbsp. canola oil

EGG WASH
1 large egg
1 Tbsp. water
1 Tbsp. sesame seeds or poppy seeds

1. Place 3 eggs in a single layer in a small saucepan; add enough cold water to cover by 1 in. Cover and quickly bring to a boil. Remove from heat. Let stand 15 minutes.

2. Rinse eggs in cold water and place in ice water until completely cooled. Drain; dye hard-boiled eggs with food coloring, following package directions. Let stand until completely dry.

3. In bread machine pan, place the first 7 bread ingredients in the order suggested by manufacturer. Select dough setting. Check dough after 5 minutes of mixing; add 1-2 Tbsp. additional milk or flour if needed.

4. When cycle is completed, turn dough onto a lightly floured surface. Punch down dough; divide into thirds. Roll each into a 15-in. rope. Place ropes on a greased baking sheet and braid. Shape into a ring. Pinch ends to seal. Lightly coat dyed eggs with oil; arrange on braid, tucking them carefully between ropes. For egg wash, whisk egg with water. Brush over dough; sprinkle with sesame seeds.

5. Cover with a kitchen towel; let rise in a warm place until almost doubled, about 30 minutes. Preheat oven to 350°.

6. Bake until golden brown, 30-35 minutes. Remove from the pan to a wire rack to cool. Refrigerate leftovers.

1 PIECE: 157 cal., 5g fat (2g sat. fat), 75mg chol., 264mg sod., 21g carb. (2g sugars, 1g fiber), 6g pro.

TO PREPARE DOUGH BY HAND: In a large bowl, mix the sugar, yeast, salt and 1 cup flour. In a small saucepan, heat the milk and butter to 120°-130°. Add to the dry ingredients; beat on medium speed 2 minutes. Add the eggs; beat on high 2 minutes. Stir in enough remaining flour to form a soft dough (dough will be sticky). Turn dough onto a floured surface; knead until smooth and elastic, 6-8 minutes. Place in a greased bowl, turning once to grease the top. Cover and let rest 1 hour. Shape and bake as directed.

A BIT NUTTY BOSTON BROWN BREAD

Hearty and dense, my homemade Boston brown bread includes hazelnuts for a taste twist. Thick slices pair well with just about anything, from soups and stews to roasts and casseroles.
—*Lorraine Caland, Shuniah, ON*

PREP: 30 MIN. • **BAKE:** 45 MIN. + COOLING
MAKES: 2 LOAVES (12 PIECES EACH)

3 **cups whole wheat flour**	2½ **cups buttermilk**
1 **cup all-purpose flour**	1 **cup molasses**
2½ **tsp. baking soda**	1 **cup golden raisins**
1 **tsp. salt**	¾ **cup chopped hazelnuts**

1. In a large bowl, combine the flours, baking soda and salt. In a small bowl, whisk the buttermilk and molasses. Stir into dry ingredients just until moistened. Fold in raisins and nuts. Transfer to 2 greased 8x4-in. loaf pans.

2. Bake at 350° for 45-50 minutes or until a toothpick inserted in center comes out clean. Cool for 10 minutes before removing from pans to wire racks.

1 PIECE: 159 cal., 3g fat (0 sat. fat), 1mg chol., 263mg sod., 31g carb. (13g sugars, 3g fiber), 4g pro.

SOUR CREAM BLUEBERRY MUFFINS

When we were kids, Mom helped warm us up on chilly mornings by making a batch of her blueberry muffins. Now I'm in college and enjoy doing the same for friends.
—*Tory Ross, Cincinnati, OH*

PREP: 15 MIN. • **BAKE:** 20 MIN. • **MAKES:** 1 DOZEN

2 **cups biscuit/baking mix**
¾ **cup plus 2 Tbsp. sugar, divided**
2 **large eggs, room temperature**
1 **cup sour cream**
1 **cup fresh or frozen blueberries**

1. Preheat oven to 375°. In a large bowl, combine biscuit mix and ¾ cup sugar. In a small bowl, combine eggs and sour cream; stir into the dry ingredients just until combined. Fold in blueberries.

2. Fill greased muffin cups three-fourths full. Sprinkle with the remaining sugar. Bake until a toothpick inserted in muffin comes out clean, 20-25 minutes. Cool 5 minutes before removing from pan to a wire rack.

1 MUFFIN: 195 cal., 7g fat (3g sat. fat), 48mg chol., 272mg sod., 29g carb. (16g sugars, 1g fiber), 3g pro.

SWEDISH PUFF COFFEE CAKE

Some of my most treasured childhood memories include waking up to the
heavenly scent of this almond-glazed coffee cake in the oven.
—Mary Shenk, DeKalb, IL

PREP: 35 MIN. • BAKE: 30 MIN. + COOLING • MAKES: 12 SERVINGS

1　cup all-purpose flour
½　cup cold butter, cubed
2　Tbsp. ice water

TOPPING
1　cup water
½　cup butter
1　tsp. almond extract
1　cup all-purpose flour
3　large eggs

GLAZE
1　cup confectioners' sugar
2　Tbsp. butter, softened
1　Tbsp. 2% milk
1　tsp. almond extract
1　cup sweetened
　　shredded coconut

1. Preheat oven to 375°. Place flour in a small bowl; cut in butter until crumbly. Gradually add ice water, tossing with a fork until dough holds together when pressed. On an ungreased baking sheet, press dough into a 10-in. circle.

2. For the topping, in a large saucepan, bring the water and butter to a rolling boil. Remove from heat; stir in almond extract. Add the flour all at once and beat until blended. Cook over medium heat until mixture pulls away from sides of pan and forms a ball, stirring vigorously. Remove from heat; let stand 5 minutes.

3. Add the eggs, 1 at a time, beating well after each addition until smooth. Continue beating until mixture is smooth and shiny; spread over pastry.

4. Bake 30-35 minutes or until lightly browned. Cover loosely with foil during the last 5 minutes if needed to prevent overbrowning. Remove from pan to a wire rack to cool completely.

5. For the glaze, in a small bowl, beat the confectioners' sugar, butter, milk and extract until smooth. Spread over top; sprinkle with coconut.

1 PIECE: 326 cal., 21g fat (14g sat. fat), 98mg chol., 160mg sod., 30g carb. (12g sugars, 1g fiber), 4g pro.

CINNAMON SWIRL BREAKFAST BREAD

The recipe for these pretty, rich-tasting loaves came from my aunt many years ago.
These days, I use my bread machine for easier preparation.
—*Peggy Burdick, Burlington, MI*

PREP: 20 MIN. + RISING • BAKE: 30 MIN. • MAKES: 2 LOAVES (16 PIECES EACH)

1 cup warm 2% milk
(70° to 80°)
¼ cup water (70° to 80°)
2 large eggs,
room temperature
¼ cup butter, softened
1 tsp. salt
¼ cup sugar
5 cups bread flour
2¼ tsp. active dry yeast

FILLING
2 Tbsp. butter, melted
⅓ cup sugar
1 Tbsp. ground cinnamon

GLAZE
1 cup confectioners' sugar
½ tsp. vanilla extract
4 to 5 tsp. 2% milk

1. In bread machine pan, place the first 8 ingredients in order suggested by manufacturer. Select dough setting (check the dough after 5 minutes of mixing; add 1-2 Tbsp. water or flour if needed).

2. When cycle is completed, turn the dough onto a lightly floured surface; divide in half. Roll each portion into a 10x8-in. rectangle. Brush with butter. Combine the sugar and cinnamon; sprinkle over dough.

3. Roll up tightly jelly-roll style, starting with a short side. Pinch the seams and ends to seal. Place seam side down in 2 greased 9x5-in. loaf pans. Cover and let rise in a warm place until doubled, about 1 hour. Preheat oven to 350°.

4. Bake for 25 minutes. Cover with foil; bake until golden brown, 5-10 minutes longer. Remove bread from the pans to wire racks to cool completely.

5. In a large bowl, combine the confectioners' sugar, vanilla and enough milk to achieve the desired consistency; drizzle over warm loaves.

1 PIECE: 121 cal., 3g fat (2g sat. fat), 20mg chol., 104mg sod., 22g carb. (7g sugars, 1g fiber), 3g pro.

MINI SWEET POTATO SCONES
WITH ROSEMARY & BACON

I grow my own sweet potatoes, and I'm always trying to think of new ways to use them. I created these goodies on a whim—and was thrilled with the results! I like to combine the dry ingredients, cut in the butter and stir in the crumbled bacon the night before. Then I just cover and refrigerate the mixture overnight and proceed with the directions the next day. In addition to saving time in the morning, this helps the rosemary and bacon flavor come through, and chilling the butter (in the mix) produces tender scones.

—Sue Gronholz, Beaver Dam, WI

PREP: 30 MIN. • **BAKE:** 15 MIN. • **MAKES:** 16 SCONES

2½ **cups all-purpose flour**
½ **cup sugar**
2½ **tsp. baking powder**
1½ **tsp. pumpkin pie spice or
    ground cinnamon**
1½ **tsp. minced fresh
    rosemary or ½ tsp. dried
    rosemary, crushed**
½ **tsp. salt**
¼ **tsp. baking soda**
½ **cup cold butter**
4 **bacon strips, cooked and
    crumbled**
½ **cup mashed sweet
    potatoes**
¼ **cup plain Greek yogurt**
1 **large egg, room
    temperature**
2 **Tbsp. maple syrup**

TOPPING
1 **Tbsp. 2% milk**
1 **Tbsp. sugar**

1. Preheat oven to 425°. In a large bowl, whisk first 7 ingredients. Cut in the butter until the mixture resembles coarse crumbs. Stir in the bacon. In another bowl, whisk sweet potatoes, yogurt, egg and maple syrup until blended; stir into the crumb mixture just until combined.

2. Turn onto a floured surface; knead gently 10 times. Divide the dough in half. Pat each half into a 6-in. circle. Cut each into 8 wedges. Place wedges on a greased baking sheet. Brush with milk; sprinkle with sugar. Bake until golden brown, 12-14 minutes. Serve warm.

FREEZE OPTION: Freeze the cooled scones in freezer containers. To use, thaw before serving or, if desired, reheat on a baking sheet in a preheated 350° oven until warmed, 3-4 minutes.

1 SCONE: 184 cal., 7g fat (4g sat. fat), 30mg chol., 261mg sod., 26g carb. (9g sugars, 1g fiber), 3g pro.

HAWAIIAN CHEESE BREAD

My mother's friend brought her cheesy Hawaiian bread to a party at work, and after one bite, Mom knew she had to have the recipe. With constant nagging, she eventually got it! Simple and fast, the mouthwatering loaf is a hit with everyone at every kind of get-together.
—*Amy McIlvain, Wilmington, DE*

PREP: 15 MIN. • BAKE: 25 MIN. • MAKES: 16 SERVINGS

- 1 loaf (1 lb.) Hawaiian sweet bread
- 1 block (8 oz.) Swiss cheese
- 3 slices red onion, chopped
- ½ cup butter, melted
- 3 garlic cloves, minced
- 1 tsp. salt

1. Cut bread diagonally into 1-in. slices to within 1 in. of bottom. Repeat cuts in the opposite direction. Cut the Swiss cheese into ¼-in. slices; cut the slices into small pieces. Insert into bread. Combine the onion, butter, garlic and salt; spoon over bread.

2. Wrap loaf in foil. Bake at 350° for 25-30 minutes or until the cheese is melted. Serve warm.

1 SERVING: 199 cal., 12g fat (7g sat. fat), 38mg chol., 314mg sod., 17g carb. (6g sugars, 1g fiber), 7g pro.

MOM'S CHOCOLATE BREAD

We had this divine streusel-topped bread on holidays and other family occasions. Whenever I have a loaf baking, the aroma takes me back to those special times.
—*Rachel Rhodes, Princeton, NC*

PREP: 10 MIN. • BAKE: 30 MIN. + COOLING • MAKES: 1 LOAF (12 PIECES)

- 4 Tbsp. sugar, divided
- 3 Tbsp. all-purpose flour
- 1 Tbsp. cold butter
- 1 to 3 Tbsp. ground cinnamon
- 1 tube (8 oz.) refrigerated crescent rolls
- ⅔ cup semisweet chocolate chips
- 1 Tbsp. butter, melted

1. Preheat oven to 375°. For streusel, in a small bowl, mix 3 Tbsp. sugar and flour; cut in the butter until crumbly. Reserve half the streusel for topping. Stir the cinnamon and remaining sugar into remaining streusel.

2. Unroll crescent dough into a long rectangle; press perforations to seal. Sprinkle with chocolate chips and cinnamon mixture. Roll up jelly-roll style, starting with a long side; pinch the seam to seal. Fold roll in half lengthwise; transfer to a greased 8x4-in. loaf pan. Brush with butter; sprinkle with reserved streusel.

3. Bake until golden brown, 30-35 minutes. Cool in pan 10 minutes before removing to a wire rack to cool completely.

1 PIECE: 164 cal., 9g fat (4g sat. fat), 5mg chol., 165mg sod., 21g carb. (11g sugars, 2g fiber), 2g pro.

MASHED POTATO DOUGHNUTS

On cold winter days, a double batch of these doughnuts welcomed us six kids home from school.
—*Tammy Evans, Nepean, ON*

PREP: 20 MIN. + CHILLING • **COOK:** 25 MIN. • **MAKES:** 2 DOZEN

1 pkg. (¼ oz.) active
　dry yeast
1 cup warm buttermilk
　(110° to 115°)
1½ cups warm mashed
　potatoes (without added
　milk and butter)
3 large eggs, room
　temperature
⅓ cup butter, melted
3 cups sugar, divided
4 tsp. baking powder
1½ tsp. baking soda
1 tsp. salt
1 tsp. ground nutmeg
6 cups all-purpose flour
　Oil for deep-fat frying
½ tsp. ground cinnamon

1. In a large bowl, dissolve the yeast in the warm buttermilk. Add the mashed potatoes, eggs and butter. Add 2 cups sugar, baking powder, baking soda, salt, nutmeg and 3 cups flour. Beat until smooth. Stir in enough remaining flour to form a soft dough. Do not knead. Cover and refrigerate for 2 hours.

2. Turn the dough onto a floured surface; divide into fourths. Roll each portion to ½-in. thickness. Cut with a floured 3-in. doughnut cutter.

3. In an electric skillet or deep-fat fryer, heat oil to 375°. Fry doughnuts, a few at a time, until golden brown on both sides. Drain on paper towels. Combine remaining 1 cup sugar and cinnamon; roll doughnuts in cinnamon-sugar while warm.

1 DOUGHNUT: 295 cal., 8g fat (2g sat. fat), 30mg chol., 309mg sod., 52g carb. (26g sugars, 1g fiber), 5g pro.

SWISS & CARAWAY FLATBREADS

My mom discovered this rustic flatbread many years ago and always made it for
us on Christmas Eve. Now I bake loaves for my own family throughout the year.
—*Diane Berger, Sequim, WA*

PREP: 20 MIN. + RISING • **BAKE:** 10 MIN. • **MAKES:** 2 LOAVES (16 PIECES EACH)

2 loaves (1 lb. each) frozen
　bread dough, thawed
¼ cup butter, melted
¼ cup canola oil
1 Tbsp. dried minced onion
1 Tbsp. Dijon mustard
2 tsp. caraway seeds
1 tsp. Worcestershire
　sauce
1 Tbsp. dry sherry, optional
2 cups shredded Swiss
　cheese

1. On a lightly floured surface, roll each portion of dough into a 15x10-in. rectangle. Transfer to 2 greased 15x10x1-in. baking pans. Cover with kitchen towels; let rise in a warm place until doubled, about 45 minutes.

2. Preheat oven to 425°. Using fingertips, press several dimples into dough. In a small bowl, whisk the melted butter, oil, onion, mustard, caraway seeds, Worcestershire sauce and, if desired, sherry until blended; brush over dough. Sprinkle with cheese. Bake until golden brown, 10-15 minutes. Serve warm.

FREEZE OPTION: Cut the cooled flatbreads into pieces. Freeze in freezer containers. To use, reheat flatbreads on an ungreased baking sheet in a preheated 425° oven until heated through.

1 PIECE: 134 cal., 6g fat (2g sat. fat), 10mg chol., 199mg sod., 14g carb. (1g sugars, 1g fiber), 5g pro.

MASHED POTATO
DOUGHNUTS

LEMON POPOVERS WITH PECAN HONEY BUTTER

Bring a little bit of sunshine to your day with honey butter and delicate lemon flavor. These golden brown bites make a nice addition to dinner, but I like them best for breakfast with a bowl of fruit and yogurt.

—*Joan Hallford, N. Richland Hills, TX*

PREP: 10 MIN. • BAKE: 25 MIN. • MAKES: 6 SERVINGS

- 2 **large eggs, room temperature**
- 1 **cup 2% milk**
- 1 **cup all-purpose flour**
- ½ **tsp. salt**
- 5 **Tbsp. finely chopped toasted pecans, divided**
- ¾ **tsp. grated lemon zest**
- 2 **tsp. lemon juice**
- 6 **Tbsp. butter, softened**
- 6 **Tbsp. honey**

1. Preheat oven to 450°. In a large bowl, whisk eggs and milk until blended. Whisk in the flour and salt until smooth (do not overbeat). Stir in 3 Tbsp. pecans, lemon zest and lemon juice.

2. Generously grease a 6-cup popover pan with nonstick spray; fill cups half full with batter. Bake 15 minutes. Reduce oven setting to 350° (do not open oven door). Bake until deep golden brown, 10-15 minutes longer (do not underbake).

3. Meanwhile, combine the butter, honey and remaining 2 Tbsp. pecans. Immediately remove the popovers from the pan to a wire rack. Pierce side of each popover with a sharp knife to let steam escape. Serve immediately with pecan honey butter.

1 POPOVER WITH ABOUT 2 TBSP. HONEY BUTTER: 325 cal., 18g fat (9g sat. fat), 96mg chol., 332mg sod., 36g carb. (20g sugars, 1g fiber), 6g pro.

FROM GRANDMA'S KITCHEN: Traditionally, popover pans are heated in the oven before they are greased and filled with batter. Try this trick to give your popovers an extra-crisp golden exterior with a higher rise.

HURRY-UP BISCUITS

When I was young, my mom would prepare her homemade biscuits with fresh cream she got from a local farmer. My family loves a batch warm from the oven.
—*Beverly Sprague, Baltimore, MD*

TAKES: 30 MIN. • MAKES: 1 DOZEN

3 cups all-purpose flour
4 tsp. baking powder
4 tsp. sugar
1 tsp. salt
2 cups heavy
   whipping cream

1. Preheat oven to 375°. In a large bowl, whisk the flour, baking powder, sugar and salt. Add cream; stir just until moistened.

2. Drop by ¼ cupfuls 1 in. apart onto greased baking sheets. Bake until the bottoms are golden brown, 17-20 minutes. Serve warm.

1 BISCUIT: 256 cal., 15g fat (9g sat. fat), 54mg chol., 346mg sod., 26g carb. (2g sugars, 1g fiber), 4g pro.

TOFFEE APPLE CINNAMON BUNS

This recipe was my dad's favorite growing up. He would sit and watch his mother sprinkle the sweet filling over the dough, carefully roll it up and cut it into rounds. The anticipation waiting for the buns to finish baking was almost too much for him to bear!
—*Jeanne Holt, St. Paul, MN*

PREP: 30 MIN. • BAKE: 25 MIN. • MAKES: 8 SERVINGS

1 medium Granny Smith
   apple, peeled and
   chopped
1 Tbsp. thawed apple juice
   concentrate
⅔ cup plus 2 Tbsp. sugar,
   divided
1½ tsp. ground cinnamon
3¼ cups all-purpose flour
1¼ tsp. baking powder
½ tsp. baking soda
½ tsp. salt
1¼ cups buttermilk
6 Tbsp. butter, melted,
   divided
¼ cup brickle toffee bits

GLAZE
1½ cups confectioners' sugar
3 Tbsp. thawed apple juice
   concentrate
2 Tbsp. brickle toffee bits

1. Preheat oven to 400°. In a microwave-safe bowl, combine the apple and apple juice concentrate; microwave, covered, on high for 1-2 minutes or until tender. Drain; cool slightly. In a small bowl, mix ⅔ cup sugar and cinnamon.

2. In a large bowl, whisk flour, baking powder, baking soda, salt and remaining sugar. Stir in buttermilk and 2 Tbsp. melted butter just until moistened. Turn onto a lightly floured surface; knead until smooth, 2-4 minutes.

3. Roll dough into a 12x9-in. rectangle. Brush with 2 Tbsp. melted butter to within ½ in. of edges; sprinkle with sugar mixture, apple and toffee bits. Roll up jelly-roll style, starting with a long side; pinch seam to seal. Cut into 8 slices.

4. Place in a greased 9-in. square or round baking pan, cut side down. Brush with remaining melted butter. Bake 22-28 minutes or until golden brown.

5. Cool 5 minutes on a wire rack. In a small bowl, mix the confectioners' sugar and apple juice concentrate until smooth. Spread over the buns; sprinkle with toffee bits. Serve warm.

1 BUN: 525 cal., 13g fat (7g sat. fat), 28mg chol., 498mg sod., 96g carb. (56g sugars, 2g fiber), 7g pro.

OATMEAL
YEAST BREAD

GRANDMA'S SECRET

This bread is delicious with a simple drizzle of honey or a pat of butter, but you can also top it with jam, a tart citrus marmalade, honey cinnamon butter, or any flavored butter.

OATMEAL YEAST BREAD

Memories of the warm, inviting aromas that greeted me after school always come rushing back when this bread is baking. With a lightly sweet flavor, crispy crust and hearty texture, it was one of Mom's special treats for us.
—*Gloria Murtha, West Mifflin, PA*

PREP: 25 MIN. + RISING • BAKE: 35 MIN. • MAKES: 2 LOAVES (16 PIECES EACH)

1 can (12 oz.) evaporated milk
½ cup water
2 Tbsp. shortening
2 cups plus 2 tsp. old-fashioned oats, divided
⅓ cup packed brown sugar
1½ tsp. salt
1 pkg. (¼ oz.) active dry yeast
1 cup warm water (110° to 115°)
5 to 5½ cups all-purpose flour
1 large egg, room temperature, beaten

1. In a saucepan over medium heat, bring milk, water and shortening to a boil. Meanwhile, combine 2 cups oats, brown sugar and salt in a bowl. Add the milk mixture; let stand until mixture reaches 110°-115°. In a small bowl, dissolve the yeast in the warm water; add to the oat mixture. Add 3 cups flour; beat until smooth. Add enough remaining flour to form a soft dough.

2. Turn onto a floured surface; knead until smooth and elastic, 6-8 minutes. Place in a greased bowl, turning once to grease the top. Cover and let rise in a warm place until doubled, about 1 hour. Punch the dough down; divide in half. Shape into 2 loaves; transfer to greased 8x4-in. loaf pans. Cover and let rise until doubled, about 40 minutes. Preheat oven to 350°.

3. Brush with egg; sprinkle with the remaining oats. Bake until golden, 35-40 minutes. Remove from pans; cool on wire racks.

1 PIECE: 123 cal., 2g fat (1g sat. fat), 10mg chol., 125mg sod., 22g carb. (4g sugars, 1g fiber), 4g pro.

SOUR CREAM CUT-OUT BISCUITS

PICTURED ON PAGE 66

After trying different ways to prepare biscuits without being completely satisfied, I stirred in some sour cream. Success! Split while warm, butter and enjoy.
—*Lorraine Caland, Shuniah, ON*

TAKES: 30 MIN. • MAKES: 10 BISCUITS

2 cups all-purpose flour
2 Tbsp. sugar
3 tsp. baking powder
½ tsp. salt
½ tsp. baking soda
1 cup sour cream
1 Tbsp. butter, melted

1. Preheat oven to 425°. In a large bowl, whisk the flour, sugar, baking powder, salt and baking soda. Stir in the sour cream just until moistened.

2. Turn onto a lightly floured surface; knead gently 8-10 times. Pat or roll dough to ½-in. thickness; cut with a floured 2¼-in. biscuit cutter. Place 1 in. apart on an ungreased baking sheet. Bake until golden brown, 10-12 minutes. Brush biscuits with melted butter; serve warm.

1 BISCUIT: 159 cal., 6g fat (4g sat. fat), 9mg chol., 343mg sod., 22g carb. (3g sugars, 1g fiber), 3g pro.

MOM'S OVEN-BARBECUED RIBS,
PAGE 106

GRANDMA'S FAVORITE

MAIN COURSES

Whether served for a weekday family dinner or the
biggest holiday feast of the year, Grandma's signature
entrees are the crowning glory on the table.

SASSY SOUTHWEST STUFFED SHELLS

When I was a child, my mom whipped up her zippy stuffed shells frequently. When I was older and came across her recipe on an index card, I quickly copied it. I've made very few changes because I want to keep all of the wonderful taste I remember.
—*Kellie Braddell, West Point, CA*

PREP: 45 MIN. • **BAKE:** 35 MIN. • **MAKES:** 8 SERVINGS

24 uncooked jumbo
   pasta shells
½ lb. lean ground beef
   (90% lean)
½ lb. lean ground pork
1 large carrot, shredded
3 green onions, chopped
3 garlic cloves, minced
2 cans (4 oz. each) chopped
   green chiles
2 cups shredded Mexican
   cheese blend, divided
1 can (6 oz.) french-fried
   onions, divided
¼ cup minced fresh cilantro
1 jar (16 oz.) picante sauce
2 cans (8 oz. each)
   tomato sauce
1 cup water

1. Preheat oven to 350°. Cook pasta according to the package directions for al dente. Drain and rinse in cold water.

2. Meanwhile, in a large skillet, cook beef and pork over medium heat until no longer pink, breaking into crumbles, 8-10 minutes; drain. Add carrot, green onions and garlic; cook 1 minute longer. Stir in green chiles, 1 cup cheese, half of the fried onions and the cilantro. In a large bowl, combine picante sauce, tomato sauce and water; stir 1 cup picante mixture into pan.

3. Spread 1 cup of the remaining picante mixture into a greased 13x9-in. baking dish. Fill pasta shells with meat mixture; place in baking dish, overlapping ends slightly. Top with the remaining sauce. Cover and bake 30 minutes. Uncover; top with remaining 1 cup of cheese and remaining fried onions. Bake until cheese is melted, 5-10 minutes longer.

3 STUFFED SHELLS: 487 cal., 26g fat (10g sat. fat), 59mg chol., 1181mg sod., 41g carb. (5g sugars, 3g fiber), 22g pro.

HAM & POTATOES AU GRATIN

Grandma always served this dish during the holidays. When I have it now, memories of those special times at her house fill my mind. Consider preparing a double batch or even more—the reheated leftovers are just as delicious.
—*Novella Cook, Hinton, WV*

PREP: 15 MIN. • **BAKE:** 35 MIN. • **MAKES:** 2 SERVINGS

2 cups sliced peeled
   potatoes, cooked
1 cup diced cooked ham
1 Tbsp. finely chopped
   onion
⅓ cup butter, cubed
3 Tbsp. all-purpose flour
1½ cups milk
1 cup shredded
   cheddar cheese
¾ tsp. salt
   Dash white pepper
   Minced fresh parsley

1. In a greased 1-qt. baking dish, combine potatoes, ham and onion; set aside.

2. In a saucepan, melt the butter over medium heat; stir in flour until smooth. Gradually add milk. Bring to a boil; cook and stir for 2 minutes or until mixture is thickened and bubbly. Add cheese, salt and pepper; stir until cheese is melted. Pour over the potato mixture and stir gently to mix.

3. Bake, uncovered, at 350° for 35-40 minutes or until bubbly. Garnish with parsley.

1 CUP: 872 cal., 59g fat (37g sat. fat), 204mg chol., 2526mg sod., 53g carb. (11g sugars, 3g fiber), 35g pro.

SASSY SOUTHWEST
STUFFED SHELLS

BRACIOLE

In our family, braciole was reserved for birthdays and holidays. When Grandma was done cooking the meat, she would call us into the kitchen to watch her lift the big roll onto the cutting board and slice it. The pinwheels of beef, topped with her signature sauce, were the main attraction on the table.

—*Cookie Curci, San Jose, CA*

PREP: 35 MIN. • COOK: 1¼ HOURS • MAKES: 6 SERVINGS

- 1 beef flank steak (1½ lbs.)
- 4 Tbsp. olive oil, divided
- ½ cup soft bread crumbs
- ½ cup minced fresh parsley
- ½ cup grated Parmesan cheese
- 2 garlic cloves, minced
- 1 tsp. dried oregano
- ½ tsp. salt, divided
- ½ tsp. pepper, divided
- 1 medium onion, chopped
- 2 cans (15 oz. each) tomato sauce
- ½ cup water
- 1 tsp. Italian seasoning
- ½ tsp. sugar
- Hot cooked spaghetti, optional

1. Flatten steak to ½-in. thickness. Rub with 1 Tbsp. oil. Combine the bread crumbs, parsley, cheese, garlic, oregano, ¼ tsp. salt and ¼ tsp. pepper. Spoon over beef to within 1 in. of the edges; press down. Roll up jelly-roll style, starting with a long side; tie with kitchen string.

2. In a Dutch oven, brown meat in remaining oil on all sides. Add onion and cook until tender. Stir in the tomato sauce, water, Italian seasoning, sugar and remaining salt and pepper. Bring to a boil. Reduce heat; cover and simmer for 70-80 minutes or until meat is tender.

3. Remove the meat from sauce and discard string. Cut into thin slices; serve with sauce and If desired, spaghetti and additional grated Parmesan cheese and minced fresh parsley.

2 SLICES: 330 cal., 20g fat (6g sat. fat), 54mg chol., 1028mg sod., 13g carb. (4g sugars, 2g fiber), 25g pro.

"This was my first braciole. My husband is Italian, and he said it was better than his mother's! This one was easy to prepare and so moist and delicious. It tasted even better the next day."
—BLINKSMOM, TASTEOFHOME.COM

HONEY HOISIN CHICKEN & POTATOES

When I was young, Tutu (my grandma) cooked up this dinner that blends Asian and American flavors. The potatoes are delicious drizzled with the pan juices.
—*Janet Yee, Phoenix, AZ*

PREP: 10 MIN. • BAKE: 50 MIN. • MAKES: 4 SERVINGS

4 medium Yukon Gold potatoes (about 1¾ lbs.), cut into 1-in. pieces
1 large onion, cut into 1-in. pieces
½ cup hoisin sauce
3 Tbsp. honey
½ tsp. salt, divided
½ tsp. pepper, divided
4 bone-in chicken thighs (about 1½ lbs.)

1. Preheat oven to 400°. Place potatoes and onion in a greased 13x9-in. baking pan. In a small bowl, mix hoisin, honey, ¼ tsp. salt and ¼ tsp. pepper; add to potato mixture and toss to coat.

2. Place the chicken over the vegetables; sprinkle with remaining salt and pepper. Roast 50-60 minutes or until potatoes are tender and a thermometer inserted in chicken reads 170°-175°, basting occasionally with pan juices.

FREEZE OPTION: Cool the chicken mixture. Freeze in freezer containers. To use, partially thaw in refrigerator overnight. Heat through slowly in a covered skillet until a thermometer inserted in chicken reads 165°, stirring occasionally; add broth or water if necessary.

1 CHICKEN THIGH WITH 1 CUP POTATO MIXTURE AND 3 TBSP. SAUCE: 561 cal., 16g fat (4g sat. fat), 82mg chol., 910mg sod., 75g carb. (27g sugars, 6g fiber), 29g pro.

MOM'S FRIED RICE

For a heartier main dish, add chopped shrimp, chicken or steak to your fried rice. I sometimes toss in pea pods for extra color and crunch. However you make this, it turns out delicious.
—*Carey Hunt, Portland, OR*

TAKES: 25 MIN. • MAKES: 4 SERVINGS

1 tsp. canola oil
1 large egg, beaten
8 bacon strips, chopped
1 cup chopped fresh mushrooms
8 green onions, thinly sliced
3 cups leftover cooked rice
1 cup bean sprouts
1 cup frozen peas, thawed
¼ cup reduced-sodium soy sauce

1. In a large skillet, heat oil over medium-high heat. Pour the egg into the pan. As egg sets, lift edges, letting uncooked portion flow underneath. When egg is completely cooked, remove to a plate. Set aside.

2. In the same skillet, cook bacon over medium heat until crisp. Using a slotted spoon, remove to paper towels; drain, reserving 2 Tbsp. drippings. Saute mushrooms and onions in the drippings. Stir in the rice, bean sprouts, peas, soy sauce and bacon. Chop egg into small pieces; stir into the pan and heat through.

1½ CUPS: 368 cal., 15g fat (5g sat. fat), 73mg chol., 984mg sod., 44g carb. (3g sugars, 4g fiber), 14g pro.

KABOBLESS CHICKEN
& VEGETABLES

KABOBLESS CHICKEN & VEGETABLES

As the primary caregiver for my grandma, I'm always on the lookout for healthy recipes.
This sheet-pan dinner of marinated chicken, zucchini, tomatoes and
more is like eating kabobs without the skewer.
—*Chelsea Madren, Anaheim, CA*

PREP: 10 MIN. + MARINATING • BAKE: 45 MIN. • MAKES: 6 SERVINGS

½ cup olive oil
½ cup balsamic vinegar
2 tsp. lemon-pepper
 seasoning
2 tsp. Italian seasoning
2 lbs. boneless skinless
 chicken breasts, cut into
 1-in. pieces
2 medium yellow summer
 squash, sliced
2 medium zucchini, sliced
1 medium carrot, sliced
1 cup grape tomatoes

1. In a large bowl, combine the oil, vinegar, lemon-pepper and Italian seasoning. Pour half the marinade into a separate bowl or shallow dish. Add chicken; turn to coat. Cover and refrigerate overnight. Cover and refrigerate remaining marinade.

2. Preheat oven to 350°. Line a 15x10x1-in. baking pan with foil. Drain the chicken, discarding that marinade. Place the squash, zucchini, carrot and tomatoes in the pan in a single layer. Place chicken on top of vegetables; pour reserved marinade over top. Cook until chicken is no longer pink and vegetables are tender, 45-60 minutes. Let stand 5 minutes before serving.

1 SERVING: 305 cal., 15g fat (3g sat. fat), 84mg chol., 158mg sod., 9g carb. (7g sugars, 2g fiber), 32g pro. **DIABETIC EXCHANGES:** 4 lean meat, 2 fat, 1 vegetable.

LEMON GRILLED SALMON

I enjoy salmon year-round by grilling it when the weather permits and by broiling
it when the weather doesn't. A savory marinade that includes dill gives
the tender, flaky fish mouthwatering flavor.
—*Aelita Kivirist, Glenview, IL*

PREP: 10 MIN. + MARINATING • BAKE: 15 MIN. • MAKES: 6 SERVINGS

2 tsp. snipped fresh dill or
 ¾ tsp. dill weed
½ tsp. lemon-pepper
 seasoning
½ tsp. salt, optional
¼ tsp. garlic powder
1 salmon fillet (1½ lbs.)
¼ cup packed brown sugar
3 Tbsp. chicken broth
3 Tbsp. canola oil
3 Tbsp. reduced-sodium
 soy sauce
3 Tbsp. finely chopped
 green onions
1 small lemon, thinly sliced
2 onion slices, separated
 into rings

1. Sprinkle dill, lemon-pepper, salt if desired and garlic powder over salmon. In a bowl or shallow dish, combine the brown sugar, chicken broth, oil, soy sauce and green onions; add salmon and turn to coat. Cover and refrigerate for 1 hour, turning once.

2. Drain and discard marinade. Grill salmon skin side down, over medium heat; arrange lemon and onion slices over the top. Cover and cook for 15-20 minutes or until fish flakes easily with a fork.

NOTE: The salmon can be broiled instead of grilled. Place the fillet on a greased broiler pan. Broil 3-4 in. from the heat for 6-8 min. or until fish flakes easily with a fork.

1 PIECE: 280 cal., 17g fat (3g sat. fat), 67mg chol., 633mg sod., 7g carb. (6g sugars, 0 fiber), 23g pro.

MOM'S OVEN-BARBECUED RIBS
PICTURED ON PAGE 98

My mom made this Sunday supper for us when we were growing up. Just a handful of basic ingredients are all you need for the zesty sauce that coats the ribs. Now I prepare them for my own family, and everyone's eyes light up when I bring the platter to the table.
—*Yvonne White, Williamson, NY*

PREP: 10 MIN. • BAKE: 2¾ HOURS • MAKES: 6 SERVINGS

3 to 4 lbs. country-style pork ribs
1½ cups water
1 cup ketchup
⅓ cup Worcestershire sauce
1 tsp. salt
1 tsp. chili powder
½ tsp. onion powder
⅛ tsp. hot pepper sauce

Preheat oven to 350°. Place ribs in a greased roasting pan. Bake, uncovered, for 45 minutes. Meanwhile, in a saucepan, combine remaining ingredients. Bring to a boil; cook for 1 minute. Drain ribs. Spoon sauce over ribs. Cover and bake for 1½ hours. Uncover; bake 30 minutes longer, basting once.

1 SERVING: 289 cal., 14g fat (5g sat. fat), 86mg chol., 1084mg sod., 14g carb. (4g sugars, 1g fiber), 27g pro.

SAVORY BRAISED CHICKEN WITH VEGETABLES

Here's a wonderful home-style dinner you'll want to have year-round. Pick up a fresh baguette to serve as a side—it's perfect for soaking up every last bit of savory broth.
—*Michelle Collins, Lake Orion, MI*

PREP: 15 MIN. • COOK: 40 MIN. • MAKES: 6 SERVINGS

½ cup seasoned bread crumbs
6 boneless skinless chicken breast halves (4 oz. each)
2 Tbsp. olive oil
1 can (14½ oz.) beef broth
2 Tbsp. tomato paste
1 tsp. poultry seasoning
½ tsp. salt
½ tsp. pepper
1 lb. fresh baby carrots
1 lb. sliced fresh mushrooms
2 medium zucchini, sliced
Sliced French bread baguette, optional

1. Place bread crumbs in a shallow bowl. Dip chicken breasts in bread crumbs to coat both sides; shake off excess.

2. In a Dutch oven, heat oil over medium heat. Add the chicken in batches; cook 2-4 minutes on each side or until browned. Remove chicken from pan.

3. Add broth, tomato paste and seasonings to same pan; cook over medium-high heat, stirring to loosen browned bits from pan. Add vegetables and chicken; bring to a boil. Reduce heat; simmer, covered, 25-30 minutes or until the vegetables are tender and a thermometer inserted in the chicken reads 165°. If desired, serve with baguette.

1 CHICKEN BREAST HALF WITH 1 CUP VEGETABLE MIXTURE: 247 cal., 8g fat (1g sat. fat), 63mg chol., 703mg sod., 16g carb. (6g sugars, 3g fiber), 28g pro. DIABETIC EXCHANGES: 3 lean meat, 2 vegetable, 1 fat, ½ starch.

SLOW-COOKED TURKEY WITH HERBED STUFFING

I'm all for special holiday meals, but I love finding ways to cut down the prep work. This recipe replaces a whole turkey with a turkey breast so it'll fit in a slow cooker. I add my grandma's easy stuffing for a family-pleasing feast that's stress-free.
—*Camille Beckstrand, Layton, UT*

PREP: 20 MIN. • COOK: 3 HOURS + STANDING • MAKES: 8 SERVINGS

1 boneless skinless turkey breast half (2 lbs.) or 2 lbs. turkey breast tenderloins
1 jar (12 oz.) turkey gravy, divided
1 can (10½ oz.) reduced-fat reduced-sodium condensed cream of mushroom soup, undiluted
½ tsp. salt
½ tsp. poultry seasoning
¼ tsp. pepper
1 medium Granny Smith apple, finely chopped
2 celery ribs, thinly sliced
1 small onion, finely chopped
1 cup sliced fresh mushrooms, optional
6 cups seasoned stuffing cubes

1. Place the turkey in a 5- or 6-qt. slow cooker. Whisk ¼ cup gravy, condensed soup and seasonings. Cover and refrigerate remaining gravy. Stir apple, celery, onion and, if desired, mushrooms into gravy mixture. Stir in stuffing cubes; spoon over turkey. Cook, covered, on low until a thermometer reads 165° and the meat is tender, 3-4 hours.

2. Remove the turkey from slow cooker; tent with foil. Let stand 10 minutes before slicing. Warm remaining gravy. Serve with turkey and stuffing.

4 OZ. COOKED TURKEY WITH ¾ CUP STUFFING AND 2 TBSP. GRAVY: 324 cal., 4g fat (1g sat. fat), 70mg chol., 1172mg sod., 38g carb. (5g sugars, 3g fiber), 32g pro.

ROUND STEAK ITALIANO

I've loved my mother's round steak since I was a child. The dense gravy is especially flavorful, and the potatoes alongside make for a complete and satisfying meal.
—*Deanne Stephens, McMinnville, OR*

PREP: 15 MIN. • COOK: 7 HOURS • MAKES: 8 SERVINGS

2 lbs. beef top round steak
1 can (8 oz.) tomato sauce
2 Tbsp. onion soup mix
2 Tbsp. canola oil
2 Tbsp. red wine vinegar
1 tsp. ground oregano
½ tsp. garlic powder
¼ tsp. pepper
8 medium potatoes
(7 to 8 oz. each)
1 Tbsp. cornstarch
1 Tbsp. cold water

1. Cut the steak into serving-sized pieces; place in a 5-qt. slow cooker. In a large bowl, combine the tomato sauce, soup mix, oil, vinegar, oregano, garlic powder and pepper; pour over the meat. Scrub and pierce the potatoes; place over meat. Cover and cook on low for 7 to 8 hours or until meat and potatoes are tender.

2. Remove the meat and potatoes; keep warm. For the gravy, pour the cooking juices into a small saucepan; skim fat. Combine the cornstarch and cold water until smooth; gradually stir into juices. Bring to a boil; cook and stir for 2 minutes or until thickened. Serve with meat and potatoes.

1 SERVING: 357 cal., 7g fat (2g sat. fat), 64mg chol., 329mg sod., 42g carb. (4g sugars, 4g fiber), 31g pro. DIABETIC EXCHANGES: 3 lean meat, 2½ starch, ½ fat.

SPANISH RICE WITH CHICKEN & PEAS

When I was a kid, Mom prepared certain favorite dinners on a weekly basis. This was Wednesday! We always looked forward to the juicy chicken and zippy rice.
—*Josee Lanzi, New Port Richey, FL*

PREP: 15 MIN. • COOK: 30 MIN. • MAKES: 6 SERVINGS

1 lb. boneless skinless chicken breasts, cut into 1½-in. pieces
1 Tbsp. all-purpose flour
½ tsp. pepper
½ tsp. salt, divided
4 tsp. plus 1 Tbsp. olive oil, divided
1 small sweet red pepper, chopped
1 small onion, chopped
1 celery rib, chopped
1½ cups uncooked long grain rice
1 tsp. ground cumin
1 tsp. chili powder
2¼ cups chicken broth
1 can (14½ oz.) diced tomatoes, undrained
1 cup frozen peas, thawed

1. In a small bowl, toss the chicken with flour, pepper and ¼ tsp. salt. In a Dutch oven, heat 4 tsp. oil over medium-high heat. Brown chicken, stirring occasionally; remove from pan.

2. In same pan, heat remaining oil over medium heat. Add pepper, onion and celery; cook and stir until onion is tender, 2-4 minutes. Add rice, cumin, chili powder and remaining salt; stir to coat rice. Stir in remaining ingredients; bring to a boil. Reduce heat; simmer, covered, 10 minutes.

3. Place browned chicken over rice (do not stir in). Cook, covered, until the rice is tender and the chicken is cooked through, about 5 minutes longer.

1½ CUPS: 367 cal., 8g fat (1g sat. fat), 44mg chol., 755mg sod., 50g carb. (5g sugars, 4g fiber), 22g pro. DIABETIC EXCHANGES: 3 starch, 2 lean meat, 1 vegetable, 1 fat.

ROUND STEAK
ITALIANO

GRANDMA'S SECRET

This recipe is easy to cut in half. Label and freeze leftover tomato sauce —or better yet, freeze the sauce mixture (with oil, seasonings, etc.), and you'll save a few steps next time.

CRESCENT TURKEY CASSEROLE

How do you make a dinner of turkey and vegetables appealing to kids? You turn it into a pie, of course! Mine has home-style taste but is ready to go on the table in just 30 minutes.
—*Daniela Essman, Perham, MN*

TAKES: 30 MIN. • **MAKES:** 4 SERVINGS

½ cup mayonnaise
2 Tbsp. all-purpose flour
1 tsp. chicken bouillon
  granules
⅛ tsp. pepper
¾ cup 2% milk

2 cups frozen mixed
  vegetables (about 10 oz.),
  thawed
1½ cups cubed cooked
  turkey breast
1 tube (4 oz.) refrigerated
  crescent rolls

1. Preheat oven to 375°. In a saucepan, mix first 4 ingredients until smooth; gradually stir in milk. Bring to a boil over medium heat; cook and stir until thickened, about 2 minutes. Add the vegetables and turkey; cook and stir until heated through. Transfer to a greased 8-in. square baking pan.

2. Unroll crescent dough and separate into 8 triangles; arrange over turkey mixture. Bake until casserole is heated through and topping is golden brown, 15-20 minutes.

1 PIECE: 453 cal., 28g fat (6g sat. fat), 48mg chol., 671mg sod., 26g carb. (7g sugars, 3g fiber), 22g pro.

TURKEY BISCUIT POTPIE: In a bowl, combine turkey breast, thawed mixed vegetables, one 10¾-oz. can condensed cream of chicken soup and ¼ tsp. dried thyme. Place in a greased 9-in. deep-dish pie plate. Mix 1 cup biscuit/baking mix, ½ cup milk and 1 lightly beaten large egg; spoon over top. Bake at 400° for 25-30 minutes.

TURKEY ASPARAGUS CASSEROLE: In a bowl, combine turkey breast, 1 thawed 10-oz. package frozen cut asparagus, one 10¾-oz. can condensed cream of chicken soup and ¼ cup water. Bake at 350° for 30 minutes, topping with one 2.8-oz. can french-fried onions during the last 5 minutes.

DAD'S SUNDAY ROAST

My father was a good friend of the local butcher, Mr. Mason, who always saved the preferred cut for his best customer. To please Dad, the roast had to be large enough so that he could count on leftovers for sandwiches the following week.
—*Mary Lewis, Memphis, TN*

PREP: 20 MIN. + STANDING • BAKE: 3½ HOURS • MAKES: 10-12 SERVINGS

1 beef rump roast or bottom round roast (5 to 6 lbs.)
½ cup cider vinegar
Salt and pepper to taste
1 cup water

GRAVY
½ cup all-purpose flour
1 cup cold water
1 tsp. browning sauce, optional
Salt and pepper to taste

1. Place roast in a deep roasting pan, fat side up; pour vinegar over roast. Let stand for 15 minutes. Sprinkle with salt and pepper. Add water to pan.

2. Cover and bake at 400° for 3½ hours or until meat is tender, adding additional water if needed. About 15 minutes before roast is done, uncover to brown the top.

3. Remove roast to a serving platter and keep warm; skim fat from pan juices. Pour juices into measuring cup, adding water if needed to measure 3 cups.

4. Mix the flour and cold water until smooth; stir into pan juices. Bring to a boil. Reduce heat; cook and stir for 1-2 minutes or until thickened. Stir in browning sauce if desired. Season with salt and pepper. Serve gravy with roast.

8 OZ. COOKED MEAT: 261 cal., 9g fat (3g sat. fat), 113mg chol., 61mg sod., 5g carb. (1g sugars, 0 fiber), 38g pro.

GRILLED SHRIMP SCAMPI

When I was in second grade, my class put together a cookbook. I saw this shrimp recipe from one of my friends, and I thought my mom would like it. I was right!
—*Peggy Roos, Minneapolis, MN*

PREP: 15 MIN. + MARINATING • GRILL: 10 MIN. • MAKES: 6 SERVINGS

2 Tbsp. olive oil
2 Tbsp. lemon juice
3 garlic cloves, minced
¼ tsp. salt
¼ tsp. pepper
1½ lbs. uncooked jumbo shrimp, peeled and deveined
Hot cooked jasmine rice
Minced fresh parsley

1. In a large bowl, whisk the first 5 ingredients. Add shrimp; toss to coat. Refrigerate, covered, 30 minutes.

2. Thread the shrimp onto 6 metal or soaked wooden skewers. Grill, covered, over medium heat or broil 4 in. from the heat 6-8 minutes or until shrimp turn pink, turning once. Serve with rice; sprinkle with parsley.

1 SKEWER: 118 cal., 4g fat (1g sat. fat), 138mg chol., 184mg sod., 1g carb. (0 sugars, 0 fiber), 18g pro. DIABETIC EXCHANGES: 2 meat, ½ fat.

HAM LOAF

HAM LOAF

I copied this recipe exactly the way Grandma had written it in her worn cookbook.
The only difference now is that I can't get home-smoked ham like those
Grandpa used to cure in his smokehouse. But that never matters
to hungry folks at the table—this loaf is a winner every time!
—*Esther Mishler, Hollsopple, PA*

PREP: 15 MIN. • BAKE: 70 MIN. • MAKES: 8 SERVINGS

2 **large eggs**
1 **cup 2% milk**
1 **cup dry bread crumbs**
¼ **tsp. pepper**
1½ **lb. ground**
   fully cooked ham
½ **lb. ground pork**

GLAZE
⅓ **cup packed brown sugar**
¼ **cup cider vinegar**
½ **tsp. ground mustard**
2 **Tbsp. water**

1. Preheat oven to 350°. In a large bowl, beat the eggs; add milk, bread crumbs and pepper. Add ham and pork; mix gently but thoroughly. Transfer to a 9x5-in. loaf pan. Bake 30 minutes.

2. Meanwhile, combine the glaze ingredients; spoon over loaf. Bake until a thermometer inserted in loaf reads 145°, 40 minutes longer, basting occasionally with glaze.

1 PIECE: 393 cal., 23g fat (8g sat. fat), 115mg chol., 1241mg sod., 21g carb. (11g sugars, 1g fiber), 25g pro.

MOM'S TURKEY TETRAZZINI

Looking for good old-fashioned, stick-to-your-ribs comfort food? Here's a hearty
classic guaranteed to warm up your family body and soul.
—*Judy Batson, Tampa, FL*

PREP: 25 MIN. • BAKE: 25 MIN. + STANDING • MAKES: 6 SERVINGS

1 **pkg. (12 oz.) fettuccine**
½ **lb. sliced fresh**
   mushrooms
1 **medium onion, chopped**
¼ **cup butter, cubed**
3 **Tbsp. all-purpose flour**
1 **cup white wine or**
   chicken broth
3 **cups 2% milk**
3 **cups cubed**
   cooked turkey
¾ **tsp. salt**
½ **tsp. pepper**
½ **tsp. hot pepper sauce**
½ **cup shredded**
   Parmesan cheese
   Paprika, optional

1. Preheat oven to 375°. Cook fettuccine according to the package directions.

2. Meanwhile, in a large skillet, saute the mushrooms and onion in butter until tender. Stir in flour until blended; whisk in wine until smooth, about 2 minutes. Slowly whisk in the milk. Bring to a boil; cook and stir until thickened. Stir in the turkey, salt, pepper and pepper sauce.

3. Drain fettuccine. Layer half of the fettuccine, turkey mixture and cheese in a greased 13x9-in. baking dish. Repeat layers. Sprinkle with paprika if desired.

4. Cover and bake 25-30 minutes or until heated through. Let stand 10 minutes before serving.

1 CUP: 516 cal., 17g fat (9g sat. fat), 87mg chol., 596mg sod., 53g carb. (10g sugars, 4g fiber), 37g pro.

BROILED SALMON WITH MEDITERRANEAN LENTILS

When I was a volunteer firefighter, I kept in shape by weight training and eating nutrition-packed dishes such as this one. Now I'm a stay-at-home mom and still make this salmon. It helps give me the energy I need to chase the kids!
—*Dawn E. Bryant, Thedford, NE*

PREP: 15 MIN. • COOK: 55 MIN. • MAKES: 4 SERVINGS

1 small carrot, julienned
¼ cup chopped onion
1 Tbsp. olive oil
½ cup dried lentils, rinsed
½ cup dried green split peas
2 garlic cloves, minced
2 tsp. capers, drained
2½ cups water
½ tsp. salt
½ tsp. pepper
2 Tbsp. lemon juice

SALMON
4 salmon fillets (4 oz. each)
Butter-flavored cooking spray
¼ tsp. salt
⅛ tsp. pepper

1. In a small saucepan, saute the carrot and onion in oil until tender. Add the lentils, peas, garlic and capers; cook and stir 3 minutes longer.

2. Add the water, salt and pepper. Bring to a boil. Reduce heat; cover and simmer for 45-50 minutes or until tender. Stir in the lemon juice.

3. Spritz fillets with butter-flavored spray; sprinkle with salt and pepper. Broil 4-6 in. from the heat for 7-9 minutes or until fish flakes easily with a fork. Serve with lentil mixture.

1 SERVING: 422 cal., 16g fat (3g sat. fat), 67mg chol., 568mg sod., 33g carb. (4g sugars, 14g fiber), 35g pro.

SLOPPY JOE BISCUIT CUPS

As a busy teacher, I rely on convenience items such as refrigerated dough for quick dinner prep on weeknights. I've brought my sloppy joe cups to school and shared the recipe many times.
—*Julie Ahern, Waukegan, IL*

TAKES: 30 MIN. • MAKES: 10 BISCUIT CUPS

1 lb. lean ground beef (90% lean)
¼ cup each finely chopped celery, onion and green pepper
½ cup barbecue sauce
1 tube (12 oz.) refrigerated flaky biscuits (10 count)
½ cup shredded cheddar cheese

1. Heat oven to 400°. In a large skillet, cook beef and vegetables over medium heat until the beef is no longer pink, 5-7 minutes, breaking up beef into crumbles; drain. Stir in barbecue sauce; bring to a boil. Reduce heat; simmer, uncovered, 2 minutes, stirring occasionally.

2. Separate dough into 10 biscuits; flatten to 5-in. circles. Press onto bottoms and up sides of greased muffin cups. Fill with the beef mixture.

3. Bake until biscuits are golden brown, 9-11 minutes. Sprinkle with cheese; bake until cheese is melted, 1-2 minutes longer.

2 BISCUIT CUPS : 463 cal., 22g fat (8g sat. fat), 68mg chol., 1050mg sod., 41g carb. (16g sugars, 1g fiber), 25g pro.

PRESSURE-COOKER
WINE-BRAISED BEEF SHANKS

I adapted slow-cooker beef shanks so I could prepare them in a pressure cooker instead. Pairing the tender meat with egg noodles or rice makes a meal that reminds me of Grandma's house.
—*Helen Nelander, Boulder Creek, CA*

PREP: 30 MIN. • **COOK:** 40 MIN. + RELEASING • **MAKES:** 6 SERVINGS

3   beef shanks (14 oz. each)
1   tsp. salt
1   tsp. canola oil
1   small onion, chopped
1   medium carrot, chopped
1   medium green pepper, chopped

1   cup dry red wine or beef broth
1   cup beef broth
1   lemon slice
1   Tbsp. cornstarch
1   Tbsp. water

1. Sprinkle the beef with salt. Select saute on a 6-qt. electric pressure cooker. Adjust for medium heat; add oil. When oil is hot, brown beef in batches. Press cancel. Return all to pressure cooker. Add onion, carrot, green pepper, wine, broth and lemon.

2. Lock lid; close pressure-release valve. Adjust to pressure-cook on high for 40 minutes. Allow the pressure to naturally release for 10 minutes, then quick-release any remaining pressure. Press cancel. Remove the meat and vegetables from pressure cooker; keep warm. Discard lemon.

3. Skim fat from cooking juices. Select saute setting and adjust for low heat. In a small bowl, mix the cornstarch and water until smooth; stir into cooking juices. Simmer, stirring constantly, until thickened, 1-2 minutes. Serve with beef and vegetables.

3 OZ. COOKED BEEF WITH ½ CUP SAUCE: 172 cal., 5g fat (2g sat. fat), 51mg chol., 592mg sod., 5g carb. (2g sugars, 1g fiber), 23g pro. **DIABETIC EXCHANGES:** 3 lean meat.

VEGETARIAN CABBAGE ROLLS

This mouthwatering meatless entree comes from my 89-year-old grandmother,
who cooks a lot with grains, particularly bulgur. Even meat lovers say
she makes vegetarian dishes taste like a treat!
—*Michelle Dougherty, Lewiston, ID*

PREP: 30 MIN. • **BAKE:** 15 MIN. • **MAKES:** 8 CABBAGE ROLLS

1½ **cups chopped
  fresh mushrooms**
 1 **cup diced zucchini**
 ¾ **cup chopped
  green pepper**
 ¾ **cup chopped
  sweet red pepper**
 ¾ **cup vegetable broth**
 ½ **cup bulgur**
 1 **tsp. dried basil**
 ½ **tsp. dried marjoram**
 ½ **tsp. dried thyme**
 ¼ **tsp. pepper**
 1 **large head cabbage**
 6 **Tbsp. shredded
  Parmesan cheese,
  divided**
 2 **tsp. lemon juice**
 1 **can (8 oz.) tomato sauce**
 ⅛ **tsp. hot pepper sauce**

1. In a large saucepan, combine the first 10 ingredients. Bring to a boil over medium heat. Reduce heat; cover and simmer for 5 minutes. Remove from the heat; let stand for 5 minutes.

2. Meanwhile, cook cabbage in boiling water just until leaves fall off head. Set aside 8 large leaves for rolls (refrigerate remaining cabbage for another use). Cut out the thick vein from each leaf, making a V-shape cut. Overlap cut ends before filling. Stir 4 Tbsp. Parmesan cheese and lemon juice into vegetable mixture.

3. Place a heaping ⅓ cupful on each cabbage leaf; fold in sides. Starting at an unfolded edge, roll to completely enclose filling.

4. Combine tomato sauce and hot pepper sauce; pour ⅓ cup into a 2-qt. baking dish. Place cabbage rolls in dish; spoon remaining sauce over top. Cover and bake at 400° for 15 minutes or until heated through. Sprinkle with remaining Parmesan cheese.

2 CABBAGE ROLLS: 142 cal., 3g fat (1g sat. fat), 5mg chol., 675mg sod., 25g carb. (0 sugars, 6g fiber), 8g pro. **DIABETIC EXCHANGES:** 2 vegetable, 1 starch.

GARLIC BEEF STROGANOFF

As a mom who works full time, I take advantage of my slow cooker whenever possible. This stroganoff is perfect because I can get it ready in the morning before the kids get up.
—*Erika Anderson, Wausau, WI*

PREP: 20 MIN. • **COOK:** 7 HOURS • **MAKES:** 6 SERVINGS

2 tsp. beef bouillon granules
1 cup boiling water
1 can (10¾ oz.) condensed cream of mushroom soup, undiluted
2 jars (4½ oz. each) sliced mushrooms, drained
1 large onion, chopped
3 garlic cloves, minced
1 Tbsp. Worcestershire sauce
1½ lbs. beef top round steak, cut into thin strips
2 Tbsp. canola oil
1 pkg. (8 oz.) cream cheese, cubed
Hot cooked noodles
Minced fresh parsley, optional

1. In a 3-qt. slow cooker, dissolve beef bouillon in boiling water. Add the soup, mushrooms, onion, garlic and Worcestershire sauce. In a skillet, brown beef in oil.

2. Transfer to the slow cooker. Cover and cook on low until the meat is tender, 7-8 hours. Stir in cream cheese until smooth. Serve with noodles and, if desired, minced parsley.

1 SERVING: 383 cal., 24g fat (10g sat. fat), 104mg chol., 991mg sod., 12g carb. (4g sugars, 2g fiber), 29g pro.

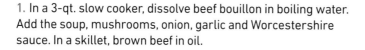

EASTERN SHORE CRAB CAKES

Here in Delaware, we're surrounded by an abundance of fresh seafood. I've found that the secret to fantastic crab cakes is using fresh crab meat, not adding too much filler and not breaking up the crab too much. This recipe meets all of those requirements!
—*Cynthia Bent, Newark, DE*

TAKES: 25 MIN. • **MAKES:** 3 SERVINGS

1 egg, lightly beaten
½ cup dry bread crumbs
½ cup mayonnaise
¾ tsp. seafood seasoning
½ tsp. lemon juice
½ tsp. Worcestershire sauce
⅛ tsp. white pepper
1 lb. fresh lump crabmeat
2 Tbsp. canola oil

1. In a large bowl, combine the egg, bread crumbs, mayonnaise, seafood seasoning, lemon juice, Worcestershire sauce and pepper. Fold in crab. Shape into 6 patties.

2. In a large skillet, cook crab cakes in oil for 4-5 minutes on each side or until browned.

2 CRAB CAKES: 599 cal., 44g fat (6g sat. fat), 235mg chol., 952mg sod., 13g carb. (1g sugars, 1g fiber), 35g pro.

BALSAMIC ROASTED CHICKEN THIGHS WITH ROOT VEGETABLES

I will always remember the way my grandmother's house smelled every Sunday when she made her amazing roasted chicken and vegetables. Now I prepare it myself, and the heartwarming flavors instantly take me back to my childhood.

—Erin Chilcoat, Central Islip, NY

PREP: 15 MIN. + MARINATING • BAKE: 35 MIN. • MAKES: 6 SERVINGS

- 4 Tbsp. olive oil, divided
- 3 Tbsp. stone-ground mustard
- 2 Tbsp. balsamic vinaigrette
- ¾ tsp. kosher salt, divided
- ¾ tsp. freshly ground pepper, divided
- 6 bone-in chicken thighs (about 2¼ lbs.)
- 4 medium parsnips, peeled and cut into ½-in. pieces
- 1 medium sweet potato, peeled and cut into ½-in. pieces
- 4 shallots, chopped
- ¼ tsp. caraway seeds
- 4 Tbsp. minced fresh parsley, divided
- 3 bacon strips, cooked and crumbled, divided

1. In a bowl, whisk 3 Tbsp. oil, mustard, vinaigrette and ½ tsp. each salt and pepper until blended. Add chicken, turning to coat. Refrigerate, covered, 6 hours or overnight.

2. Preheat oven to 425°. Place the chicken, skin side up, on half of a greased 15x10x1-in. baking pan. Place parsnips and sweet potato in a large bowl; add shallots, caraway seeds and the remaining oil, salt and pepper and toss to combine. Arrange in a single layer on remaining half of pan.

3. Roast chicken and vegetables 20 minutes. Stir vegetables; roast chicken and vegetables until a thermometer inserted in the chicken reads 170°-175° and the vegetables are tender, 15-20 minutes longer.

4. Transfer vegetables to a bowl; toss with 2 Tbsp. parsley and half of the bacon. Serve chicken with vegetables; sprinkle chicken with the remaining parsley and bacon.

1 SERVING: 480 cal., 27g fat (6g sat. fat), 85mg chol., 604mg sod., 33g carb. (10g sugars, 5g fiber), 27g pro.

"I used parchment paper for easy cleanup. The chicken skin came out nice and crispy, and the vegetables were extra flavorful. I'm sure that the bacon would be a great addition, but I didn't take the time to add it. The recipe is a winner even without it."
—SUSANFOOTE, TASTEOFHOME.COM

GREEK-STYLE CHICKEN
WITH GREEN BEANS

GREEK-STYLE CHICKEN WITH GREEN BEANS

My Greek grandmother used to make the most delicious green beans with a lemon-tomato twist. Whenever I prepare this recipe, I think of her. The juices from the chicken lend extra flavor to the beans, but they're delicious alone as a side dish, too.
—*Elizabeth Lindemann, Driftwood, TX*

PREP: 20 MIN. • COOK: 4 HOURS • MAKES: 4 SERVINGS

1 lb. fresh green beans, trimmed
2 large tomatoes, chopped
1 medium onion, chopped
1 cup chicken broth
¼ cup snipped fresh dill
2 to 3 Tbsp. lemon juice
2 garlic cloves, minced
4 bone-in chicken thighs (about 1½ lbs.)
1 Tbsp. olive oil
¾ tsp. salt
¼ tsp. pepper
Optional: Lemon wedges and additional snipped fresh dill

1. Combine the first 7 ingredients in a 5- or 6-qt. slow cooker. Top with chicken. Drizzle with oil; sprinkle with salt and pepper. Cook, covered, on low until a thermometer inserted in chicken reads 170°-175°, 4-6 hours.

2. Preheat broiler. Place chicken on a greased rack in a broiler pan. Broil 4-6 in. from heat until golden brown, 3-4 minutes. Serve with bean mixture and, if desired, lemon wedges and additional fresh dill.

1 SERVING: 324 cal., 18g fat (5g sat. fat), 82mg chol., 769mg sod., 16g carb. (7g sugars, 6g fiber), 26g pro.

LINGUINE WITH HAM & SWISS CHEESE

Pasta, ham, cheese and a creamy sauce come together for an easy baked entree that never fails to please. It was one of my grandma's favorites to serve at parties and potlucks.
—*Mary Savor, Woodburn, IN*

PREP: 15 MIN. • BAKE: 50 MIN. • MAKES: 8 SERVINGS

8 oz. uncooked linguine, broken in half
2 cups cubed fully cooked ham
1 can (10¾ oz.) condensed cream of mushroom soup, undiluted
2½ cups shredded Swiss cheese, divided
1 cup sour cream
1 medium onion, chopped
½ cup finely chopped green pepper
2 Tbsp. butter, melted

1. Cook the linguine according to package directions; drain. Meanwhile, in a large bowl, combine the ham, soup, 2 cups cheese, sour cream, onion, green pepper and butter. Add the pasta; toss to coat.

2. Transfer to a greased 13x9-in. baking dish. Cover and bake at 350° for 35 minutes. Uncover; sprinkle with remaining cheese. Bake until cheese is melted, 15-20 minutes longer.

1 CUP: 402 cal., 23g fat (12g sat. fat), 68mg chol., 797mg sod., 27g carb. (3g sugars, 2g fiber), 22g pro.

SLOW COOKER BEEF TIPS

With a rich gravy, this mouthwatering dinner tastes like one of my childhood favorites. I cook the beef tips with mushrooms and serve it all over mashed potatoes, brown rice or noodles.

—Amy Lents, Grand Forks, ND

PREP: 25 MIN. • COOK: 6¼ HOURS • MAKES: 4 SERVINGS

½ **lb. sliced baby portobello mushrooms**
1 **small onion, halved and sliced**
1 **beef top sirloin steak (1 lb.), cubed**
½ **tsp. salt**
¼ **tsp. pepper**
2 **tsp. olive oil**
⅓ **cup dry red wine or beef broth**
2 **cups beef broth**
1 **Tbsp. Worcestershire sauce**
2 **Tbsp. cornstarch**
¼ **cup cold water**
   Hot cooked mashed potatoes

1. Place mushrooms and onion in a 3-qt. slow cooker. Sprinkle beef with salt and pepper. In a large skillet, heat 1 tsp. oil over medium-high heat; brown meat in batches, adding more oil as needed. Transfer meat to slow cooker.

2. Add wine to skillet, stirring to loosen browned bits from pan. Stir in broth and Worcestershire sauce; pour over meat. Cook, covered, on low 6-8 hours or until meat is tender.

3. In a small bowl, mix cornstarch and cold water until smooth; gradually stir into slow cooker. Cook, covered, on high until gravy is thickened, 15-30 minutes. Serve with mashed potatoes.

1 CUP: 212 cal., 7g fat (2g sat. fat), 46mg chol., 836mg sod., 8g carb. (2g sugars, 1g fiber), 27g pro. **DIABETIC EXCHANGES:** 3 lean meat, ½ starch, ½ fat.

FROM GRANDMA'S KITCHEN: The best cuts of meat for making beef tips are sirloin, as this recipe calls for, or top round. However, because this is a slow-cooked recipe that will tenderize tougher cuts of meat, you can use stew meat in a pinch or to save money.

ITALIAN PASTA SAUCE

When my daughter got married, her new husband made something extra-special for their wedding buffet—a huge batch of his grandmother's thick, flavorful pasta sauce. She brought the recipe from Italy nearly 100 years ago.
—Judy Braun, Juneau, WI

PREP: 25 MIN. • **COOK:** 2½ HOURS • **MAKES:** 20 SERVINGS

4 lbs. ground beef
1 lb. bulk Italian sausage
1 large onion, finely chopped
3 celery ribs, finely chopped
4 garlic cloves, minced
2 Tbsp. olive oil
3 cans (28 oz. each) crushed tomatoes in puree
3 cans (6 oz. each) tomato paste
3 cups chicken or beef broth
1 lb. fresh mushrooms, sliced
¾ cup minced fresh parsley
1 Tbsp. sugar
2 to 3 tsp. salt
½ tsp. pepper
½ tsp. ground allspice, optional
Hot cooked pasta

1. In a Dutch oven or soup kettle, cook and crumble the beef in 2 batches over medium heat until no longer pink; drain and set aside. Cook and crumble the sausage over medium heat until no longer pink; drain and set aside. In the same pan, saute the onion, celery and garlic in oil until vegetables are tender.

2. Return the beef and sausage to pan. Add the next 9 ingredients, including allspice if desired, and bring to a boil. Reduce the heat; cover and simmer until sauce reaches desired thickness, stirring occasionally, 2-3 hours. Serve over pasta.

FREEZE OPTION: Freeze the cooled sauce in freezer containers. To use, partially thaw in the refrigerator overnight. Heat through in a saucepan, stirring occasionally. Add water if necessary.

1 CUP: 284 cal., 15g fat (5g sat. fat), 57mg chol., 821mg sod., 16g carb. (9g sugars, 3g fiber), 23g pro.

SHRIMP-STUFFED POBLANO PEPPERS

My mom enjoys seafood and a little bit of spice, so I decided to surprise her
by creating a main dish of shrimp-stuffed poblanos. She loved them!

—*Tina Garcia-Ortiz, Tampa, FL*

PREP: 35 MIN. • **BAKE:** 10 MIN. • **MAKES:** 8 SERVINGS

4 large poblano peppers
2 Tbsp. butter,
 melted, divided
1 tsp. coarsely ground
 pepper
½ tsp. kosher salt
1 small onion,
 finely chopped
2 celery ribs, chopped
4 oz. cream cheese,
 softened
1 lb. chopped cooked
 peeled shrimp
1¾ cups shredded Mexican
 cheese blend
1½ cups cooked rice
2 Tbsp. lemon juice
2 tsp. dried cilantro flakes
½ tsp. onion powder
½ tsp. garlic powder

TOPPING

1 cup panko bread crumbs
¼ cup grated Parmesan
 cheese
2 Tbsp. butter, melted

1. Cut the peppers in half lengthwise and discard seeds. Place peppers, cut side down, in an ungreased 15x10x1-in. baking pan. Brush with 1 Tbsp. butter; sprinkle with pepper and salt. Bake, uncovered, at 350° for 10-15 minutes or until tender.

2. Meanwhile, in a large skillet, saute the onion and celery in the remaining butter until tender. Stir in cream cheese until melted. Add the shrimp, cheese blend, rice, lemon juice and seasonings; heat through. Spoon into pepper halves.

3. Place in an ungreased 15x10x1-in. baking pan. Combine topping ingredients; sprinkle over peppers. Bake, uncovered, at 350° for 10-15 minutes or until topping is golden brown.

1 STUFFED PEPPER HALF: 361 cal., 21g fat (13g sat. fat), 153mg chol., 541mg sod., 20g carb. (2g sugars, 2g fiber), 23g pro.

"I tried this recipe for stuffed peppers yesterday. They were delicious! My husband had two servings, which is something he very rarely does. It's a keeper."
—DENISE62ARIZONA, TASTEOFHOME.COM

MOM'S PAELLA

I enjoy cooking traditional foods from around the world, especially those that call for lots of rice. Like my mom, I often prepare this paella for special Sunday get-togethers.
—*Ena Quiggle, Goodhue, MN*

PREP: 10 MIN. • **COOK:** 40 MIN. • **MAKES:** 8 SERVINGS

1½ cups cubed cooked chicken

1 cup cubed fully cooked ham

½ cup sliced fully cooked smoked sausage (¼-in. slices)

1 medium onion, chopped

1 small green pepper, chopped

4 Tbsp. olive oil, divided

¼ cup pimiento-stuffed olives, halved

½ cup raisins, optional

1 cup uncooked converted rice

2 garlic cloves, minced

3 tsp. ground turmeric

1½ tsp. curry powder

2¼ cups chicken broth

1½ cups frozen mixed vegetables

1. In a large skillet, saute the chicken, ham, sausage, onion and green pepper in 2 Tbsp. oil for 3-5 minutes or until onion is tender. Add olives and raisins if desired. Cook 2-3 minutes longer or until heated through, stirring occasionally; remove meat and vegetable mixture from pan and keep warm.

2. In the same skillet, saute rice in remaining oil for 2-3 minutes or until lightly browned. Stir in the garlic, turmeric and curry. Return meat and vegetables to pan; toss lightly. Add broth and mixed vegetables; bring to a boil. Reduce heat; cover and simmer for 25-30 minutes or until rice is tender.

1 CUP: 258 cal., 14g fat (3g sat. fat), 39mg chol., 711mg sod., 19g carb. (3g sugars, 3g fiber), 15g pro.

MY BRAZILIAN FEIJOADA

When I found out a co-worker's mother used to make him feijoada, his favorite dish, I surprised him with my own version. If you like, use ham hocks instead of sausage, or lean white meat instead of red meat.
—*Christiane Counts, Webster, TX*

PREP: 20 MIN. + SOAKING • COOK: 7 HOURS • MAKES: 10 SERVINGS

8 oz. dried black beans
   (about 1 cup)
2 lbs. boneless pork
   shoulder butt roast,
   trimmed and cut into
   1-in. cubes
3 bone-in beef short ribs
   (about 1½ lbs.)
4 bacon strips, cooked
   and crumbled
1¼ cups diced onion
3 garlic cloves, minced
1 bay leaf
¾ tsp. salt
¾ tsp. pepper
1½ cups chicken broth
1 cup water
½ cup beef broth
8 oz. smoked sausage,
   cut into ½-in. slices
   Orange sections
   Hot cooked rice, optional

1. Rinse and sort beans; soak according to package directions. Meanwhile, place pork roast, short ribs and bacon in a 6-qt. slow cooker. Add onion, garlic, bay leaf and seasonings; pour chicken broth, water and beef broth over meat. Cook, covered, on high 2 hours.

2. Stir in beans and sausage. Cook, covered, on low 5-6 hours, until meat and beans are tender. Discard bay leaf. Remove short ribs. When cool enough to handle, remove the meat from bones; discard bones. Shred meat with 2 forks; return to slow cooker. Top servings with orange sections. If desired, serve with hot cooked rice.

1 SERVING: 481 cal., 27g fat (11g sat. fat), 123mg chol., 772mg sod., 17g carb. (2g sugars, 4g fiber), 41g pro.

FROM GRANDMA'S KITCHEN: Feijoada is a versatile stew of beans, various meats and sausages that's typically served over rice. Having originated in Portugal, feijoada is the national dish of Brazil.

CRUNCHY TUNA SURPRISE

Here's a tried-and-true recipe from my Grandma Mollie's kitchen. With my busy lifestyle, I appreciate quick and easy family-pleasers such as this one.
—*Lisa Le Sage, Wauwatosa, WI*

TAKES: 30 MIN. • MAKES: 4 SERVINGS

1 can (12 oz.) tuna, drained
   and flaked
1½ cups cooked rice
1 can (10¾ oz.) condensed
   cream of mushroom
   soup, undiluted
½ cup 2% milk
¼ cup minced fresh parsley
¾ cup crushed cornflakes
2 Tbsp. butter, melted

1. In a large bowl, combine the first 5 ingredients. Transfer to a greased shallow 1½-qt. baking dish.

2. Combine the cornflake crumbs and butter; sprinkle over the top. Bake, uncovered, at 350° for 25-30 minutes or until bubbly.

1 CUP: 341 cal., 11g fat (5g sat. fat), 52mg chol., 945mg sod., 39g carb. (4g sugars, 2g fiber), 21g pro.

MOM'S CELERY SEED BRISKET

Here's my advice: Keep a close eye on this tangy pot of goodness.
It's been fine-tuned to perfection and tends to vanish at gatherings!
—*Aysha Schurman, Ammon, ID*

PREP: 20 MIN. • **COOK:** 8 HOURS • **MAKES:** 8 SERVINGS

1 fresh beef brisket
   (3 to 4 lbs.)
1 can (28 oz.) Italian
   crushed tomatoes
1 large red onion, chopped
2 Tbsp. red wine vinegar
2 Tbsp. Worcestershire
   sauce
4 garlic cloves, minced
1 Tbsp. brown sugar
1 tsp. celery seed
1 tsp. pepper
½ tsp. salt
½ tsp. ground cumin
½ tsp. liquid smoke
4 tsp. cornstarch
3 Tbsp. cold water

1. Place brisket in a 5-qt. slow cooker. In a large bowl, combine tomatoes, onion, vinegar, Worcestershire sauce, garlic, brown sugar, celery seed, pepper, salt, cumin and liquid smoke. Pour over beef. Cover and cook on low until meat is tender, 8-10 hours.

2. Remove the meat to a serving platter; keep warm. In a large saucepan, combine the cornstarch and cold water until smooth. Gradually stir in 4 cups cooking liquid. Bring to a boil; cook and stir until thickened, 2 minutes. Slice brisket across the grain; serve with gravy.

FREEZE OPTION: Place individual portions of the sliced brisket in freezer containers; top with the gravy. Cool and freeze. To use, partially thaw in refrigerator overnight. Heat through in a covered saucepan, stirring occasionally; add water if necessary.

5 OZ. COOKED MEAT WITH ½ CUP GRAVY: 262 cal., 7g fat (3g sat. fat), 72mg chol., 425mg sod., 10g carb. (5g sugars, 1g fiber), 36g pro. DIABETIC EXCHANGES: 5 lean meat, 1 vegetable.

"This was really good. I didn't have a brisket in the freezer so I used a round roast. I also substituted fire-roasted diced tomatoes for the Italian crushed. There were no leftovers. Big hit with the family."
—EZONDII, TASTEOFHOME.COM

CITRUS HERB TURKEY

When it came to roasting a turkey, my grandma had the magic touch. She would wrap hers in foil and cook it on low heat for 8 hours so it would bake up juicy and tender. This version doesn't take as long—but I think it's just as good!

—Portia Gorman, Los Angeles, CA

PREP: 40 MIN. • **BAKE:** 2½ HOURS + STANDING • **MAKES:** 16 SERVINGS

1 pkg. (1 oz.) fresh rosemary, divided
1 pkg. (1 oz.) fresh thyme, divided
¾ cup softened unsalted butter, divided
1 turkey (12 to 14 lbs.)
2 tsp. seasoned salt
½ tsp. garlic powder
½ tsp. pepper
1 medium apple, chopped
1 medium orange, chopped
1 small red onion, chopped
1 small sweet orange pepper, chopped

1. Preheat oven to 400°. Line a roasting pan with 3 pieces of heavy-duty foil (pieces should be long enough to cover the turkey). Mince half the rosemary and thyme from each package (about ¼ cup total). In a small bowl, beat ½ cup butter and minced herbs until blended. With fingers, carefully loosen the skin from turkey breast; rub the butter mixture under the skin. Secure skin to underside of breast with toothpicks. Mix seasoned salt, garlic powder and pepper; sprinkle over turkey and inside turkey cavity.

2. Cube remaining butter. In a large bowl, combine butter, apple, orange, onion, orange pepper and remaining herb sprigs; spoon inside cavity. Tuck wings under turkey; tie drumsticks together. Place turkey in prepared pan, breast side up.

3. Bring edges of foil over turkey to cover. Roast, covered, 1 hour. Carefully open foil and fold it down. Reduce oven to 325°. Roast, uncovered, 1½-2 hours longer or until a thermometer inserted in thickest part of thigh reads 170°-175°. Cover loosely with foil if turkey browns too quickly.

4. Remove turkey from oven; tent with foil. Let stand 20 minutes before carving. Discard fruit mixture from cavity. If desired, skim fat and thicken pan drippings for gravy. Serve with turkey.

7 OZ. COOKED TURKEY: 488 cal., 27g fat (11g sat. fat), 207mg chol., 322mg sod., 3g carb. (2g sugars, 1g fiber), 55g pro.

ITALIAN PAN-FRIED CHICKEN

My Italian grandmother passed down her classic recipe for pan-fried chicken, and I've prepared it countless times. Over the years, I've made only slight modifications because her dish was already simple, satisfying and delicious.

—*Karen Mahlke, Estero, FL*

PREP: 15 MIN. • **COOK:** 40 MIN. • **MAKES:** 6 SERVINGS

- **6 bone-in chicken thighs (about 2¼ lbs.)**
- **½ tsp. pepper**
- **1½ tsp. minced fresh rosemary or ½ tsp. dried rosemary, crushed**
- **¾ tsp. minced fresh oregano or ¼ tsp. dried oregano**
- **¼ tsp. minced fresh basil or ⅛ tsp. dried basil**
- **2 Tbsp. olive oil**
- **9 garlic cloves, minced and divided**
- **¾ cup red wine vinegar**
- **¼ cup balsamic vinegar**
- **1 Tbsp. chicken base**
- **½ cup chardonnay or chicken broth**
- **1 Tbsp. heavy whipping cream**
- **1 Tbsp. cold butter**

1. Sprinkle chicken with pepper. Combine rosemary, oregano and basil; sprinkle half the herb mixture over chicken. In a large skillet over medium heat, place chicken, skin side down, in oil. Brown chicken on both sides. Add 8 garlic cloves; cook 1 minute longer. Stir in vinegars and chicken base. Cook, covered, on low heat until a thermometer reads 170°-175°, 15-20 minutes.

2. Remove the chicken to a serving platter; keep warm. Add the chardonnay to pan; increase heat to medium-high. Bring to a boil; cook, uncovered, until the liquid is reduced by half, 8-10 minutes, stirring to loosen browned bits from pan. Strain sauce. Return to pan and add remaining garlic clove and herb mixture; heat through. Stir in cream; remove from heat. Whisk in butter until creamy. If needed, return pan briefly to very low heat to soften butter. (Do not allow butter to melt completely or the sauce may separate.) Serve with chicken. If desired, garnish with additional rosemary and basil.

1 SERVING: 317 cal., 22g fat (6g sat. fat), 89mg chol., 425mg sod., 8g carb. (3g sugars, 0 fiber), 23g pro.

AIR-FRYER SALMON PATTIES

On days when we were working late on the family farm, my mom often fixed her salmon patties for a quick dinner. Feel free to add some chopped green or red peppers to the mixture.

—Bonnie Evans, Cameron, NC

TAKES: 25 MIN. • MAKES: 3 SERVINGS

⅓ cup finely chopped onion
1 large egg, beaten
5 saltines, crushed
½ tsp. Worcestershire sauce
¼ tsp. salt
⅛ tsp. pepper
1 can (14¾ oz.) salmon, drained, bones and skin removed
Cooking spray

1. Preheat air fryer to 375°. In a large bowl, combine the first 6 ingredients. Crumble salmon over mixture and mix lightly but thoroughly. Shape into 6 patties.

2. Arrange patties on greased tray in air-fryer basket; spritz with cooking spray. Cook until set and golden brown, 6-8 minutes.

2 PATTIES: 285 cal., 12g fat (3g sat. fat), 172mg chol., 876mg sod., 6g carb. (1g sugars, 0 fiber), 36g pro.

GRANDMA SCHWARTZ'S ROULADEN

My Grandpa Schwartz was a German butcher, and this beef recipe from Grandma was one of his (and our) favorite dishes. We think it's best served with mashed potatoes made with butter and sour cream.

—Lynda Sharai, Summer Lake, OR

PREP: 35 MIN. • COOK: 6 HOURS • MAKES: 6 SERVINGS

3 bacon strips, chopped
1½ lbs. beef top round steak
2 Tbsp. Dijon mustard
3 medium carrots, quartered lengthwise
6 dill pickle spears
¼ cup finely chopped onion
1 cup sliced fresh mushrooms
1 small parsnip, peeled and chopped
1 celery rib, chopped
1 can (10¾ oz.) condensed golden cream of mushroom soup, undiluted
⅓ cup dry red wine
2 Tbsp. Worcestershire sauce
2 Tbsp. minced fresh parsley

1. In a large skillet, cook bacon over medium heat until crisp. Remove to paper towels with a slotted spoon; drain, reserving drippings.

2. Meanwhile, cut steak into 6 serving-size pieces; pound with a meat mallet to ¼-in. thickness. Spread the tops with mustard. Top each with 2 carrot pieces and 1 pickle spear; sprinkle with onion. Roll up each from a short side and secure with toothpicks.

3. In a large skillet, brown the roll-ups in the bacon drippings over medium-high heat. Place roll-ups in a 4-qt. slow cooker. Top with mushrooms, parsnip, celery and cooked bacon.

4. In a small bowl, whisk soup, wine and Worcestershire sauce. Pour over the top. Cover and cook on low until the beef is tender, 6-8 hours. Sprinkle with parsley.

1 SERVING: 288 cal., 11g fat (3g sat. fat), 74mg chol., 1030mg sod., 14g carb. (4g sugars, 3g fiber), 28g pro.

**GRANDMA'S
SECRET**
Instead of using an air fryer, you
can fry these salmon patties on the
stovetop in a little cooking oil until
set and golden brown. Serve them
with mac 'n' cheese and
a green veggie.

AIR-FRYER
SALMON PATTIES

GREEK SAUSAGE & PEPPERS

Every year for Christmas Eve, I prepare this family-favorite dinner with my grandma and mom. After doing the chopping and slicing, we toss most of the ingredients into the slow cooker, turn it on and let it cook. The house smells amazing, and we have wonderful comfort food on a chilly holiday.
—*Debbie Vair, Wake Forest, NC*

PREP: 30 MIN. • **COOK:** 5½ HOURS • **MAKES:** 12 SERVINGS

4 lbs. loukaniko or other smoked sausage, cut into ½-in. slices

1 each large sweet yellow, orange and red peppers, chopped

1 large sweet onion, chopped

2 cups beef stock

1 whole garlic bulb, minced

1 Tbsp. minced fresh oregano or 1 tsp. dried oregano

1 tsp. coarse sea salt

1 tsp. coarsely ground pepper

3 to 3½ cups cherry tomatoes

Hot cooked rice, optional

In a 7- or 8-qt. slow cooker, combine the sausage, sweet peppers, onion, beef stock, garlic, oregano, salt and pepper. Cook, covered, on low until vegetables are tender, 5-6 hours. Add tomatoes; cook until wilted, about 30 minutes longer. If desired, serve with rice.

1¼ CUPS: 504 cal., 41g fat (17g sat. fat), 101mg chol., 1958mg sod., 10g carb. (7g sugars, 2g fiber), 23g pro.

LEMON CHICKEN PASTA

Here's my twist on the lemony chicken and rice my mother used to make. In my quick update, I saute lightly breaded chicken breasts and serve them over capellini pasta.
—*Aileen Rivera, Bronx, NY*

PREP: 30 MIN. • COOK: 15 MIN. • MAKES: 6 SERVINGS

4 boneless skinless chicken breast halves (6 oz. each)
1 tsp. salt, divided
¼ tsp. plus ⅛ tsp. pepper, divided
½ cup all-purpose flour
8 oz. uncooked capellini or angel hair pasta
3 Tbsp. olive oil, divided
¼ cup peeled and thinly sliced garlic cloves (about 12 cloves)
1 cup white wine or chicken broth
2 Tbsp. lemon juice
½ cup grated Parmigiano-Reggiano cheese
⅓ cup plus 3 Tbsp. minced fresh parsley, divided
   Lemon wedges, optional

1. Pound chicken with a meat mallet to ¼-in. thickness. Sprinkle with ½ tsp. salt and ¼ tsp. pepper. Place flour in a shallow bowl. Dip chicken in flour to coat both sides; shake off excess.

2. Cook pasta according to the package directions for al dente. Meanwhile, in a large skillet, heat 2 Tbsp. oil over medium heat. Add chicken; cook 2-3 minutes on each side or until no longer pink. Remove and keep warm.

3. In same pan, heat remaining oil over medium heat; add garlic. Cook and stir 30-60 seconds or until the garlic is lightly browned. Add wine to pan; increase heat to medium-high. Cook, stirring to loosen browned bits from pan, until liquid is reduced by half. Stir in lemon juice.

4. Drain pasta, reserving ½ cup pasta water; place in a large bowl. Add cheese, ⅓ cup parsley, half of the garlic mixture, and the remaining salt and pepper; toss to combine, adding enough reserved pasta water to moisten the pasta. Serve with chicken. Drizzle with remaining garlic mixture; sprinkle with remaining parsley. If desired, serve with lemon wedges.

1 SERVING: 403 cal., 12g fat (3g sat. fat), 68mg chol., 577mg sod., 35g carb. (2g sugars, 2g fiber), 31g pro. DIABETIC EXCHANGES: 4 lean meat, 2 starch, 1½ fat.

"The flavor is delicate but still rich with garlic. Works fine with fettuccine or, in a pinch, other types of pasta."
—NH-RESCUE, TASTEOFHOME.COM

CHERRY TOMATO
PASTA WITH AVOCADO
SAUCE, PAGE 173

GRANDMA'S FAVORITE
SIDE DISHES

Be prepared to be wowed by the amazingly delicious
accompaniments in this chapter. On Grandma's table,
side dishes are anything but a side note!

PIZZA BEANS

Take this pizza-inspired dish to your next party—you'll hear raves! A larger serving
of these beans can even make a delicious main course alongside a green salad.
—Taste of Home *Test Kitchen*

PREP: 20 MIN. • COOK: 6 HOURS • MAKES: 20 SERVINGS

1   **lb. bulk Italian sausage**
2   **cups chopped celery**
2   **cups chopped onion**
1   **can (14½ oz.) cut**
    green beans, drained
1   **can (14½ oz.) cut**
    wax beans, drained
1   **can (16 oz.) kidney beans,**
    rinsed and drained
1   **can (16 oz.) butter beans,**
    drained
1   **can (15 oz.) pork**
    and beans
3   **cans (8 oz. each)**
    pizza sauce
    Optional toppings:
    Grated Parmesan
    cheese, minced fresh
    oregano and crushed
    red pepper flakes

In a large skillet, brown sausage over medium heat until no longer pink, breaking it into crumbles. Transfer to a 5-qt. slow cooker with a slotted spoon. Add the celery and onion to the skillet; cook until softened, about 5 minutes. Drain. Add vegetable mixture and the next 6 ingredients to slow cooker; mix well. Cover and cook on low until bubbly, 6-8 hours. If desired, serve with toppings.

FREEZE OPTION: Freeze the cooled beans in freezer containers. To use, partially thaw in the refrigerator overnight. Heat through in a saucepan, stirring occasionally; add a little water or broth if necessary.

¾ CUP: 142 cal., 6g fat (2g sat. fat), 12mg chol., 542mg sod., 17g carb. (4g sugars, 5g fiber), 7g pro.

MOM'S POTATO PANCAKES

These old-fashioned potato pancakes are fluffy inside and crispy outside, just like Mom's.
She got her recipe from Grandma, and it's been a favorite for many years.
—Dianne Esposite, New Middletown, OH

TAKES: 30 MIN. • MAKES: 6 SERVINGS

4   **cups shredded peeled**
    potatoes (about 4 large
    potatoes)
1   **large egg, lightly beaten**
3   **Tbsp. all-purpose flour**
1   **Tbsp. grated onion**
1   **tsp. salt**
¼   **tsp. pepper**
    Oil for frying
    Optional: Chopped
    parsley, applesauce
    and sour cream

1. Rinse shredded potatoes in cold water; drain well, squeezing to remove excess water. Place in a large bowl. Stir in egg, flour, onion, salt and pepper.

2. In a large nonstick skillet, heat ¼ in. oil over medium heat. Working in batches, drop potato mixture by ⅓ cupfuls into oil; press to flatten slightly. Fry both sides until golden brown; drain on paper towels. Serve immediately. If desired, sprinkle with parsley and top with applesauce and sour cream.

2 PANCAKES: 171 cal., 7g fat (1g sat. fat), 31mg chol., 411mg sod., 24g carb. (1g sugars, 2g fiber), 3g pro.

PIZZA
BEANS

GRANDMA'S
SECRET

Don't feel like using your slow cooker? These pizza beans can be made in the oven instead. Simply bake the beans at 325° until bubbly (about 1½ hours).

GREEN BEAN & POTATO SALAD

For family reunions, my mom would bring everybody's favorite
bean and potato salad tossed in a homemade dressing.
Now I'm the one who carries on the tradition.
—*Connie Dicavoli, Shawnee, KS*

PREP: 15 MIN. • **COOK:** 20 MIN. + CHILLING • **MAKES:** 10 SERVINGS

- **2 lbs. red potatoes (about 6 medium), cubed**
- **1 lb. fresh green beans, trimmed and halved**
- **1 small red onion, halved and thinly sliced**
- **¼ cup chopped fresh mint, optional**

DRESSING
- **½ cup canola oil**
- **¼ cup white vinegar**
- **2 Tbsp. lemon juice**
- **1 tsp. salt**
- **½ tsp. garlic powder**
- **¼ tsp. pepper**

1. Place potatoes in a 6-qt. stockpot; add water to cover. Bring to a boil. Reduce heat; cook, uncovered, 10-15 minutes or until tender, adding beans during the last 4 minutes of cooking. Drain.

2. Transfer potatoes and beans to a large bowl; add onion and, if desired, mint. In a small bowl, whisk the dressing ingredients until blended. Pour over the potato mixture; toss gently to coat. Refrigerate, covered, at least 2 hours before serving.

¾ CUP: 183 cal., 11g fat (1g sat. fat), 0 chol., 245mg sod., 19g carb. (2g sugars, 3g fiber), 3g pro. **DIABETIC EXCHANGES:** 2½ fat, 1 starch.

LEMON MUSHROOM ORZO

Here's a pasta dish we've enjoyed both chilled and hot. The orzo gets a pleasant
twist from the lemon, and the toasted pecans add a nice crunch.
—*Shelly Nelson, Akeley, MN*

TAKES: 25 MIN. • **MAKES:** 12 SERVINGS

- **1 pkg. (16 oz.) orzo pasta**
- **3 Tbsp. olive oil, divided**
- **¾ lb. sliced fresh mushrooms**
- **¾ cup chopped pecans, toasted**
- **½ cup minced fresh parsley**
- **1 tsp. grated lemon zest**
- **3 Tbsp. lemon juice**
- **1 tsp. salt**
- **½ tsp. pepper**

1. Cook the orzo according to package directions. Meanwhile, in a large cast-iron or other heavy skillet, heat 2 Tbsp. oil over medium-high heat. Add mushrooms; cook and stir until tender and lightly browned. Drain orzo.

2. In a large bowl, place the orzo, mushroom mixture, pecans, parsley, lemon zest, lemon juice, salt, pepper and remaining oil; toss to combine.

¾ CUP: 225 cal., 9g fat (1g sat. fat), 0 chol., 202mg sod., 31g carb. (2g sugars, 2g fiber), 6g pro. **DIABETIC EXCHANGES:** 2 starch, 1½ fat.

CREAMY RANCH PASTA

I came up with this side while preparing food for a bridal shower. It was party day and I needed to take some shortcuts! Everyone loves the easy Parmesan ranch white sauce, and you can throw in veggies you have on hand.
—*Merry Graham, Newhall, CA*

PREP: 25 MIN. • **BAKE:** 30 MIN. • **MAKES:** 8 SERVINGS

2½ cups uncooked bow tie pasta
2 cups (8 oz.) shredded Italian cheese blend
1¼ cups grated Parmesan cheese, divided
1 cup (8 oz.) sour cream
1 cup ranch salad dressing
1 pkg. (10 oz.) frozen chopped spinach, thawed and squeezed dry or 2 cups chopped fresh spinach
2 slices day-old French bread (½ in. thick)
1 Tbsp. olive oil
1 tsp. grated lemon zest
1 tsp. dried parsley flakes
¼ tsp. garlic salt

1. Preheat oven to 350°. Cook the bow tie pasta according to the package directions.

2. In a large bowl, mix Italian cheese blend, 1 cup Parmesan cheese, sour cream and salad dressing. Drain pasta; add to the cheese mixture. Fold in spinach. Transfer to a greased 13x9-in. baking dish.

3. Tear French bread into pieces; place in a food processor. Cover and pulse until crumbs form. Toss bread crumbs with oil, lemon zest, parsley, garlic salt and remaining ¼ cup Parmesan cheese. Sprinkle over pasta mixture.

4. Bake, covered, 25 minutes. Uncover; bake until golden brown and bubbly, 5-10 minutes.

¾ CUP: 436 cal., 30g fat (12g sat. fat), 40mg chol., 841mg sod., 25g carb. (3g sugars, 2g fiber), 15g pro.

AIR-FRYER CANDIED ACORN SQUASH SLICES

My grandma always served her simple but yummy acorn squash at Thanksgiving. She passed the recipe down to me, and now I make it in my air fryer.
—*Rita Addicks, Weimar, TX*

PREP: 15 MIN. • **COOK:** 15 MIN./BATCH • **MAKES:** 6 SERVINGS

2 medium acorn squash
⅔ cup packed brown sugar
½ cup butter, softened

1. Preheat air fryer to 350°. Cut squash in half lengthwise; remove and discard the seeds. Cut each half crosswise into ½-in. slices; discard the ends. In batches, arrange squash in a single layer on greased tray in air-fryer basket. Cook until just tender, 5 minutes per side.

2. Combine the brown sugar and butter; spread over squash. Cook 3 minutes longer.

NOTE: If you don't have an air fryer, you can make this recipe in an oven.

1 SERVING: 320 cal., 16g fat (10g sat. fat), 41mg chol., 135mg sod., 48g carb. (29g sugars, 3g fiber), 2g pro.

CRANBERRY
APPLE STUFFING

CRANBERRY APPLE STUFFING

One Thanksgiving, I couldn't find the stuffing recipe I planned to use, so I improvised and created a cranberry version. I got a wonderful compliment from my cousin Sandy, a die-hard fan of traditional stuffing. She said mine was the best she'd ever tasted!
—*Beverly A. Norris, Evanston, WY*

PREP: 30 MIN. • **BAKE:** 30 MIN. • **MAKES:** 12 SERVINGS

¾ **lb. bulk Italian sausage**
2 **celery ribs,**
 finely chopped
1 **small onion,**
 finely chopped
6 **garlic cloves, minced**
1 **can (14½ oz.) chicken**
 broth
½ **cup butter, cubed**
1 **pkg. (12 oz.) seasoned**
 stuffing cubes
1½ **cups chopped apples**
1 **cup dried cranberries**
½ **cup slivered almonds**
1½ **tsp. dried sage leaves**
1½ **tsp. dried thyme**
⅛ **tsp. pepper**
 Dash salt
1 **to 1½ cups apple cider**
 or juice

1. Preheat oven to 350°. In a Dutch oven, cook sausage, celery, onion and garlic over medium heat until sausage is no longer pink; drain. Add broth, stirring to loosen browned bits from pan. Add butter; cook and stir until butter is melted. Remove from the heat.

2. Stir in stuffing cubes, apples, cranberries, almonds, sage, thyme, pepper, salt and enough cider to reach desired moistness. Transfer to a greased 13x9-in. baking dish.

3. Cover and bake 25 minutes. Uncover; bake until lightly browned, 5-10 minutes.

¾ CUP: 338 cal., 17g fat (7g sat. fat), 36mg chol., 809mg sod., 40g carb. (16g sugars, 4g fiber), 8g pro.

"Awesome recipe! Everyone raves about it when we make it. We've even made it with gluten-free stuffing cubes and it's still delicious! "
—AUDRA13, TASTEOFHOME.COM

COLCANNON IRISH POTATOES

My mother came from Ireland as a teen and cooked traditional dishes such as this one. It's a fantastic way to get my family to eat more veggies—cabbage is hidden in Grandma's potatoes!
—*Marie Pagel, Lena, WI*

TAKES: 30 MIN. • **MAKES:** 10 SERVINGS

2½ **lbs. potatoes (about**
 6 medium), peeled and
 cut into 1-in. pieces
2 **cups chopped cabbage**
1 **large onion, chopped**
1 **tsp. salt**
¼ **tsp. pepper**
¼ **cup butter, softened**
1 **cup 2% milk**

1. Place the potatoes in a 6-qt. stockpot; add water to cover. Bring to a boil. Reduce heat to medium; cook, covered, until potatoes are almost tender, 8-10 minutes.

2. Add cabbage and onion; cook, covered, until cabbage is tender, 5-7 minutes. Drain; return to the pot. Add salt and pepper; mash to desired consistency, gradually adding butter and milk.

¾ CUP: 129 cal., 5g fat (3g sat. fat), 14mg chol., 290mg sod., 19g carb. (4g sugars, 2g fiber), 3g pro. **DIABETIC EXCHANGES:** 1 starch, 1 fat.

GRANDMA'S CLASSIC POTATO SALAD

When I asked my grandmother how old this potato salad recipe is, she told me that her mom used to prepare it when Grandma was a little girl. It has definitely stood the test of time.

—*Kimberly Wallace, Dennison, OH*

PREP: 25 MIN. • COOK: 20 MIN. + CHILLING • MAKES: 10 SERVINGS

6 medium potatoes, peeled and cubed
¼ cup all-purpose flour
1 Tbsp. sugar
1½ tsp. salt
1 tsp. ground mustard
1 tsp. pepper
¾ cup water
2 large eggs, beaten
¼ cup white vinegar
4 hard-boiled large eggs, divided use
2 celery ribs, chopped
1 medium onion, chopped
Sliced green onions, optional

1. Place potatoes in a large saucepan and cover with water. Bring to a boil. Reduce heat; cover and cook until tender, 15-20 minutes. Drain and cool to room temperature.

2. Meanwhile, in a small heavy saucepan, combine flour, sugar, salt, mustard and pepper. Gradually stir in water until smooth. Cook and stir over medium-high heat until thickened and bubbly. Reduce heat; cook and stir 2 minutes longer.

3. Remove from the heat. Stir a small amount of the hot mixture into beaten eggs; return all to the pan, stirring constantly. Bring to a gentle boil; cook and stir 2 minutes longer. Remove from the heat and cool completely. Gently stir in vinegar.

4. Chop and refrigerate 1 hard-boiled egg; chop the remaining 3 hard-boiled eggs. In a large bowl, combine the potatoes, celery, chopped onion and eggs; add the dressing and stir until blended. Refrigerate until chilled. Garnish with reserved chopped egg and, if desired, sliced green onions.

¾ CUP: 144 cal., 3g fat (1g sat. fat), 112mg chol., 402mg sod., 23g carb. (3g sugars, 2g fiber), 6g pro. **DIABETIC EXCHANGES:** 1½ starch, ½ fat.

BUTTERED NOODLES

Here's a quick side people ask for again and again. I dress up egg noodles with two kinds of cheese and a few other basic ingredients.
—*Heather Nalley, Easley, SC*

TAKES: 20 MIN. • MAKES: 4 SERVINGS

2¼ cups uncooked
  egg noodles
¼ cup shredded part-skim
  mozzarella cheese
2 Tbsp. butter, melted
2 Tbsp. grated Parmesan
  cheese
2 tsp. minced fresh parsley
¼ tsp. salt
¼ tsp. garlic powder
⅛ tsp. pepper

Cook the noodles according to package directions; drain. Transfer to a serving bowl. Immediately add the remaining ingredients and toss to coat.

¾ CUP: 165 cal., 9g fat (5g sat. fat), 40mg chol., 290mg sod., 16g carb. (1g sugars, 1g fiber), 6g pro.

FROM GRANDMA'S KITCHEN: If you don't have the egg noodles this recipe calls for, simply use another pasta shape or type. For example, try fettuccine, spaghetti, pappardelle or rigatoni.

APPLE & GORGONZOLA SALAD

I added the gorgonzola to this tangy dressing my grandmother used to make. Once I also mistakenly marinated the apples in the dressing for a few hours. It tasted so good that now I do it every time.
—*Pat Ferjancsik, Santa Rosa, CA*

PREP: 15 MIN. + CHILLING • MAKES: 2 SERVINGS

½ cup heavy
  whipping cream
¼ cup red wine vinegar
¼ tsp. salt
¼ tsp. pepper
1 medium red apple,
  thinly sliced
½ cup crumbled
  Gorgonzola cheese
2 cups torn curly endive

1. In a small bowl, whisk the cream, vinegar, salt and pepper. Stir in the apple and cheese. Cover and refrigerate for at least 1 hour.

2. Divide endive between 2 plates; top with apple mixture.

1 SERVING: 358 cal., 30g fat (20g sat. fat), 107mg chol., 709mg sod., 16g carb. (7g sugars, 4g fiber), 8g pro.

MINTY PEAS & ONIONS

When Mother was in a hurry and needed a quick side dish, she turned to the peas and onions recipe from my grandmother. Besides being easy to prepare, it complemented many different main courses and pleased everyone at the table.
—*Santa D'Addario, Jacksonville, FL*

TAKES: 20 MIN. • MAKES: 8 SERVINGS

2 **large onions, cut into ½-in. wedges**
½ **cup chopped sweet red pepper**
2 **Tbsp. canola oil**
2 **pkg. (16 oz. each) frozen peas**
2 **Tbsp. minced fresh mint or 2 tsp. dried mint**

In a large skillet, saute the onions and red pepper in oil until onions just begin to soften. Add peas; cook, uncovered, stirring occasionally, for 10 minutes or until heated through. Stir in mint and cook for 1 minute.

1 SERVING: 134 cal., 4g fat (1g sat. fat), 0 chol., 128mg sod., 19g carb. (9g sugars, 6g fiber), 6g pro. DIABETIC EXCHANGES: 1 starch, 1 fat.

SCALLOPED SWEET CORN CASSEROLE

I grew up enjoying my grandma's sweet corn casserole. Now I love treating my own children and grandchildren to that home-style comfort food.
—*Lonnie Hartstack, Clarinda, IA*

PREP: 25 MIN. • BAKE: 50 MIN. • MAKES: 8 SERVINGS

4 **tsp. cornstarch**
⅔ **cup water**
¼ **cup butter, cubed**
3 **cups fresh or frozen corn**
1 **can (5 oz.) evaporated milk**
¾ **tsp. plus 1½ tsp. sugar, divided**
½ **tsp. plus ¾ tsp. salt, divided**
3 **large eggs**
¾ **cup 2% milk**
¼ **tsp. pepper**
3 **cups cubed bread**
1 **small onion, chopped**
1 **cup Rice Krispies, slightly crushed**
3 **Tbsp. butter, melted**

1. Preheat oven to 350°. In a small bowl, mix the cornstarch and water until smooth. In a large saucepan, heat butter over medium heat. Stir in corn, evaporated milk, ¾ tsp. sugar and ½ tsp. salt; bring just to a boil. Stir in cornstarch mixture; return to a boil, stirring constantly. Cook and stir 1-2 minutes or until thickened; cool slightly.

2. In a large bowl, whisk the eggs, milk, pepper and the remaining sugar and salt until blended. Stir in bread, onion and corn mixture. Transfer to a greased 8-in. square or 1½-qt. baking dish.

3. Bake, uncovered, 40 minutes. In a small bowl, toss the Rice Krispies with the melted butter; sprinkle over casserole. Bake 10-15 minutes longer or until golden brown.

FREEZE OPTION: Cool the unbaked casserole, reserving the Rice Krispies topping for baking; cover and freeze. To use, partially thaw in refrigerator overnight. Remove from refrigerator 30 minutes before baking. Preheat oven to 350°. Bake casserole as directed, increasing the time as necessary to heat through and for a thermometer inserted in center to read 165°.

⅔ CUP: 258 cal., 15g fat (8g sat. fat), 104mg chol., 604mg sod., 26g carb. (9g sugars, 2g fiber), 8g pro.

MINTY PEAS
& ONIONS

CELERY GRATIN

My grandmother had a knack for turning simple ingredients into something memorable. Here's just one delicious example!
—*David Ross, Spokane Valley, WA*

PREP: 25 MIN. • BAKE: 25 MIN. • MAKES: 8 SERVINGS

½ cup butter, divided
6 Tbsp. all-purpose flour
1 cup whole milk
1 cup heavy whipping cream
¾ cup shredded Swiss cheese
½ tsp. salt

½ tsp. pepper
Dash ground nutmeg
8 celery ribs, cut into 1-in. pieces
½ cup chopped celery leaves
6 slices white bread, crusts removed

1. Preheat oven to 375°. In a large saucepan, melt 6 Tbsp. butter over medium heat. Stir in the flour until smooth; gradually whisk in milk and heavy cream. Bring to a boil, stirring constantly; cook and stir until thickened, 3-4 minutes. Stir in cheese, salt, pepper and nutmeg until combined. Stir in celery and leaves; transfer to a greased 13x9-in. baking dish.

2. Tear bread into pieces and place in a food processor or blender. Cover and pulse until crumbs form. Transfer to a large bowl. Melt remaining 2 Tbsp. butter. Drizzle over bread crumbs; toss to coat. Sprinkle over celery mixture.

3. Bake until bubbly and topping is golden brown, 25-30 minutes. If desired, sprinkle with additional celery leaves.

⅔ CUP: 331 cal., 27g fat (17g sat. fat), 77mg chol., 390mg sod., 16g carb. (4g sugars, 1g fiber), 7g pro.

HOMEMADE FETTUCCINE

Indulge in a taste of Italy by making your own from-scratch fettuccine—no pasta maker required!
—Taste of Home *Test Kitchen*

PREP: 1¼ HOURS + STANDING • MAKES: 1¼ LBS.

3½ to 4 cups semolina flour
1 tsp. salt
1 cup warm water

1. Combine 3½ cups flour and salt in a large bowl. Make a well in center. Pour water into well and stir together, forming a ball.

2. Turn onto a floured surface; knead until smooth and elastic, 8-10 minutes, adding remaining flour if necessary to keep dough from sticking to surface and hands (dough will be stiff). Shape into a rectangle; cover and let rest for 30 minutes.

3. Divide the dough into fourths. On a floured surface, roll each portion into a 16x8-in. rectangle. Dust dough with flour to prevent sticking while rolling. Cut crosswise into ⅛-in. slices. Separate noodles onto clean towels; let dry overnight (let dry in the shape the noodles will be stored in). Package dry pasta.

4. To cook fettuccine: Fill a Dutch oven three-fourths full with water. Bring to a boil. Add noodles; cook, uncovered, until tender, 8-10 minutes. Drain.

2 OZ.: 210 cal., 1g fat (0 sat. fat), 0 chol., 237mg sod., 43g carb. (1g sugars, 2g fiber), 7g pro.

SEASONED BEANS & TOMATOES

For years, Grandma Wasnock made these spiced green beans on Christmas Day. When my aunt served them at her daughter's wedding, we found out the recipe came from a handmade cookbook my aunt received at her bridal shower.
—John Wasnock, Medina, NY

TAKES: 15 MIN. • MAKES: 4-6 SERVINGS

1 medium onion, diced
2 Tbsp. canola oil
2 cups fresh or frozen green beans, thawed
1 can (14½ oz.) diced tomatoes, undrained
2 Tbsp. sugar
¼ tsp. salt
¼ tsp. ground cloves
⅛ tsp. pepper

In a skillet, saute onion in oil until tender. Stir in the remaining ingredients. Bring to a boil. Reduce heat; cook, uncovered, over medium-low heat until the green beans are tender. Serve with a slotted spoon.

¾ CUP: 92 cal., 5g fat (1g sat. fat), 0 chol., 189mg sod., 12g carb. (9g sugars, 3g fiber), 2g pro.

HOMEMADE POTATO GNOCCHI

My Italian mom still has the bowl that her mother used for mixing gnocchi dough.
Grandma treated family and friends to these homemade potato dumplings on special occasions.
—*Tina Mirilovich, Johnstown, PA*

PREP: 30 MIN. • **COOK:** 10 MIN./BATCH • **MAKES:** 8 SERVINGS

4 medium potatoes,
  peeled and quartered
1 egg, lightly beaten
1½ tsp. salt, divided
1¾ to 2 cups all-purpose
  flour
3 qt. water
  Spaghetti sauce, warmed
  Optional: grated
  Parmesan cheese,
  crushed red pepper
  flakes and fresh herbs,
  such as basil, oregano
  or parsley

1. Place the potatoes in a saucepan and cover with water. Bring to a boil. Reduce heat; cover and cook for 15-20 minutes or until tender. Drain and mash.

2. Place 2 cups mashed potatoes in a large bowl (save any remaining mashed potatoes for another use). Stir in the egg and 1 tsp. salt. Gradually beat in flour until blended (dough will be firm and elastic).

3. Turn onto a lightly floured surface; knead 15 times. Roll into ½-in.-wide ropes. Cut ropes into 1-in. pieces. Press down with a lightly floured fork.

4. In a Dutch oven, bring the water and remaining salt to a boil. Add the gnocchi in small batches; cook for 8-10 minutes or until gnocchi float to the top and are cooked through. Remove with a slotted spoon. Serve immediately with spaghetti sauce. Top with desired toppings.

1 SERVING: 159 cal., 1g fat (0 sat. fat), 27mg chol., 674mg sod., 33g carb. (1g sugars, 2g fiber), 5g pro.

FROM GRANDMA'S KITCHEN: It's best to store gnocchi uncooked. It will last about 5 days in the refrigerator or about 1 month in the freezer. To freeze, place uncooked gnocchi on a baking tray in the freezer. Transfer to zip-top bags once frozen.

CREAMY BLUEBERRY GELATIN SALAD

With refreshing fruit and a fluffy topping, Mom's gelatin salad was a must
on our holiday menus. Now it's become a favorite with my grandchildren, too.
—*Sharon Hoefert, Greendale, WI*

PREP: 30 MIN. + CHILLING • MAKES: 15 SERVINGS

2 pkg. (3 oz. each)
grape gelatin
2 cups boiling water
1 can (21 oz.) blueberry pie
filling
1 can (20 oz.) unsweetened
crushed pineapple,
undrained

TOPPING
1 pkg. (8 oz.) cream cheese,
softened
1 cup sour cream
½ cup sugar
1 tsp. vanilla extract
½ cup chopped walnuts

1. In a large bowl, dissolve the gelatin in the boiling water. Cool for 10 minutes. Stir in pie filling and pineapple until blended. Transfer to a 13x9-in. dish. Cover and refrigerate until partially set, about 1 hour.

2. For topping, in a small bowl, combine the cream cheese, sour cream, sugar and vanilla. Carefully spread over gelatin; sprinkle with walnuts. Cover and refrigerate until firm.

1 PIECE: 221 cal., 10g fat (5g sat. fat), 27mg chol., 76mg sod., 29g carb. (26g sugars, 1g fiber), 4g pro.

STRAWBERRY GELATIN SALAD: Prepare gelatin salad with strawberry gelatin and pie filling instead of grape and blueberry. Stir in 1¼ cups chilled lemon-lime soda instead of the pineapple. Top if desired.

CHERRY COLA SALAD: Prepare gelatin salad with cherry gelatin and pie filling instead of grape and blueberry. Substitute 20 oz. crushed pineapple (drained) for undrained pineapple and add ¾ cup chilled cola. Omit topping.

DAD'S BAKED BEANS

I automatically reach for Dad's recipe when I need to serve baked beans
for any occasion. The reason is simple—they're the best I've ever tasted!
—*Kimberly Wallace, Dennison, OH*

PREP: 15 MIN. • BAKE: 1 HOUR • MAKES: 8 SERVINGS

3 cans (15½ oz. each) great
northern beans, rinsed
and drained
5 hot dogs, sliced
1½ cups ketchup
½ cup packed brown sugar
2 Tbsp. molasses
1 medium onion, chopped
½ tsp. ground mustard
¼ tsp. salt
¼ tsp. pepper

In an ungreased 2-qt. baking dish, combine all ingredients. Cover and bake at 350° for 1 to 1½ hours or until heated through.

¾ CUP: 344 cal., 9g fat (4g sat. fat), 16mg chol., 1322mg sod., 55g carb. (30g sugars, 8g fiber), 11g pro.

AUNT MARGARET'S SWEET POTATO CASSEROLE

My great-aunt made the most incredible sweet potato casserole for special dinners. I've lightened it up a bit, but we love it just the same.
—*Beth Britton, Fairlawn, OH*

PREP: 50 MIN. • BAKE: 50 MIN. • MAKES: 12 SERVINGS

3 lbs. sweet potatoes (about 3 large), peeled and cubed

TOPPING
¾ cup all-purpose flour
¾ cup packed brown sugar
¾ cup old-fashioned oats
⅛ tsp. salt
⅓ cup cold butter, cubed

FILLING
½ cup sugar
½ cup 2% milk
2 large eggs, lightly beaten
¼ cup butter
1 tsp. vanilla extract
2 cups miniature marshmallows

1. Preheat oven to 350°. Place sweet potatoes in a 6-qt. stockpot; add water to cover. Bring to a boil. Reduce heat; cook, uncovered, until tender, 10-12 minutes. Meanwhile, make the topping by combining the flour, brown sugar, oats and salt; cut in the cold butter until crumbly.

2. Drain potatoes; return to pan. Beat until mashed. Add sugar, milk, eggs, butter and vanilla; mash. Transfer to a broiler-safe 13x9-in. baking dish. Sprinkle topping over potato mixture.

3. Bake, uncovered, until topping is golden brown, 40-45 minutes; let stand 10 minutes. Sprinkle with marshmallows. If desired, broil 4-5 in. from heat until marshmallows are puffed and golden, 30-45 seconds.

½ CUP: 373 cal., 11g fat (6g sat. fat), 56mg chol., 134mg sod., 66g carb. (39g sugars, 4g fiber), 5g pro.

FROM GRANDMA'S KITCHEN: If you add the marshmallows to the casserole right out of the oven, they'll start to melt together and form a silky marshmallow layer.

ORZO WITH CARAMELIZED BUTTERNUT SQUASH & BACON

The year my garden produced a bumper crop of butternut squash, I tried so many new recipes to use up the bounty. This is a tasty, easy side I've enjoyed countless times since. For a main course instead, just add shrimp or shredded chicken.
—*Kallee Krong-McCreery, Escondido, CA*

PREP: 20 MIN. • **COOK:** 20 MIN. • **MAKES:** 6 SERVINGS

1½ **cups uncooked orzo pasta**
4 **bacon strips, chopped**
2 **cups cubed peeled butternut squash (½-in. cubes)**
½ **cup chopped onion**
1 **cup cut fresh or frozen cut green beans, thawed**
1 **garlic clove, minced**
1 **Tbsp. butter**
1 **tsp. garlic salt**
¼ **tsp. pepper**
¼ **cup grated Parmesan cheese**
   Minced fresh parsley

1. In a large saucepan, cook orzo according to package directions.

2. Meanwhile, in a large skillet, cook bacon over medium heat until crisp, stirring occasionally. Remove with a slotted spoon; drain on paper towels. Cook and stir squash and onion in bacon drippings until tender, 8-10 minutes. Add beans and garlic; cook 1 minute longer.

3. Drain the orzo; stir into the squash mixture. Add butter, garlic salt, pepper and reserved bacon; heat through. Sprinkle with Parmesan and parsley.

¾ CUP: 329 cal., 11g fat (4g sat. fat), 20mg chol., 533mg sod., 47g carb. (4g sugars, 3g fiber), 11g pro.

CREAMED POTATOES & PEAS

Early in June, we always helped Mom pick the first sweet peas of the season. She combined them with red potatoes and green onion for a creamy dish everyone loved.
—*Ginny Werkmeister, Tilden, NE*

PREP: 10 MIN. • **COOK:** 25 MIN. • **MAKES:** 6 SERVINGS

1 **lb. small red potatoes**
2½ **cups frozen peas**
¼ **cup butter, cubed**
1 **green onion, sliced**
¼ **cup all-purpose flour**
½ **tsp. salt**
   Dash pepper
2 **cups 2% milk**

1. Scrub and quarter the potatoes; place in a large saucepan and cover with water. Bring to a boil. Reduce heat; cover and simmer for 10 minutes. Add the peas; cook 5 minutes longer or until the vegetables are tender.

2. Meanwhile, in another large saucepan, melt butter. Add onion; saute until tender. Stir in the flour, salt and pepper until blended; gradually add milk. Bring to a boil. Reduce heat; cook and stir for 1-2 minutes or until thickened. Drain the potatoes and peas; toss with sauce.

¾ CUP: 236 cal., 11g fat (6g sat. fat), 28mg chol., 355mg sod., 28g carb. (8g sugars, 4g fiber), 8g pro.

ORZO WITH CARAMELIZED
BUTTERNUT SQUASH & BACON

SLOW-COOKER POLENTA

Take advantage of your slow cooker to enjoy an Italian classic
any day of the week—even the busiest!
—*Elisabeth Matelski, Boston, MA*

PREP: 10 MIN. • COOK: 6 HOURS • MAKES: 12 SERVINGS

13 **cups reduced-sodium chicken broth, divided**
3 **cups cornmeal**
1 **medium onion, finely chopped**
3 **garlic cloves, minced**
2 **bay leaves**
2 **tsp. salt**

1 **cup half-and-half cream**
1 **cup shredded Parmesan cheese**
¼ **cup butter, cubed**
1 **tsp. pepper**
 Additional shredded Parmesan cheese

In a 6-qt. slow cooker, combine 12 cups broth, cornmeal, onion, garlic, bay leaves and salt. Cook, covered, on low 6-8 hours, until liquid is absorbed and polenta is creamy. Remove bay leaves. Stir in cream, cheese, butter, pepper and remaining broth. If desired, serve with additional cheese.

1 CUP: 255 cal., 8g fat (5g sat. fat), 25mg chol., 1168mg sod., 34g carb. (3g sugars, 2g fiber), 9g pro.

SUPREME GREEN VEGETABLE BAKE

When my paternal grandmother passed her veggie bake recipe down to me, she included suggestions
for different ways of preparing it. She was a big inspiration for my love of cooking.
—*Priscilla Gilbert, Indian Harbour Beach, FL*

PREP: 15 MIN. • BAKE: 20 MIN. • MAKES: 8 SERVINGS

3 **large eggs, lightly beaten**
1 **can (10¾ oz.) condensed cream of mushroom soup, undiluted**
⅓ **cup mayonnaise**
1½ **cups shredded reduced-fat cheddar cheese**
1 **small onion, finely chopped**
6 **cups frozen chopped broccoli, thawed and patted dry**
1 **pkg. (10 oz.) frozen chopped spinach, thawed and squeezed dry**
1 **cup french-fried onions**

1. In a large bowl, combine the first 5 ingredients. Fold in broccoli and spinach. Transfer to a greased 13x9-in. baking dish. Sprinkle with french-fried onions.

2. Bake, uncovered, at 350° for 20-25 minutes or until a thermometer inserted in the center reads 160° and the top is lightly browned.

¾ CUP: 261 cal., 19g fat (6g sat. fat), 99mg chol., 591mg sod., 12g carb. (3g sugars, 4g fiber), 11g pro.

12-HOUR SALAD

This was Mom's scrumptious scheme to get us kids to eat vegetables! She never had any trouble
when she served this colorful, crunchy salad. The bonus was that she could
make it the night before and just refrigerate it until mealtime.
—*Dorothy Bowen, Thomasville, NC*

PREP: 20 MIN. + CHILLING • MAKES: 12 SERVINGS

8 cups torn mixed
  salad greens
1½ cups chopped celery
2 medium green peppers,
  chopped
1 medium red onion,
  chopped
2½ cups frozen peas
  (about 10 oz.), thawed
1 cup mayonnaise
1 cup sour cream
3 Tbsp. sugar
1 cup shredded
  cheddar cheese
½ lb. bacon strips, cooked
  and crumbled

1. Place greens in a 3-qt. bowl or 13x9-in. dish. Layer with celery, peppers, onion and peas.

2. Mix mayonnaise, sour cream and sugar; spread over the top. Sprinkle with cheese and bacon. Refrigerate, covered, 12 hours or overnight.

1 CUP: 280 cal., 23g fat (7g sat. fat), 22mg chol., 347mg sod., 11g carb. (6g sugars, 3g fiber), 8g pro.

*"Amazing flavors. Everyone loved this salad—it was the
first to go at our barbecue! It doesn't go soggy, it stays
fresh, and the bacon flavor goes all the way through.
I will make this again for sure."*
—MAZZYJEN, TASTEOFHOME.COM

GERMAN POTATO DUMPLINGS

Called Kartoffel Kloesse in Germany, potato dumplings are a delightful addition
to any feast, German or not. The browned butter sauce that accompanies them is delectable.
—*Arline Hofland, Deer Lodge, MT*

PREP: 40 MIN. • COOK: 10 MIN. • MAKES: 8 SERVINGS

3 lbs. medium potatoes
  (about 10), peeled
  and quartered
1 cup all-purpose flour
3 large eggs, lightly beaten
⅔ cup dry bread crumbs
1 tsp. salt
½ tsp. ground nutmeg
12 cups water

BROWNED BUTTER SAUCE
½ cup butter, cubed
1 Tbsp. chopped onion
¼ cup dry bread crumbs

1. Place the potatoes in a Dutch oven; add water to cover. Bring to a boil. Reduce heat; cook, uncovered, 15-20 minutes or until tender. Drain; transfer to a large bowl.

2. Mash potatoes. Stir in the flour, eggs, bread crumbs, salt and nutmeg. Shape into sixteen (2-in.) balls.

3. In a Dutch oven, bring water to a boil. Carefully add the dumplings. Reduce heat; simmer, uncovered, 7-9 minutes or until a toothpick inserted in center of dumplings comes out clean.

4. Meanwhile, in a small heavy saucepan, heat butter and onion over medium heat. Cook 5-7 minutes or until butter is golden brown, stirring constantly. Remove from heat; stir in bread crumbs. Serve with dumplings.

2 DUMPLINGS WITH 2 TBSP. SAUCE: 367 cal., 14g fat (8g sat. fat), 100mg chol., 524mg sod., 51g carb. (2g sugars, 5g fiber), 9g pro.

SWEET POTATO
KALE PILAF

SWEET POTATO KALE PILAF

Wild rice goes from ordinary to amazing when you stir in sweet potatoes, bacon, asparagus and kale. To save time and cut down on dishes, cook the rice in an Instant Pot and use it to saute the other ingredients, too.
—*Courtney Stultz, Weir, KS*

PREP: 15 MIN. • COOK: 1 HOUR • MAKES: 8 CUPS

1 cup uncooked wild rice
2¼ cups vegetable broth
   or water
1 tsp. olive oil
4 bacon strips, chopped
1 lb. fresh asparagus,
   trimmed and cut into
   2-in. pieces
1 large sweet potato,
   peeled and chopped
½ cup chopped red onion
1 cup chopped fresh kale
1 garlic clove, minced
½ tsp. salt
½ tsp. pepper
   Chopped fresh parsley

1. Rinse wild rice thoroughly; drain. In a large saucepan, combine broth, rice and oil; bring to a boil. Reduce heat; simmer, covered, until rice is fluffy and tender, 50-55 minutes. Drain if necessary.

2. Meanwhile, in a large skillet, cook bacon over medium heat until crisp. Remove to paper towels to drain. Add asparagus, sweet potato and onion to bacon drippings; cook and stir over medium-high heat until potatoes are crisp-tender, 8-10 minutes.

3. Stir in the kale, garlic, salt and pepper. Cook and stir until vegetables are tender, 8-10 minutes. Stir in rice and reserved bacon. Sprinkle with parsley.

¾ CUP: 156 cal., 5g fat (2g sat. fat), 7mg chol., 350mg sod., 23g carb. (5g sugars, 3g fiber), 5g pro. DIABETIC EXCHANGES: 1½ starch, 1 fat.

OLD-FASHIONED DRESSING

Remember Grandma's delicious turkey dressing? Taste it again with this family favorite you can make in your slow cooker.
—*Sherry Vink, Lacombe, AB*

PREP: 35 MIN. • COOK: 3 HOURS • MAKES: 8 SERVINGS

½ cup butter, cubed
2 celery ribs, chopped
1 cup sliced fresh
   mushrooms
1 medium onion, chopped
½ cup minced fresh parsley
2 tsp. rubbed sage
2 tsp. dried marjoram
1 tsp. dried thyme
1 tsp. poultry seasoning
½ tsp. pepper
¼ tsp. salt
6 cups cubed day-old
   white bread
6 cups cubed day-old
   whole wheat bread
1 can (14½ oz.) chicken
   broth

1. In a large skillet, melt the butter. Add the celery, mushrooms and onion; saute until tender. Stir in the seasonings. Place bread cubes in a large bowl. Stir in vegetable mixture. Add chicken broth; toss to coat.

2. Transfer to a 3-qt. slow cooker coated with cooking spray. Cover and cook on low for 3-4 hours or until heated through.

¾ CUP: 258 cal., 14g fat (8g sat. fat), 31mg chol., 714mg sod., 30g carb. (4g sugars, 4g fiber), 6g pro.

LORA'S RED BEANS & RICE

My dear mother-in-law shared this simple dish with me. The meats, beans
and veggies simmer in the slow cooker all day to savory perfection.
—Carol Simms, Madison, MS

PREP: 15 MIN. + SOAKING • COOK: 8 HOURS • MAKES: 10 SERVINGS

1 **lb. dried kidney beans
(about 2½ cups)**
2 **cups cubed fully cooked
ham (about 1 lb.)**
1 **pkg. (12 oz.) fully cooked
andouille chicken
sausage links or flavor
of choice, sliced**
1 **medium green pepper,
chopped**
1 **medium onion, chopped**
2 **celery ribs, chopped**
1 **Tbsp. hot pepper sauce**
2 **garlic cloves, minced**
1½ **tsp. salt**
Hot cooked rice

1. Place kidney beans in a large bowl; add cool water to cover.
Soak overnight.

2. Drain the beans, discarding the water; rinse with cool water.
Place beans in a greased 6-qt. slow cooker. Stir in ham, sausage,
vegetables, pepper sauce, garlic and salt. Add water to cover
by 1 in.

3. Cook, covered, on low 8-9 hours or until beans are tender.
Serve with rice.

1 CUP BEAN MIXTURE: 249 cal., 5g fat (1g sat. fat), 43mg chol.,
906mg sod., 31g carb. (2g sugars, 7g fiber), 23g pro.

MAMA'S WARM GERMAN POTATO SALAD

Every relative would arrive with food in hand when my grandmother, Mama, held family gatherings
at her home. She always made her German potato salad. She never wrote down the recipe,
so I had to re-create it from memory. I think this is just about right!
—Charlene Chambers, Ormond Beach, FL

PREP: 20 MIN. • COOK: 30 MIN. • MAKES: 12 SERVINGS

3 **lbs. small red potatoes**
⅓ **cup canola oil**
2 **Tbsp. champagne
vinegar**
1 **tsp. kosher salt**
½ **tsp. coarsely ground
pepper**
½ **English cucumber,
very thinly sliced**
2 **celery ribs, thinly sliced**
1 **small onion, chopped**
6 **bacon strips, cooked
and crumbled**
1 **Tbsp. minced fresh
parsley**

Place the red potatoes in a large saucepan; add water to cover.
Bring to a boil. Reduce the heat; cook, uncovered, until tender,
18-21 minutes. Drain; cool slightly. Peel and thinly slice. Whisk
oil, vinegar, salt and pepper. Add potatoes; toss to coat. Add the
remaining ingredients; toss to combine. Serve warm.

¾ CUP: 163 cal., 8g fat (1g sat. fat), 4mg chol., 246mg sod.,
20g carb. (2g sugars, 2g fiber), 4g pro. DIABETIC EXCHANGES:
1½ fat, 1 starch.

CAULIFLOWER DILL KUGEL

I enjoy cauliflower and kugel, so I decided to try combining
the two into one special dish. The ricotta cheese adds
a distinctive creaminess and lightness, while
shallots and herbs deepen the flavors.
—Arlene Erlbach, Morton Grove, IL

PREP: 30 MIN. • BAKE: 35 MIN. + STANDING • MAKES: 8 SERVINGS

5   Tbsp. butter, divided
1½ cups thinly sliced shallots
4   large eggs
2   cups whole-milk
    ricotta cheese
1   cup minced fresh parsley,
    divided
½   cup shredded Gruyere
    or Swiss cheese
¼   cup dill weed, divided

3   tsp. grated lemon
    zest, divided
¼   tsp. salt, divided
⅛   tsp. pepper
1   pkg. (16 oz.) frozen
    cauliflower, thawed
    and patted dry
¾   cup panko bread crumbs
½   tsp. garlic powder

1. Preheat oven to 375°. In a large skillet, heat 3 Tbsp. butter over
medium-high heat. Add shallots; cook and stir until golden brown,
3-5 minutes. Remove and set aside.

2. In a large bowl, mix the eggs, ricotta cheese, ¾ cup parsley,
shredded cheese, 3 Tbsp. dill, 2 tsp. lemon zest, ⅛ tsp. salt and
pepper. Stir in cauliflower and shallots. Transfer to a greased
8-in. square baking dish.

3. In the same skillet, heat the remaining butter. Add the bread
crumbs; cook and stir until lightly browned, 2-3 minutes. Stir
in garlic powder and the remaining parsley, dill, lemon zest and
salt. Sprinkle over cauliflower mixture.

4. Bake, uncovered, until set, 35-45 minutes. Let stand 10 minutes
before cutting. Refrigerate leftovers.

1 PIECE: 289 cal., 19g fat (11g sat. fat), 147mg chol., 343mg sod.,
16g carb. (7g sugars, 3g fiber), 16g pro.

HOMEMADE PIEROGI

Pierogi, dumplings stuffed with a filling, bring traditional comfort to the table.
This meatless version contains potatoes, onions and cream cheese.
—Diane Gawrys, Manchester, TN

PREP: 1 HOUR • COOK: 5 MIN./BATCH • MAKES: 6 DOZEN

SIDE DISHES

5 **cups all-purpose flour**
1 **tsp. salt**
1 **cup water**
3 **large eggs**
½ **cup butter, softened**

FILLING
4 **medium potatoes,**
   peeled and cubed
2 **medium onions, chopped**
2 **Tbsp. butter**
5 **oz. cream cheese,**
   softened
½ **tsp. salt**
½ **tsp. pepper**

ADDITIONAL INGREDIENTS
   (FOR EACH SERVING)
¼ **cup chopped onion**
1 **Tbsp. butter**
   Minced fresh parsley

1. In a food processor, combine flour and salt; cover and pulse to blend. Add water, eggs and butter; cover and pulse until dough forms a ball, adding an additional 1-2 Tbsp. of water or flour if needed. Let rest, covered, 15-30 minutes.

2. Place the potatoes in a large saucepan and cover with water. Bring to a boil over high heat. Reduce heat; cover and simmer until tender, 10-15 minutes. Meanwhile, in a large skillet over medium-high heat, saute onions in butter until tender.

3. Drain potatoes. Over very low heat, stir potatoes until steam has evaporated, 1-2 minutes. Press through a potato ricer or strainer into a large bowl. Stir in the cream cheese, salt, pepper and onion mixture.

4. Divide dough into 4 parts. On a lightly floured surface, roll 1 portion of dough to ⅛-in. thickness; cut with a floured 3-in. biscuit cutter. Place 2 tsp. of filling in the center of each circle. Moisten edges with water; fold in half and press edges to seal. Repeat with remaining dough and filling.

5. Bring a Dutch oven of water to a boil over high heat; add the pierogi in batches. Reduce heat to a gentle simmer; cook until pierogi float to the top and are tender, 1-2 minutes. Remove with a slotted spoon. In a large skillet, saute 4 pierogi and the onion in butter until pierogi are lightly browned and heated through; sprinkle with parsley. Repeat with remaining pierogi.

FREEZE OPTION: Place cooled pierogi on waxed paper-lined 15x10x1-in. baking pans; freeze until firm. Transfer to an airtight freezer container; freeze up to 3 months. To use, for each serving, in a large skillet, saute 4 pierogi and ¼ cup chopped onion in 1 Tbsp. butter until pierogi are lightly browned and heated through; sprinkle with minced fresh parsley.

4 PIEROGI: 373 cal., 22g fat (13g sat. fat), 86mg chol., 379mg sod., 38g carb. (3g sugars, 2g fiber), 6g pro.

GRANDMA'S SECRET
Pierogi dough needs to be boiled before it is fried to ensure the dough is cooked all the way through. Frying also gives the dough a better texture and golden color.

DAD'S CREAMED PEAS & PEARL ONIONS

When I was growing up, it was a tradition to have creamed peas with pearl onions as part of our Thanksgiving and Christmas dinners. My dad would not be a happy camper if he sat at the table and didn't see this dish—it was his favorite! I made it for my own family, and now my daughter does the same for hers.

—*Nancy Heishman, Las Vegas, NV*

TAKES: 25 MIN. • **MAKES:** 6 SERVINGS

5 cups frozen peas (about 20 oz.), thawed and drained
2 cups frozen pearl onions (about 9 oz.), thawed and drained
2 celery ribs, finely chopped
¾ cup chicken broth
½ tsp. salt
½ tsp. pepper
½ tsp. dried thyme
½ cup sour cream
10 bacon strips, cooked and crumbled
¾ cup salted cashews

In a large skillet, combine the first 7 ingredients; bring to a boil. Reduce heat to medium; cook, uncovered, until the onions are tender and most of liquid is evaporated, 8-10 minutes, stirring occasionally. Remove from heat; stir in sour cream. Top with bacon and cashews.

¾ CUP: 322 cal., 18g fat (6g sat. fat), 19mg chol., 783mg sod., 26g carb. (10g sugars, 7g fiber), 14g pro.

"This recipe is so delicious! I prepared it for a cookout on Memorial Day, and there was almost nothing left after everyone ate their fill."
—APRILF, TASTEOFHOME.COM

GOLDEN BEET CURRY RISOTTO WITH CRISPY BEET GREENS

I was delighted to find golden beets at the farmers market and knew they'd be perfect in a risotto recipe I was working on. With the baked crispy beet greens, it's a vibrant side that will steal the show.

—*Merry Graham, Newhall, CA*

PREP: 30 MIN. • **COOK:** 50 MIN. • **MAKES:** 6 SERVINGS

3 medium fresh golden beets and beet greens
3 Tbsp. melted coconut oil, divided
¾ tsp. sea salt, divided
5 cups reduced-sodium chicken broth
1 cup chopped leeks (white portion only)
1 tsp. curry powder
1 tsp. garlic salt
1 cup medium pearl barley
½ cup white wine or unsweetened apple juice
1 cup grated Manchego cheese
3 Tbsp. lemon juice (Meyer lemons preferred)
4 tsp. grated lemon zest, divided
¼ tsp. coarsely ground pepper
¼ cup chopped fresh parsley
Lemon slices

1. Preheat oven to 350°. Wash and trim beet greens, removing the stems; dry with paper towels. Place the greens in a single layer on parchment-lined baking sheets. Brush with 1 Tbsp. coconut oil; sprinkle with ¼ tsp. sea salt. Bake until dry and crisp, 15-18 minutes. Set aside.

2. Meanwhile, peel and dice the beets. In a large saucepan, bring chicken broth to a boil. Add beets. Reduce heat; simmer, covered, until beets are tender, 15-18 minutes. Remove beets with a slotted spoon. Keep broth hot.

3. In another large saucepan, heat the remaining coconut oil over medium heat. Add the leeks; cook and stir 2-3 minutes. Add the curry powder, garlic salt and remaining sea salt; cook, stirring, until leeks are tender, 2-3 minutes. Increase heat to medium-high. Add the barley; stir constantly until lightly toasted, 2-3 minutes. Add wine; stir until liquid has evaporated.

4. Add enough broth, about 1 cup, to cover barley. Reduce heat to medium; cook and stir until broth is absorbed. Add remaining broth, ½ cup at a time, cooking and stirring until broth is absorbed after each addition. Stir in beets with last addition of broth. Cook until barley is tender but firm to the bite and risotto is creamy, 25-30 minutes.

5. Remove from heat. Stir in cheese, lemon juice, 2½ tsp. grated lemon zest and pepper. Transfer to a serving dish. Sprinkle with parsley and remaining lemon zest. Serve with crispy beet greens and lemon slices.

⅔ CUP: 314 cal., 14g fat (11g sat. fat), 19mg chol., 1238mg sod., 37g carb. (7g sugars, 8g fiber), 12g pro.

CALICO
BEANS

CALICO BEANS

Need to satisfy big appetites? Packed full of ground beef and bacon, these beans
are an especially hearty side and can even make a main course.
—*Betty Claycomb, Alverton, PA*

PREP: 25 MIN. • BAKE: 45 MIN. • MAKES: 10 SERVINGS

1 lb. lean ground beef
(90% lean)
1 small onion, chopped
1 can (21 oz.) pork
and beans
1 can (16 oz.) kidney beans,
rinsed and drained
1 can (16 oz.) butter beans,
rinsed and drained
½ cup packed brown sugar
½ cup ketchup
4 bacon strips, cooked
and crumbled
1 Tbsp. cider vinegar
1 tsp. prepared mustard
1 tsp. salt

1. Preheat oven to 325°. In a large skillet, cook the ground beef
and onion over medium heat until the beef is no longer pink,
5-7 minutes, breaking up beef into crumbles; drain. Stir in the
remaining ingredients. Transfer to a greased 2-qt. cast-iron pan
or baking dish.

2. Bake, uncovered, until the beans are as thick as desired,
45-60 minutes.

1 SERVING: 260 cal., 5g fat (2g sat. fat), 32mg chol., 826mg sod.,
39g carb. (19g sugars, 7g fiber), 18g pro.

MUSHROOMS MARSALA WITH BARLEY

Here's a tasty mashup of chicken Marsala and mushroom barley soup. The ingredients go in my
slow cooker for a filling vegetarian dish that can be served with or without the barley.
—*Arlene Erlbach, Morton Grove, IL*

PREP: 20 MIN. • COOK: 4¼ HOURS • MAKES: 6 SERVINGS

1½ lbs. baby portobello
mushrooms, cut into
¾-in. chunks
1 cup thinly sliced shallots
3 Tbsp. olive oil
½ tsp. minced fresh thyme
¾ cup Marsala wine,
divided
3 Tbsp. reduced-fat
sour cream
2 Tbsp. all-purpose flour
1½ tsp. grated lemon zest
¼ tsp. salt
¼ cup crumbled
goat cheese
¼ cup minced fresh parsley
2½ cups cooked barley

1. In a 4- or 5-qt. slow cooker, combine mushrooms, shallots,
olive oil and thyme. Add ¼ cup Marsala wine. Cook, covered,
on low about 4 hours, until vegetables are tender.

2. Stir in sour cream, flour, lemon zest, salt and remaining ½ cup
Marsala. Cook, covered, on low 15 minutes longer. Sprinkle with
goat cheese and parsley. Serve with hot cooked barley.

¾ CUP MUSHROOMS WITH ABOUT ⅓ CUP BARLEY: 235 cal., 9g fat
(2g sat. fat), 7mg chol., 139mg sod., 31g carb. (6g sugars, 5g fiber),
7g pro. DIABETIC EXCHANGES: 2 starch, 2 fat, 1 vegetable.

FROM GRANDMA'S KITCHEN: Marsala is an Italian wine fortified
with alcohol. Its distinctive flavor is found in many Italian desserts,
entrees and side dishes. You can substitute red or white wine, beer
or broth for the Marsala, but take note—making such a substitution
will change the flavor dramatically.

FINNISH CAULIFLOWER

After my Finnish grandmother passed away, I found a large index card in a box of her trinkets.
I had the writing translated, and it turned out to be this festive cauliflower casserole.
—*Judy Batson, Tampa, FL*

PREP: 20 MIN. • BAKE: 30 MIN. • MAKES: 8 SERVINGS

2 **cups cubed day-old rye bread**
1 **small head cauliflower, cut into florets**
2 **Tbsp. butter**
1 **tsp. caraway seeds**
3 **cups shredded sharp cheddar cheese**
4 **large eggs, beaten**
1 **cup flat beer or nonalcoholic beer**
1 **tsp. ground mustard**
½ **tsp. ground coriander**
¼ **tsp. pepper**

1. Place the bread in a 15x10x1-in. baking pan; bake at 300° for 15-20 minutes or until crisp. In a large skillet, saute cauliflower in butter with the caraway seeds until tender. Remove from the heat; stir in bread and cheese. Transfer to a greased 11x7-in. baking dish.

2. In a small bowl, whisk the eggs, beer, mustard, coriander and pepper. Pour over bread mixture. Bake at 350° for 30-35 minutes or until a knife inserted in the center comes out clean.

1 SERVING: 261 cal., 18g fat (12g sat. fat), 158mg chol., 387mg sod., 10g carb. (3g sugars, 2g fiber), 14g pro.

CHEESY BEANS & RICE

To accommodate my dad's special dietary needs years ago, Mom adapted an old recipe
and came up with a lighter beans-and-rice dish. It's been a dinnertime hit
for a long time. Even my kids are fans—and they can be quite picky!
—*Linda Rindels, Littleton, CO*

PREP: 15 MIN. • BAKE: 35 MIN. • MAKES: 6 SERVINGS

1 **cup uncooked brown rice**
1 **can (16 oz.) kidney beans, rinsed and drained**
1 **large onion, chopped**
1 **Tbsp. canola oil**
1 **can (14½ oz.) diced tomatoes and green chilies, undrained**
2 **tsp. chili powder**
¼ **tsp. salt**
1¼ **cups shredded reduced-fat cheddar cheese, divided**

1. Cook rice according to package directions. Transfer to a large bowl; add the beans. In a nonstick skillet, saute the onion in oil for 4-5 minutes. Stir in the tomatoes, chili powder and salt. Bring to a boil; remove from the heat.

2. In a 2-qt. baking dish coated with cooking spray, layer a third of the rice mixture, cheese and tomato mixture. Repeat layers. Layer with remaining rice mixture and tomato mixture.

3. Cover and bake at 350° for 30 minutes or until heated through. Uncover; sprinkle with remaining cheese. Bake 5-10 minutes longer or until cheese is melted.

1 CUP: 306 cal., 7g fat (3g sat. fat), 13mg chol., 470mg sod., 47g carb. (0 sugars, 9g fiber), 15g pro. **DIABETIC EXCHANGES:** 2½ starch, 2 lean meat, 1 vegetable.

PEAS PLEASE ASIAN NOODLES

As the name implies, my Asian-inspired pasta salad doubles up on the peas for some serious crunch and sweetness.

—Catherine Cassidy, Milwaukee, WI

TAKES: 20 MIN. • MAKES: 8 SERVINGS

12 oz. uncooked Japanese soba noodles or whole wheat spaghetti
¼ cup water
1 cup fresh snow peas or sugar snap peas, trimmed
3 cups ice water
¾ cup frozen green peas, thawed
1 small cucumber, chopped
3 green onions, finely chopped

SAUCE
¼ cup creamy peanut butter
3 Tbsp. orange juice
3 Tbsp. white or rice vinegar
3 Tbsp. soy sauce
4 tsp. sesame oil or tahini
4 tsp. canola oil
1 Tbsp. garlic powder
2 to 3 tsp. hot pepper sauce
2¼ tsp. sugar

TOPPINGS
½ cup chopped fresh cilantro
Sesame seeds, toasted

1. Cook the noodles according to package directions. Meanwhile, in a small saucepan, bring ¼ cup water to a boil over medium-high heat. Add snow peas; cook, uncovered, just until crisp-tender, 1-2 minutes. Drain; immediately drop snow peas into ice water. Remove and pat dry.

2. Drain noodles; rinse with cold water and drain again. Combine noodles with snow peas, green peas, cucumber and green onions.

3. In another bowl, whisk together the sauce ingredients until blended; pour over noodles and vegetables. Toss to coat. To serve, sprinkle with cilantro and sesame seeds.

1 CUP: 264 cal., 9g fat (1g sat. fat), 0 chol., 740mg sod., 39g carb. (4g sugars, 2g fiber), 10g pro.

"I was unsure about this recipe at first, but my husband likes anything peanut butter, so I decided to try it. So glad I did! It's delicious! My hubby loved it. He went back for seconds and asked to have it for his lunch for work."
—JETLUVS2COOK, TASTEOFHOME.COM

SMOKY MACARONI & CHEESE

I discovered this recipe years ago in a magazine, and I kept tweaking the ingredients until I found the perfect combination. You can make it in the oven, but grilling or smoking is the real way to go.
—*Stacey Dull, Gettysburg, OH*

PREP: 40 MIN. • GRILL: 20 MIN. + STANDING • MAKES: 2 CASSEROLES (8 SERVINGS EACH)

- 6 **cups small pasta shells**
- 12 **oz. Velveeta, cut into small cubes**
- 2 **cups shredded smoked cheddar cheese, divided**
- 1 **cup shredded cheddar cheese**
- 1 **cup 2% milk**
- 4 **large eggs, lightly beaten**
- ¾ **cup heavy whipping cream**
- ⅔ **cup half-and-half cream**
- ½ **cup shredded provolone cheese**
- ½ **cup shredded Colby-Monterey Jack cheese**
- ½ **cup shredded pepper jack cheese**
- 1 **tsp. salt**
- ½ **tsp. pepper**
- ½ **tsp. smoked paprika**
- ½ **tsp. liquid smoke, optional**
  Dash cayenne pepper, optional
- 8 **bacon strips, cooked and crumbled, optional**

1. Preheat grill or smoker to 350°. Cook the pasta according to package directions for al dente. Drain and transfer to a large bowl. Stir in Velveeta, 1 cup smoked cheddar, cheddar cheese, milk, eggs, heavy cream, half-and-half cream, provolone, Colby-Monterey Jack, pepper jack, salt, pepper, paprika and, if desired, liquid smoke and cayenne pepper.

2. Transfer to 2 greased 13x9-in. baking pans; sprinkle with the remaining 1 cup smoked cheddar cheese. Place on grill or smoker rack. Grill or smoke, covered, until a thermometer reads at least 160°, 20-25 minutes, rotating the pans partway through cooking. Do not overcook. Let stand 10 minutes before serving; if desired, sprinkle with bacon.

1 CUP: 403 cal., 23g fat (13g sat. fat), 117mg chol., 670mg sod., 30g carb. (4g sugars, 1g fiber), 18g pro.

FROM GRANDMA'S KITCHEN: Turn this side dish into an easy entree by stirring in cooked chicken, grilled pork, last night's taco meat or even leftover breakfast sausages.

GLAZED JULIENNED CARROTS

Mom's glazed carrots have just enough butter and sugar in them to bring out the veggie's natural sweetness. Beyond that, you'll need only water, salt and thyme to get a wonderful side on the table.
—*Mary Lou Boyce, Wilmington, DE*

TAKES: 20 MIN. • MAKES: 8 SERVINGS

- 2 **lbs. carrots, julienned**
- ⅓ **cup butter, cubed**
- ¼ **cup sugar**
- ¼ **cup water**
- ½ **tsp. salt**
  Fresh thyme sprigs, optional

In a large skillet, combine all ingredients. Cover and cook over medium heat for 7-10 minutes or until carrots are crisp-tender. Serve with a slotted spoon. If desired, sprinkle with thyme.

¾ CUP: 140 cal., 8g fat (5g sat. fat), 20mg chol., 264mg sod., 18g carb. (14g sugars, 3g fiber), 1g pro. DIABETIC EXCHANGES: 2 vegetable, 1½ fat, ½ starch.

SMOKY MACARONI
& CHEESE

AIR-FRYER BEETS WITH ORANGE GREMOLATA & GOAT CHEESE

My grandma would grow beets and then either pickle or can them. I like to roast them in an air fryer and add fresh herbs, a splash of citrus and tangy goat cheese. The colorful side dish is delicious whether served warm or chilled.

—*Courtney Archibeque, Greeley, CO*

PREP: 25 MIN. • **COOK:** 45 MIN. + COOLING • **MAKES:** 12 SERVINGS

- 3 **medium fresh golden beets (about 1 lb.)**
- 3 **medium fresh beets (about 1 lb.)**
- 2 **Tbsp. lime juice**
- 2 **Tbsp. orange juice**
- ½ **tsp. fine sea salt**
- 1 **Tbsp. minced fresh parsley**
- 1 **Tbsp. minced fresh sage**
- 1 **garlic clove, minced**
- 1 **tsp. grated orange zest**
- 3 **Tbsp. crumbled goat cheese**
- 2 **Tbsp. sunflower kernels**

1. Preheat air fryer to 400°. Scrub the beets and trim tops by 1 in. Place beets on a double thickness of heavy-duty foil (about 24x12 in.). Fold foil around beets, sealing tightly. Place in a single layer on tray in air-fryer basket. Cook until tender, 45-55 minutes. Open foil carefully to allow steam to escape.

2. When cool enough to handle, peel, halve and slice beets; place in a serving bowl. Add the lime juice, orange juice and salt; toss to coat. Combine parsley, sage, garlic and orange zest; sprinkle over beets. Top with goat cheese and sunflower kernels. Serve warm or chilled.

¾ CUP: 49 cal., 1g fat (0 sat. fat), 2mg chol., 157mg sod., 9g carb. (6g sugars, 2g fiber), 2g pro.

CHERRY TOMATO PASTA WITH AVOCADO SAUCE
PICTURED ON PAGE 136

Heart-healthy avocado makes this pasta indulgent without being overly rich. The flavorful sauce is dairy-free but so luscious that your guests will think there's cream hiding in there. Even the texture and consistency call to mind traditional cream-based sauces.
—*Julie Peterson, Crofton, MD*

TAKES: 30 MIN. • MAKES: 10 SERVINGS

- 1 pkg. (14½ oz.) protein-enriched rotini (about 3½ cups uncooked)
- 2 medium ripe avocados, peeled and pitted
- 1 cup fresh spinach
- ¼ cup loosely packed basil leaves
- 2 garlic cloves, halved
- 2 Tbsp. lime juice
- ½ tsp. kosher salt
- ¼ tsp. coarsely ground pepper
- ⅓ cup olive oil
- 1 cup assorted cherry tomatoes, halved
- ½ cup pine nuts
  Optional: Shredded Parmesan cheese, shredded mozzarella cheese and grated lime zest

1. Cook the rotini according to package directions for al dente. Meanwhile, place the avocados, spinach, basil, garlic, lime juice, salt and pepper in a food processor; pulse until chopped. Continue processing while gradually adding oil in a steady stream.

2. Drain rotini; transfer to a large bowl. Add avocado mixture and tomatoes; toss to coat. Sprinkle with pine nuts, and add toppings as desired.

¾ CUP: 314 cal., 18g fat (2g sat. fat), 0 chol., 125mg sod., 32g carb. (2g sugars, 5g fiber), 9g pro.

FROM GRANDMA'S KITCHEN: Avocado sauce may turn slightly brown, which is natural and normal. However, the lime juice in the sauce will help slow the browning process.

GERMAN-STYLE SPINACH
We children never had to be told to eat our spinach at Grandma's house! Her recipe reflects her Austrian heritage and always pleases everyone at the table.
—*Joan Hutter, Warwick, RI*

TAKES: 20 MIN. • MAKES: 8 SERVINGS

- 2 pkg. (10 oz. each) frozen chopped spinach
- 1 large onion, chopped
- 2 garlic cloves, minced
- 2 Tbsp. butter
- 6 bacon strips, cooked and crumbled
- ½ tsp. ground nutmeg
- ½ tsp. salt
  Pepper to taste

Cook the spinach according to the package directions. Drain well and set aside. Saute the onion and garlic in butter in a large skillet until tender. Stir in the spinach, bacon, nutmeg, salt and pepper; heat through.

¾ CUP: 70 cal., 5g fat (3g sat. fat), 12mg chol., 279mg sod., 3g carb. (1g sugars, 1g fiber), 3g pro.

GRANDMA'S
PRESSURE-COOKER
CHICKEN NOODLE SOUP,
PAGE 182

GRANDMA'S FAVORITE

SOUPS & STEWS

Get a pot simmering and ladle up some chowder,
bisque, chili or other specialty from Grandma.
Whatever you choose, it's a bowl of pure comfort.

SAUCY INDIAN-STYLE CHICKEN & VEGETABLES

Warm naan flatbreads make the perfect side for this easy Indian dish. Feel free to add more or less tikka masala sauce according to your taste.
—*Erica Polly, Sun Prairie, WI*

PREP: 15 MIN. • COOK: 4 HOURS • MAKES: 8 SERVINGS

2 medium sweet potatoes, peeled and cut into 1½-in. pieces
2 Tbsp. water
2 medium sweet red peppers, cut into 1-in. pieces
3 cups fresh cauliflowerets
2 lbs. boneless skinless chicken thighs, cubed
2 jars (15 oz. each) tikka masala curry sauce
¾ tsp. salt
Minced fresh cilantro, optional
Naan flatbreads, warmed

1. Microwave sweet potatoes and water, covered, on high just until potatoes begin to soften, 3-4 minutes.

2. In a 5- or 6-qt. slow cooker, combine vegetables and chicken; add sauce and salt. Cook, covered, on low 4-5 hours or until meat is tender. If desired, top with cilantro. Serve with warmed naan.

FREEZE OPTION: Omitting the cilantro, freeze cooled chicken and vegetable mixture in freezer containers. To use, partially thaw in the refrigerator overnight. Microwave, covered, on high in a microwave-safe dish until heated through, stirring gently; add water if necessary. If desired, sprinkle with cilantro. Serve with warmed naan.

1¼ CUPS: 334 cal., 15g fat (4g sat. fat), 80mg chol., 686mg sod., 25g carb. (12g sugars, 5g fiber), 25g pro. DIABETIC EXCHANGES: 3 lean meat, 2 fat, 1½ starch.

CABBAGE & BEEF SOUP

When I was young, I helped my parents with the chores on our small farm. Lunchtime was always a treat when Mom picked fresh vegetables from the garden and simmered them in her big soup pot. Now I enjoy the same meal with my own homegrown veggies.
—*Ethel Ledbetter, Canton, NC*

PREP: 10 MIN. • COOK: 70 MIN. • MAKES: 12 SERVINGS (3 QT.)

1 lb. lean ground beef (90% lean)
½ tsp. garlic salt
¼ tsp. garlic powder
¼ tsp. pepper
2 celery ribs, chopped
1 can (16 oz.) kidney beans, rinsed and drained
½ medium head cabbage, chopped
1 can (28 oz.) diced tomatoes, undrained
3½ cups water
4 tsp. beef bouillon granules
Minced fresh parsley

1. In a Dutch oven, cook beef over medium heat until no longer pink, breaking it into crumbles; drain. Stir in the remaining ingredients except parsley.

2. Bring to a boil. Reduce heat; cover and simmer for 1 hour. Garnish with parsley.

1 CUP: 116 cal., 3g fat (1g sat. fat), 19mg chol., 582mg sod., 11g carb. (3g sugars, 3g fiber), 11g pro. DIABETIC EXCHANGES: 1 starch, 1 lean meat.

FROM GRANDMA'S KITCHEN: Cooking for two? Freeze this soup in serving-size portions you can enjoy months later.

SAUCY INDIAN-STYLE
CHICKEN & VEGETABLES

TANGY BEAN SOUP

My family loves all the zippy southwestern flavor in this bean soup.
I love it even more because it cooks while I'm at work. When I get
home, I quickly mix together the cheesy cornmeal dumplings,
toss them in and serve a complete dinner in a bowl.
—*Joan Hallford, N. Richland Hills, TX*

PREP: 15 MIN. • **COOK:** 6½ HOURS • **MAKES:** 6 SERVINGS

2 cans (14½ oz. each)
   chicken broth
1 pkg. (16 oz.) frozen
   mixed vegetables
1 can (15 oz.) black beans,
   rinsed and drained
1 can (15 oz.) pinto beans,
   rinsed and drained
1 can (14½ oz.) diced
   tomatoes, undrained
1 medium onion, chopped
1 Tbsp. chili powder
1 Tbsp. minced
   fresh cilantro
4 garlic cloves, minced
¼ tsp. pepper

CORNMEAL DUMPLINGS
½ cup all-purpose flour
½ cup shredded
   cheddar cheese
⅓ cup cornmeal
1 Tbsp. sugar
1 tsp. baking powder
1 large egg,
   room temperature
2 Tbsp. whole milk
2 tsp. canola oil

1. In a 5-qt. slow cooker, combine the first 10 ingredients. Cover
and cook on low until vegetables are tender, 6-8 hours.

2. For dumplings, combine the flour, cheese, cornmeal, sugar and
baking powder in a large bowl. In another bowl, combine the egg,
milk and oil; add to dry ingredients just until moistened (batter
will be stiff).

3. Drop by heaping tablespoonful onto the soup. Cover and
cook on high (without lifting cover) until a toothpick inserted
in a dumpling comes out clean, about 30 minutes.

1 CUP: 334 cal., 6g fat (3g sat. fat), 46mg chol., 774mg sod.,
55g carb. (11g sugars, 12g fiber), 16g pro.

CONFETTI CHOWDER

Grandma always said that if you add a little color to your meal, folks will eat up a storm. This was one of her favorite recipes. She served mugs of the colorful chowder to help warm us up as we sat cross-legged before the crackling fireplace in her kitchen.

—*Rose Bomba, Lisbon, NH*

TAKES: 30 MIN. • **MAKES:** 8 SERVINGS (2 QT.)

3 Tbsp. butter
1 cup chopped carrots
1 cup diced zucchini
1 cup broccoli florets
½ cup chopped onion
½ cup chopped celery
¼ cup all-purpose flour
½ tsp. salt
½ tsp. pepper
¼ tsp. sugar
3 cups whole milk
1 cup chicken broth
1 cup whole kernel corn
1 cup diced fully cooked ham
½ cup peas
1 jar (2 oz.) sliced pimiento, drained
1 cup shredded cheddar cheese

1. Melt the butter in a Dutch oven. Add the carrots, zucchini, broccoli, onion and celery; cook and stir for about 5 minutes or until crisp-tender. Sprinkle the flour, salt, pepper and sugar over vegetables; mix well.

2. Stir in milk and chicken broth; cook and stir until thickened and bubbly. Add the corn, ham, peas and pimiento; cook and stir until heated through. Remove from the heat; stir in cheese until melted.

1 CUP: 237 cal., 13g fat (8g sat. fat), 48mg chol., 762mg sod., 17g carb. (9g sugars, 2g fiber), 12g pro.

"This is a wonderful, hearty and wholesome chowder. I took it to a potluck lunch for the seniors at the YMCA, and it was enjoyed by everyone."
—JUDYDERKOWSKI, TASTEOFHOME.COM

MUSHROOM &
BROCCOLI SOUP

MUSHROOM & BROCCOLI SOUP

One of my daughters doesn't eat meat, and the other struggles to get enough fiber.
This recipe does double duty! It helps give them both the nutrition they need in a meal they love.
—*Maria Davis, Flower Mound, TX*

PREP: 20 MIN. • COOK: 45 MIN. • MAKES: 8 SERVINGS (1½ QT.)

1 **bunch broccoli**
  (about 1½ lbs.)
1 **Tbsp. canola oil**
½ **lb. sliced fresh**
  mushrooms
1 **Tbsp. reduced-sodium**
  soy sauce
2 **medium carrots,**
  finely chopped
2 **celery ribs,**
  finely chopped
¼ **cup finely chopped onion**
1 **garlic clove, minced**
1 **carton (32 oz.)**
  vegetable broth
2 **cups water**
2 **Tbsp. lemon juice**

1. Cut broccoli florets into bite-sized pieces. Peel and chop stalks.

2. In a large saucepan, heat oil over medium-high heat; saute the mushrooms until tender, 4-6 minutes. Stir in soy sauce; remove from pan.

3. In same pan, combine broccoli stalks, carrots, celery, onion, garlic, broth and water; bring to a boil. Reduce heat; simmer, uncovered, until vegetables are softened, 25-30 minutes.

4. Puree soup using an immersion blender. Or cool slightly and puree soup in a blender; return to pan. Stir in broccoli florets and mushrooms; bring to a boil. Reduce heat to medium; cook until broccoli is tender, 8-10 minutes, stirring occasionally. Stir in the lemon juice.

¾ CUP: 69 cal., 2g fat (0 sat. fat), 0 chol., 574mg sod., 11g carb. (4g sugars, 3g fiber), 4g pro. **DIABETIC EXCHANGES:** 2 vegetable, ½ fat.

KNOEPHLA SOUP

Mom served German Knoephla (pronounced nip-fla) soup when I was growing up.
Now it's become a warm and comforting favorite in my own family.
—*Lorraine Meyers, Willow City, ND*

PREP: 20 MIN. • COOK: 40 MIN. • MAKES: 10 SERVINGS (2½ QT.)

½ **cup butter, cubed**
3 **medium potatoes,**
  peeled and cubed
1 **small onion, grated**
3 **cups 2% milk**
6 **cups water**
6 **tsp. chicken**
  or 3 vegetable
  bouillon cubes

KNOEPHLA
1½ **cups all-purpose flour**
1 **egg, beaten**
5 **to 6 Tbsp. milk**
½ **tsp. salt**
  Minced fresh parsley,
  optional

1. In a large skillet, melt the butter; cook potatoes and onion for 20-25 minutes or until tender. Add milk; heat through but do not boil. Set aside. In a Dutch oven, bring water and bouillon to a boil.

2. Meanwhile, combine the first 4 knoephla ingredients to form a stiff dough. Roll into a ½-in. rope. Cut into ¼-in. pieces and drop into boiling broth. Reduce heat; cover and simmer for 10 minutes. Add potato mixture; heat through. Sprinkle with parsley if desired.

1 CUP: 249 cal., 13g fat (8g sat. fat), 57mg chol., 762mg sod., 28g carb. (6g sugars, 1g fiber), 6g pro.

GRANDMA'S PRESSURE-COOKER CHICKEN NOODLE SOUP

PICTURED ON PAGE 174

*I adapted my grandma's recipe so I could prepare it in a pressure cooker.
I've been making home-style chicken noodle soup on a weekly basis ever since!*
—*Tammy Stanko, Greensburg, PA*

PREP: 10 MIN. • COOK: 25 MIN. + RELEASING • MAKES: 4 SERVINGS

2 tsp. olive oil
4 bone-in chicken thighs
2 medium carrots, peeled and sliced into ½-in. pieces
1½ celery ribs, sliced into ½-in. pieces
6 cups reduced-sodium chicken broth
½ tsp. salt
⅛ tsp. pepper
½ pkg. (8 oz.) uncooked fine egg noodles, cooked
Chopped fresh parsley, optional

1. Select saute setting on a 3- or 6-qt. electric pressure cooker and adjust for medium heat; add oil. Brown the chicken thighs. Press cancel. Add carrots, celery and broth to pressure cooker. Lock lid; close pressure-release valve. Adjust to pressure-cook on high for 10 minutes. Allow pressure to release naturally for 10 minutes, then quick-release any remaining pressure.

2. Stir in salt and pepper. Evenly divide noodles among 4 serving bowls; top each bowl with 1 chicken thigh and top with the broth. If desired, sprinkle with parsley.

2 CUPS SOUP WITH 1 CHICKEN THIGH: 389 cal., 29g fat (5g sat. fat), 112mg chol., 1262mg sod., 25g carb. (4g sugars, 2g fiber), 31g pro.

SPICY PEANUT SOUP

*After tasting a similar menu item at a little cafe, I knew I had to try to create
my own spicy peanut specialty at home. I think I came pretty close!*
—*Lisa Meredith, St. Paul, MN*

PREP: 35 MIN. • COOK: 20 MIN. • MAKES: 7 SERVINGS (1¾ QT.)

2 medium carrots, chopped
1 small onion, chopped
2 Tbsp. olive oil
2 garlic cloves, minced
1 large sweet potato, peeled and cubed
½ cup chunky peanut butter
2 Tbsp. red curry paste
2 cans (14½ oz. each) vegetable broth
1 can (14½ oz.) fire-roasted diced tomatoes, undrained
1 bay leaf
1 fresh thyme sprig
½ tsp. pepper
½ cup unsalted peanuts

1. In a large saucepan, cook carrots and onion in oil over medium heat for 2 minutes. Add garlic; cook 1 minute longer.

2. Stir in sweet potato; cook 2 minutes longer. Stir in peanut butter and curry paste until blended. Add the broth, tomatoes, bay leaf, thyme and pepper.

3. Bring to a boil. Reduce the heat; cover and simmer for 15-20 minutes or until sweet potatoes and carrots are tender. (Soup will appear curdled.) Discard the bay leaf and thyme sprig. Stir soup until blended. Sprinkle with peanuts.

1 CUP: 276 cal., 18g fat (3g sat. fat), 0 chol., 932mg sod., 22g carb. (9g sugars, 4g fiber), 8g pro.

EFFORTLESS BLACK BEAN CHILI

A slow-cooker cookbook gave Mom the inspiration for this chili. After a few updates, we all love it—even those of us who don't care for beans. We think it's best served over rice.
—*Amelia Gormley, Ephrata, PA*

PREP: 25 MIN. • **COOK:** 6 HOURS • **MAKES:** 6 SERVINGS (1½ QT.)

1 **lb. ground turkey**
1 **small onion, chopped**
3 **tsp. chili powder**
2 **tsp. minced fresh oregano or ¾ tsp. dried oregano**
1 **tsp. chicken bouillon granules**
1 **jar (16 oz.) mild salsa**
1 **can (15¼ oz.) whole kernel corn, drained**

1 **can (15 oz.) black beans, rinsed and drained**
1 **can (14½ oz.) diced tomatoes, undrained**
½ **cup water**
 Optional toppings: sour cream, finely chopped red onion, chopped cilantro and corn chips

1. In a large skillet, cook and crumble ground turkey with onion over medium-high heat until no longer pink, 5-7 minutes. Transfer to a 4-qt. slow cooker.

2. Stir in all remaining ingredients except toppings. Cook, covered, on low until flavors are blended, 6-8 hours. Top as desired.

1 CUP: 242 cal., 6g fat (1g sat. fat), 50mg chol., 868mg sod., 26g carb. (9g sugars, 6g fiber), 20g pro.

FROM GRANDMA'S KITCHEN: Feel free to substitute about 1¾ cups frozen corn for the canned corn called for in this recipe.

ASIAN RAMEN SHRIMP SOUP

Store-bought ramen noodles speed up the assembly of this colorful Asian soup from my mom. In just 15 minutes, you'll be ladling up brimming bowlfuls.
—*Donna Hellinger, Lorain, OH*

TAKES: 15 MIN. • **MAKES:** 4 SERVINGS

3½ cups water
1 pkg. (3 oz.) Soy Sauce ramen noodles
1 cup cooked small shrimp, peeled and deveined
½ cup chopped green onions
1 medium carrot, julienned
2 Tbsp. soy sauce

1. In a large saucepan, bring water to a boil. Set aside seasoning packet from noodles. Add the noodles to boiling water; cook and stir for 3 minutes.

2. Add shrimp, green onions, carrot, soy sauce and contents of seasoning packet. Cook until heated through, 3-4 minutes longer.

1 CUP: 148 cal., 4g fat (2g sat. fat), 83mg chol., 857mg sod., 17g carb. (2g sugars, 1g fiber), 12g pro. **DIABETIC EXCHANGES:** 1 starch, 1 lean meat.

HEARTY QUINOA & CORN CHOWDER

At her home in the Appalachian Mountains, my grandmother always served veggies straight from the garden. I updated her chowder recipe by adding quinoa and herbs.
—*Kari Napier, Louisville, KY*

PREP: 25 MIN. + STANDING • **COOK:** 15 MIN. • **MAKES:** 14 SERVINGS (¾ CUP EACH)

3 medium sweet red peppers
1 cup quinoa, rinsed
1 Tbsp. butter
1 Tbsp. olive oil
1 medium onion, chopped
2 garlic cloves, minced
⅓ cup all-purpose flour
4 cups vegetable stock
2 cups heavy whipping cream
6 medium ears sweet corn, kernels removed (about 4 cups) or 2 pkg. (10 oz.) frozen corn, thawed
1 can (15 oz.) pinto beans, rinsed and drained
2 Tbsp. minced fresh parsley
½ tsp. minced fresh thyme
1½ tsp. salt
½ tsp. pepper

1. Broil the peppers 4 in. from the heat until skins blister, about 5 minutes. With tongs, rotate peppers a quarter turn. Broil and rotate until all sides are blistered and blackened. Immediately place peppers in a large bowl; cover and let stand for 20 minutes.

2. Peel off and discard charred skin. Remove stems and seeds. Finely chop peppers.

3. Meanwhile, in a Dutch oven, cook and stir the quinoa over medium-high heat for 3-5 minutes or until lightly toasted; remove from the pan.

4. In the same pan, heat butter and oil over medium-high heat. Add onion; cook and stir until tender. Add garlic; cook 1 minute longer. Stir in flour until blended. Gradually whisk in vegetable stock and cream.

5. Add the corn, pinto beans, roasted peppers and quinoa; bring to a boil, stirring frequently. Reduce heat; simmer, uncovered, for 15-20 minutes or until quinoa is tender, stirring occasionally. Stir in the remaining ingredients.

¾ CUP: 264 cal., 16g fat (9g sat. fat), 49mg chol., 485mg sod., 27g carb. (3g sugars, 4g fiber), 6g pro.

ASIAN RAMEN
SHRIMP SOUP

HEARTY BEEF &
SWEET POTATO STEW

I have fond memories of growing up in an Italian/Irish family and learning to cook from my grandparents. This beef stew reminds me of the special dishes we used to prepare.
—*Renee Murphy, Smithtown, NY*

PREP: 40 MIN. • **BAKE:** 2 HOURS • **MAKES:** 8 SERVINGS (2½ QT.)

3 Tbsp. canola oil, divided
1½ lbs. boneless beef chuck steak, cut into 1-in. pieces
2 medium onions, chopped
2 garlic cloves, minced
2 cans (14½ oz. each) reduced-sodium beef broth
⅓ cup dry red wine or additional reduced-sodium beef broth
1 Tbsp. minced fresh thyme or 1 tsp. dried thyme
1 Tbsp. Worcestershire sauce

1 tsp. salt
¾ tsp. pepper
3 Tbsp. cornstarch
3 Tbsp. cold water
1¼ lbs. sweet potatoes (about 2 medium), cut into 1-in. cubes
1 lb. baby portobello mushrooms, halved
4 medium carrots, cut into ½-in. slices
2 medium parsnips, cut into ½-in. slices
1 medium turnip, cut into ¾-in. cubes

1. Preheat oven to 325°. In an ovenproof Dutch oven, heat 2 Tbsp. oil over medium-high heat. Brown beef in batches. Remove with a slotted spoon.

2. Add remaining oil to pan. Add onions; cook and stir 2-3 minutes or until tender. Add garlic; cook 1 minute longer. Add beef broth and wine, stirring to remove browned bits from pan. Stir in thyme, Worcestershire sauce, salt and pepper. Return beef to pan; bring to a boil. Transfer to oven; bake, covered, 1¼ hours.

3. In a small bowl, mix cornstarch and cold water until smooth; gradually stir into stew. Add sweet potatoes, mushrooms, carrots, parsnips and turnip to pan. Bake, covered, 45-60 minutes longer or until beef and vegetables are tender. If desired, strain cooking juices; skim fat. Return cooking juices to Dutch oven.

1¼ **CUPS:** 354 cal., 14g fat (4g sat. fat), 57mg chol., 586mg sod., 36g carb. (14g sugars, 6g fiber), 22g pro. **DIABETIC EXCHANGES:** 3 vegetable, 3 lean meat, 1 starch, 1 fat.

CHUNKY CHICKEN NOODLE SOUP

Craving a bowlful of comfort? Here's a home-style classic that tastes just like Grandma used to make. Feel free to change up the veggies to suit your family. My kids love carrots, so I always toss in extra.
—*Coleen Martin, Brookfield, WI*

TAKES: 25 MIN. • **MAKES:** 6 SERVINGS

½ cup finely chopped carrot
¼ cup finely chopped celery
¼ cup finely chopped onion
1 tsp. butter
6 cups chicken broth
1½ cups cubed
   cooked chicken
1 tsp. salt
½ tsp. dried marjoram
½ tsp. dried thyme
⅛ tsp. pepper
1¼ cups uncooked medium
   egg noodles
1 Tbsp. minced fresh
   parsley

Saute the carrot, celery and onion in butter in a Dutch oven until tender. Stir in the broth, chicken and seasonings. Bring to a boil. Reduce heat. Add noodles; cook for 10 minutes or until noodles are tender. Sprinkle with parsley.

1 CUP: 126 cal., 4g fat (1g sat. fat), 40mg chol., 1370mg sod., 9g carb. (2g sugars, 1g fiber), 14g pro.

"I made this for the first time when my 4-year old was sick. He loved it and claimed it's what made him better! Now he asks for it all the time. It's the only soup he likes."
—SARAHC, TASTEOFHOME.COM

GRANNY'S SPICY SOUP

Thanks to her amazing creations, my mom has become known as The Soup Lady. I'm happy to oblige whenever my children ask me to simmer up one of Granny's specialties. This recipe gets its name from the pickling spices, not from being hot.
—*Rose Rose, Akron, OH*

PREP: 10 MIN. • **COOK:** 3¼ HOURS • **MAKES:** 12 SERVINGS (ABOUT 3 QT.)

1 broiler/fryer chicken
   (3½ to 4 lbs.), cut up
8 cups water
4 to 5 celery ribs
   with leaves, diced
2 medium carrots, diced
1 large onion, diced
1 to 1½ tsp. pickling spices
1½ tsp. salt, optional
4 chicken bouillon cubes
¼ tsp. pepper
1 cup uncooked noodles

1. Place chicken and water in a large soup kettle. Cover and bring to a boil; skim fat. Reduce the heat; cover and simmer for 2 hours or until chicken falls off bone.

2. Strain the broth; return to kettle. Allow chicken to cool; debone and cut into chunks. Skim fat from broth. Return chicken to broth along with celery, carrots and onion.

3. Place the pickling spices in a tea ball or cheesecloth bag; add to soup. Bring to a boil. Reduce heat; cover and simmer for 1 hour. Remove spices; add salt if desired, bouillon, pepper and noodles. Cook for 10-15 minutes or until noodles are tender.

1 CUP: 114 cal., 3g fat (0 sat. fat), 32mg chol., 74mg sod., 9g carb. (0 sugars, 0 fiber), 14g pro. **DIABETIC EXCHANGES:** 1 vegetable, 1 lean meat, ½ starch.

TURKEY, BACON & CORN CHOWDER

This recipe transforms extra food from yesterday's holiday feast into a thick, rich, flavorful chowder that tastes like its own special treat. My grandmother almost always used her Thanksgiving leftovers and sometimes would add chopped hard-boiled eggs, too. She made her own stock with the turkey carcass, but you can use prepared chicken stock to speed up the process if you like.
—*Susan Bickta, Kutztown, PA*

PREP: 25 MIN. • COOK: 50 MIN. • MAKES: 16 SERVINGS (4 QT.)

1 lb. thick-sliced bacon strips, chopped
3 celery ribs, sliced
1 medium onion, chopped
1 medium carrot, chopped
½ cup chopped red onion
1 bay leaf
¼ cup all-purpose flour
1 carton (32 oz.) chicken stock
1 can (10½ oz.) condensed cream of chicken soup, undiluted
1 pkg. (8 oz.) cream cheese, softened
¾ cup whole milk
¾ cup heavy whipping cream
3½ cups frozen corn (about 17.5 oz.)
2½ cups cubed cooked turkey
2 cups refrigerated shredded hash brown potatoes (about 10 oz.)
¾ cup turkey gravy
1 Tbsp. dried parsley flakes
Thinly sliced green onions, optional

1. In a Dutch oven, cook the bacon over medium heat until crisp, stirring occasionally. Remove with a slotted spoon; drain on paper towels. Discard drippings, reserving ¼ cup in the pan. Add the celery, onion, carrot, red onion and bay leaf; cook and stir over medium-high heat until vegetables are tender, 8-10 minutes.

2. Stir in the flour until blended; gradually whisk in stock. Bring to a boil, stirring constantly; cook and stir 2 minutes. Add soup, cream cheese, milk and cream; mix well. Stir in corn, turkey, hash browns, gravy, parsley and ¾ cup reserved bacon; reduce heat. Cook, covered, 20 minutes, stirring occasionally.

3. Discard bay leaf. Serve with remaining bacon and, if desired, green onions.

1 CUP: 289 cal., 19g fat (9g sat. fat), 63mg chol., 603mg sod., 17g carb. (4g sugars, 2g fiber), 14g pro.

FROM GRANDMA'S KITCHEN: Have leftover chicken? Feel free to use that in place of the turkey. Rotisserie chicken would work well here, too.

AUNT FRAN'S GOULASH

When I was a young girl, Aunt Fran always made her goulash when we came to visit.
My brother and I would have been disappointed if she didn't! Now as an adult,
I like her dish even more because it's so quick and easy to make.
—*LaVergne Krones, Matteson, IL*

TAKES: 25 MIN. • MAKES: 6 SERVINGS

1½ lbs. ground beef
1 medium onion, diced
1 can (16 oz.) kidney beans,
    rinsed and drained
1 can (10¾ oz.) condensed
    tomato soup, undiluted
1 can (8 oz.) tomato sauce
1 tsp. beef bouillon
    granules
1½ cups water
    Dash pepper
8 oz. spiral pasta, cooked
    and drained
    Grated Parmesan
    cheese, optional

1. In a skillet, cook beef and onion over medium heat until no longer pink, breaking up beef into crumbles; drain and set aside.

2. In a large saucepan, combine the beans, soup, tomato sauce, bouillon, water and pepper. Add cooked noodles and beef; heat through. If desired, garnish with Parmesan cheese.

1 SERVING: 436 cal., 11g fat (5g sat. fat), 56mg chol., 816mg sod., 52g carb. (9g sugars, 6g fiber), 31g pro.

"Finally, a goulash recipe that doesn't have spaghetti sauce in it! This is much closer to what my mother used to make 45 years ago."
—CHAD68164, TASTEOFHOME.COM

OKRA & BUTTER BEAN STEW

This hearty stew served over rice is adapted from my mom's down-home Louisiana recipe.
Just one spoonful will turn an okra-hater into an okra-lover—guaranteed!
—*Kaya Mack, Wichita Falls, TX*

PREP: 25 MIN. • COOK: 45 MIN. • MAKES: 12 SERVINGS (1 CUP EACH)

7 bacon strips, chopped
1 lb. smoked sausage,
    halved and thinly sliced
1 large onion, chopped
2 small green peppers,
    chopped
3 cups water
2 cans (16 oz. each)
    butter beans, rinsed
    and drained
1 can (14½ oz.) diced
    tomatoes, undrained
1 can (12 oz.) tomato paste
1 tsp. pepper
¼ tsp. salt
1 pkg. (16 oz.) frozen
    sliced okra
    Hot cooked rice, optional

1. In a Dutch oven, cook bacon and sausage over medium heat until bacon is crisp. Remove to paper towels; drain, reserving 2 Tbsp. drippings.

2. Cook the onion and green peppers in the drippings until tender. Stir in the water, beans, tomatoes, tomato paste, pepper and salt. Bring to a boil. Reduce heat; simmer, uncovered, 10 minutes. Add bacon and sausage; cook 10 minutes longer.

3. Stir in okra. Cover and cook until okra is tender, 8-10 minutes. If desired, serve with rice.

1 CUP: 252 cal., 14g fat (6g sat. fat), 31mg chol., 901mg sod., 24g carb. (9g sugars, 7g fiber), 12g pro.

SLOW-COOKED STUFFED PEPPER STEW

Here's one of my go-to meals in winter. When my garden is full of green peppers, I dice and freeze them for the cold days to come.
—*Debbie Johnson, Centertown, MO*

PREP: 20 MIN. • COOK: 4¼ HOURS • MAKES: 8 SERVINGS (3 QT.)

1½ lbs. bulk Italian sausage
1 large onion, chopped
2 medium green peppers, chopped
2 to 4 Tbsp. brown sugar
2 tsp. beef base
½ tsp. salt
¼ tsp. pepper
2 cans (15 oz. each) tomato sauce
1 can (28 oz.) diced tomatoes, undrained
2 cups tomato juice
¾ cup uncooked instant rice

1. In a large skillet, cook the sausage and onion over medium heat until sausage is no longer pink, breaking up sausage into crumbles, 8-10 minutes; drain.

2. In a 6-qt. slow cooker, combine the sausage mixture, green peppers, brown sugar, beef base, salt, pepper, tomato sauce, tomatoes and tomato juice. Cook, covered, on low until the vegetables are tender, 4-5 hours.

3. Stir in the rice. Cook, covered, until the rice is tender, 15-20 minutes longer.

FREEZE OPTION: Freeze the cooled stew in freezer containers. To use, partially thaw in refrigerator overnight. Heat through in a saucepan, stirring occasionally; add water if necessary.

1½ CUPS: 327 cal., 20g fat (6g sat. fat), 46mg chol., 1637mg sod., 28g carb. (12g sugars, 5g fiber), 14g pro.

SMOKY & SPICY VEGETABLE BISQUE

On an ordinary day, I make this a complete meal by pairing a big bowlful with a side of bruschetta or a Caprese salad. For a special-occasion feast, I serve the bisque as my first course because it sets off the richer dishes with a bit of heat and smoke.

—*Juliana Inhofer, Rocklin, CA*

PREP: 1 HOUR • COOK: 30 MIN. • MAKES: 6 SERVINGS

2 large onions, cut into 8 wedges
4 large tomatoes, cut into 8 wedges
1 large sweet red pepper, cut into 8 wedges
4 garlic cloves, halved
¼ cup olive oil
2 cans (14½ oz. each) reduced-sodium chicken broth
½ cup fat-free half-and-half
½ cup coarsely chopped fresh basil
1 small chipotle pepper in adobo sauce, seeded
½ tsp. pepper
¼ tsp. salt
Fresh basil leaves, optional

1. Line a 15x10x1-in. baking pan with foil and coat the foil with cooking spray. Place the onions, tomatoes, red pepper and garlic in pan. Drizzle with oil and toss to coat.

2. Bake, uncovered, at 425° for 40-45 minutes or until tender and browned, stirring occasionally.

3. In a large saucepan, combine the broth, half-and-half, chopped basil, chipotle pepper, pepper, salt and roasted vegetables. Bring to a boil. Reduce heat; simmer, uncovered, for 20-25 minutes. Cool slightly.

4. In a blender, process the soup in batches until smooth. Return all to the pan; heat through. Garnish with basil leaves if desired.

1 CUP: 157 cal., 9g fat (1g sat. fat), 0 chol., 528mg sod., 15g carb. (9g sugars, 3g fiber), 5g pro.

GRANDMA'S CORN STEW

Beefy corn stew was one of my grandma's favorites. When I prepare it for my family, memories of Mom and I fixing it together always come rushing back.

—*Trisha Kaylor, Lebanon, PA*

PREP: 10 MIN. • COOK: 1 HOUR 20 MIN. • MAKES: 4 SERVINGS

1 lb. ground beef
1 medium onion, chopped
⅓ cup chopped green pepper
1 can (15¼ oz.) whole kernel corn, drained
1 can (10¾ oz.) condensed tomato soup, undiluted
1 Tbsp. Worcestershire sauce
2 tsp. sugar
1½ tsp. salt

In a large saucepan, cook beef, onion and green pepper over medium heat until the meat is no longer pink; drain. Add the remaining ingredients; bring to a boil. Reduce heat; cover and simmer for 1 hour.

1 SERVING: 333 cal., 11g fat (5g sat. fat), 56mg chol., 1746mg sod., 30g carb. (15g sugars, 4g fiber), 24g pro.

SMOKY & SPICY
VEGETABLE BISQUE

BIG BATCH CHEESEBURGER SOUP

My mother-in-law gave me her recipe for cheeseburger
soup, and I changed a few things to make it my own.
It's the perfect comfort food on a chilly evening.
—*Christina Addison, Blanchester, OH*

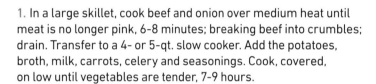

PREP: 20 MIN. • **COOK:** 7 HOURS • **MAKES:** 6 SERVINGS (2¼ QT.)

- 1 lb. lean ground beef (90% lean)
- 1 small onion, chopped
- 1¾ lbs. potatoes (about 3-4 medium), peeled and cut into ½-in. pieces
- 3 cups chicken broth
- 1½ cups whole milk
- 2 medium carrots, shredded
- 1 celery rib, finely chopped
- 1 Tbsp. dried parsley flakes
- ½ tsp. salt
- ½ tsp. dried basil
- ¼ tsp. pepper
- 1 pkg. (8 oz.) Velveeta, cubed
- ¼ cup sour cream
  Chopped fresh parsley, optional

1. In a large skillet, cook beef and onion over medium heat until meat is no longer pink, 6-8 minutes; breaking beef into crumbles; drain. Transfer to a 4- or 5-qt. slow cooker. Add the potatoes, broth, milk, carrots, celery and seasonings. Cook, covered, on low until vegetables are tender, 7-9 hours.

2. Stir in the cheese until melted. Stir in the sour cream. If desired, sprinkle with parsley.

1½ CUPS: 300 cal., 15g fat (8g sat. fat), 75mg chol., 949mg sod., 21g carb. (7g sugars, 2g fiber), 19g pro.

TURKEY SAUSAGE BEAN SOUP

Every generation of our family since my great-grandmother has enjoyed this specialty.
I've tweaked it a bit to include some of my favorite ingredients, such as celery root.
Just add a side salad and slices of artisan bread for a wonderful dinner.
—*Terrel Porter-Smith, Los Osos, CA*

PREP: 15 MIN. • COOK: 25 MIN. • MAKES: 8 SERVINGS (2 QT.)

4 **Italian turkey sausage links, casings removed**
1 **large onion, chopped**
1 **cup chopped fennel bulb**
1 **cup chopped peeled celery root or turnip**
1 **can (14½ oz.) no-salt-added diced tomatoes, undrained**
3 **cups water**
4 **bay leaves**
1 **Tbsp. reduced-sodium beef base**
2 **tsp. Italian seasoning**
½ **tsp. pepper**
2 **cans (15 oz. each) cannellini beans, rinsed and drained**
  Shaved Parmesan cheese, optional

1. In a Dutch oven, cook sausage, onion, fennel and celery root over medium heat 4-5 minutes or until sausage is no longer pink, breaking into crumbles; drain. Stir in tomatoes, water, bay leaves, beef base, Italian seasoning and pepper.

2. Bring to a boil. Reduce the heat; simmer, covered, 20 minutes or until vegetables are tender. Stir in beans; heat through. Remove bay leaves. If desired, top servings with cheese.

FREEZE OPTION: Freeze soup without cheese in freezer containers. To use, partially thaw in the refrigerator overnight. Heat through in a saucepan, stirring occasionally. If desired, top with cheese.

1 CUP: 168 cal., 4g fat (1g sat. fat), 20mg chol., 585mg sod., 22g carb. (3g sugars, 6g fiber), 11g pro. DIABETIC EXCHANGES: 1½ starch, 1 medium-fat meat.

FROM GRANDMA'S KITCHEN: No turkey sausage? No problem. Use whatever you have on hand, including ground beef.

GRANDMA'S OXTAIL STEW

This heirloom recipe is one of our family treasures. Oxtail, the meaty part of the tail of an ox (now commonly cow), requires long and slow cooking. The end result is so worth it! A bowlful of this wonderfully rich stew will warm you body and soul.
—*Bobbie Keefer, Byers, CO*

PREP: 20 MIN. • **COOK:** 10 HOURS • **MAKES:** 8 SERVINGS (3 QT.)

2 lbs. oxtails, trimmed
2 Tbsp. olive oil
4 medium carrots, sliced (about 2 cups)
1 medium onion, chopped
2 garlic cloves, minced
2 cans (14½ oz. each) diced tomatoes, undrained
1 can (15 oz.) beef broth
3 bay leaves
1 tsp. salt
1 tsp. dried oregano
½ tsp. dried thyme
½ tsp. pepper
6 cups chopped cabbage

1. In a large skillet, brown the oxtails in oil over medium heat. Remove from pan; place in a 5-qt. slow cooker.

2. Add the carrots and onion to drippings; cook and stir until just softened, 3-5 minutes. Add garlic, cook 1 minute longer. Transfer the vegetable mixture to slow cooker. Add tomatoes, broth, bay leaves, salt, oregano, thyme and pepper; stir to combine.

3. Cook, covered, on low 8 hours. Add the cabbage; cook until the cabbage is tender and the meat pulls away easily from the bones, about 2 hours longer. Remove oxtails; set aside until cool enough to handle. Remove meat from bones; discard bones and shred meat. Return meat to stew. Discard bay leaves.

FREEZE OPTION: Freeze the cooled stew in freezer containers. To use, partially thaw in the refrigerator overnight. Heat through in a saucepan, stirring occasionally; add broth if necessary.

1½ CUPS: 204 cal., 10g fat (3g sat. fat), 34mg chol., 705mg sod., 14g carb. (8g sugars, 5g fiber), 16g pro.

LEMONY MUSHROOM ORZO SOUP

Every Sunday after church, my grandmother used to make classic Greek avgolemono.
The kids and I started experimenting with different ingredients and came up with
this variation of her traditional soup. I think my yia-yia would be proud.
—*Nick Haros, Stroudsburg, PA*

PREP: 10 MIN. • COOK: 25 MIN. • MAKES: 8 SERVINGS (2¾ QT.)

2 Tbsp. butter
1 lb. sliced fresh
  button mushrooms
1 lb. sliced fresh baby
  portobello mushrooms
1 celery rib, sliced
2 cartons (32 oz. each)
  chicken broth
2 tsp. chicken bouillon
  granules
1½ cups uncooked
  orzo pasta
2 large eggs
¼ cup lemon juice
¼ tsp. pepper
  Minced fresh parsley

1. In a Dutch oven, heat butter over medium-high heat. Add the mushrooms and celery; cook and stir 6-7 minutes or until tender. Add broth and bouillon; bring to a boil. Stir in orzo; return to a boil. Cook, uncovered, 7-9 minutes or until orzo is al dente, stirring occasionally. Remove from heat; let stand 5 minutes.

2. Meanwhile, in a large bowl, whisk the eggs, lemon juice and pepper. Gradually whisk in 1½ cups of the hot broth; return all to pan, stirring constantly. Cook over medium heat until the broth is slightly thickened, stirring occasionally. (Do not allow to boil.) Top servings with parsley.

1⅓ CUPS: 225 cal., 6g fat (2g sat. fat), 59mg chol., 1243mg sod., 33g carb. (5g sugars, 2g fiber), 11g pro.

CARROT CHOWDER

My husband's grandma handed her beefy chowder recipe down to us, and it's just wonderful.
Add a basket of fresh-baked bread on the side, and you have perfection!
—*Wendy Wilkins, Prattville, AL*

PREP: 20 MIN. • COOK: 1 HOUR • MAKES: 10 SERVINGS (2½ QT.)

1 lb. ground beef, browned
  and drained
½ cup chopped celery
½ cup chopped onion
1 cup chopped
  green pepper
2½ cups grated carrots
1 can (32 oz.) tomato juice
2 cans (10½ oz. each)
  condensed cream of
  celery soup, undiluted
1½ cups water
½ tsp. garlic salt
½ tsp. dried marjoram
1 tsp. sugar
½ tsp. salt
  Shredded Monterey Jack
  cheese

In a Dutch oven, combine all ingredients except cheese. Bring to a boil; reduce heat and simmer, uncovered, about 1 hour or until vegetables are tender. Sprinkle each serving with cheese.

1 CUP: 130 cal., 5g fat (2g sat. fat), 23mg chol., 803mg sod., 11g carb. (6g sugars, 2g fiber), 10g pro.

"Love, love, love this recipe! I like to make it with leftover beef roast, and to save time you can use frozen shredded carrots from the store."
—PYNKBABIE, TASTEOFHOME.COM

CEYLON CHICKEN CURRY & RICE NOODLE SOUP

Whenever cold or flu season hit, my mother would simmer up a curried chicken rice noodle soup that was nutritious, comforting and cozy. This turmeric lemongrass version is a take on that childhood favorite and can easily be made vegan or vegetarian, too.
—*Sarita Gelner, Waunakee, WI*

PREP: 25 MIN. • COOK: 25 MIN. • MAKES: 8 SERVINGS (2½ QT.)

- 6 oz. uncooked wide rice noodles
- 2 Tbsp. ghee or olive oil, divided
- 1 lb. boneless chicken breasts, thinly sliced and cut into ½-in. pieces
- 1 medium onion, chopped
- ⅔ cup sliced fresh carrots
- 3 bay leaves
- 2 Tbsp. minced fresh gingerroot
- 1 lemongrass stalk
- 1 whole star anise
- 1 Tbsp. curry powder
- 2 tsp. ground turmeric
- 1 garlic clove, minced
- ½ tsp. salt
- ¼ tsp. cayenne pepper
- 2 anchovy fillets, minced, optional
- 2 Tbsp. white wine vinegar
- 1 carton (32 oz.) chicken broth
- 1 can (13.66 oz.) coconut milk
- 2 Tbsp. jaggery or dark brown sugar
- 1½ cups chopped fresh kale
- ½ cup cherry tomatoes, halved

1. Cook the noodles according to package directions for al dente. Meanwhile, in a Dutch oven, heat 1 Tbsp. ghee over medium-high heat. Add chicken; cook and stir until no longer pink, 4-5 minutes. Remove from pan. Cook and stir onion and carrots in remaining 1 Tbsp. ghee until tender, 12-15 minutes. Add bay leaves, ginger, lemongrass, star anise, curry powder, turmeric, garlic, salt, cayenne and, if desired, minced fillets; cook 1 minute longer.

2. Add the vinegar to the pan; cook 30 seconds, stirring to loosen browned bits from pan. Add the broth, coconut milk and jaggery. Bring to a boil; reduce heat. Add kale and tomatoes; simmer until tender, 6-8 minutes. Remove and discard bay leaves, lemongrass and star anise. Drain the noodles; stir into the soup. Add chicken; heat through.

1¼ CUPS: 316 cal., 16g fat (11g sat. fat), 46mg chol., 758mg sod., 26g carb. (6g sugars, 2g fiber), 15g pro.

CHICKPEA TORTILLA SOUP

We like to play around with the toppings we add each time we make this filling, family-friendly, vegan soup. Tortilla chips, avocado chunks, lime wedges and chopped cilantro are just a few of the fun, flavorful options.
—*Julie Peterson, Crofton, MD*

TAKES: 30 MIN. • **MAKES:** 8 SERVINGS (3 QT.)

1 Tbsp. olive oil
1 medium red onion, chopped
4 garlic cloves, minced
1 to 2 jalapeno peppers, seeded and chopped, optional
¼ tsp. pepper
8 cups vegetable broth
1 cup red quinoa, rinsed
2 cans (15 oz. each) no-salt-added chickpeas or garbanzo beans, rinsed and drained
1 can (15 oz.) no-salt-added black beans, rinsed and drained
3 medium tomatoes, chopped
1 cup fresh or frozen corn
⅓ cup minced fresh cilantro
Optional ingredients: Crushed tortilla chips, cubed avocado, lime wedges and additional chopped cilantro

Heat oil in a Dutch oven over medium-high heat. Add the red onion, garlic, jalapeno if desired, and pepper; cook and stir until tender, 3-5 minutes. Add broth and quinoa. Bring to a boil; reduce heat. Simmer, uncovered, until quinoa is tender, about 10 minutes. Add chickpeas, beans, tomatoes, corn and cilantro; heat through. If desired, serve with optional ingredients.

1½ CUPS: 289 cal., 5g fat (0 sat. fat), 0 chol., 702mg sod., 48g carb. (5g sugars, 9g fiber), 13g pro.

FROM GRANDMA'S KITCHEN: Don't skip the lime wedges—that little bit of acid really perks up the flavor of this soup.

CARAMEL-PECAN COOKIE
BUTTER BARS, PAGE 210

GRANDMA'S FAVORITE

COOKIES, BROWNIES & BARS

Any day becomes special when Grandma pulls a pan
of her freshly baked goodies from the oven. Treat your
own family and friends to these delights by the dozen.

S'MORE BACON BROWNIES

When I needed something to bring to a bacon-themed gathering, I chose these. They were a huge hit!
Guests stood in line for them. I got a kick out of seeing the adults and kids together putting
yummy toppings on their brownies and torching the marshmallow creme to toast it.
The interaction of people making their own desserts really added to the fun.
—*Lisa Benoit, Cookeville, TN*

PREP: 30 MIN. • **BAKE:** 40 MIN. + COOLING • **MAKES:** 16 SERVINGS

1 lb. bacon strips
1 pkg. (18½ oz.) caramel swirl brownie mix (8-in. square pan size), such as Ghirardelli
¼ cup water
3 Tbsp. canola oil
1 large egg, room temperature
¼ tsp. ground chipotle pepper
½ cup semisweet chocolate chips
1 cup marshmallow creme
1 cup hot caramel ice cream topping
6 whole graham crackers, coarsely chopped
   Coffee ice cream, optional

1. Preheat oven to 425°. Place a wire rack in a 15x10x1-in. baking pan. Place bacon strips in a single layer on rack. Bake until crisp, about 20 minutes. When cool enough to handle, chop bacon; set aside. Reserve 2 Tbsp. drippings.

2. Reduce oven setting to 325°. Line an 8-in. square baking pan with foil, letting the ends extend up sides; grease foil. In a large bowl, combine the brownie mix, water, oil, egg, chipotle powder and reserved bacon drippings. Stir in chocolate chips and half the chopped bacon. Transfer to the prepared pan. Swirl in the caramel packet included with the brownie mix. Bake and cool as package directs.

3. Serve brownies with marshmallow creme, caramel, graham crackers, remaining bacon and, if desired, ice cream.

1 PIECE: 335 cal., 13g fat (4g sat. fat), 23mg chol., 392mg sod., 49g carb. (37g sugars, 1g fiber), 6g pro.

CHOCOLATE-HAZELNUT MAGIC BARS

Want to update classic magic bars? Mix in hazelnuts for a new taste treat.
I like to drizzle melted Nutella spread on top for extra flair.
—*James Schend, Pleasant Prairie, WI*

PREP: 10 MIN. • **BAKE:** 30 MIN. + COOLING • **MAKES:** 16 BARS

½ cup butter, cubed
1 cup chocolate wafer crumbs
1 cup sweetened shredded coconut
1 cup dark chocolate chips
1 cup chopped hazelnuts
1 can (14 oz.) sweetened condensed milk
   Nutella, optional

Preheat oven to 350°. Melt butter in a 9-in. square baking pan. On top of melted butter, evenly sprinkle crumbs, then coconut, then chocolate chips, then hazelnuts. Pour milk over all. Do not stir. Bake until a toothpick inserted in center comes out clean, about 30 minutes. Cool several hours before cutting. If desired, drizzle with melted Nutella.

1 BAR: 305 cal., 20g fat (10g sat. fat), 24mg chol., 138mg sod., 32g carb. (27g sugars, 2g fiber), 5g pro.

GRANDMA'S SECRET

To amp up the s'more flavor of these decadent treats, use a kitchen torch to lightly toast the marshmallow creme.

S'MORE
BACON
BROWNIES

STRAWBERRY & PEACH LIME CUSTARD BARS

Whenever I did any baking, Dad would come to the kitchen and ask to sample what I made. He was always ready with a compliment. I loved having him taste test new creations, such as these bars topped with strawberries and peaches. Feel free to arrange different fruits over the custard to suit the season.

—*Carlin Tou, Chandler, AZ*

PREP: 20 MIN. + COOLING • **BAKE:** 20 MIN. + CHILLING • **MAKES:** 2 DOZEN

- 2 **cups graham cracker crumbs**
- 1 **cup all-purpose flour**
- ¾ **cup butter, softened**
- ½ **cup plus 2 Tbsp. sugar, divided**
- 5 **large egg yolks**
- 4 **oz. cream cheese, softened**
- 1 **can (14 oz.) sweetened condensed milk**
- ½ **cup lime juice**
- 2 **Tbsp. grated lime zest, divided**
- 1 **Tbsp. vanilla bean paste**
- 2½ **cups fresh strawberries, halved**
- 1 **can (15 oz.) peach halves in light syrup, drained and thinly sliced**
- 2 **tsp. ground cinnamon**

1. Preheat oven to 350°. Line a 13x9-in. baking pan with nonstick foil; set aside. In a large bowl, beat the graham cracker crumbs, flour, butter and ½ cup sugar until combined. Press onto bottom of prepared pan. Bake until lightly browned, 10-15 minutes. Cool on a wire rack.

2. In a large bowl, beat egg yolks and cream cheese until smooth. Beat in sweetened condensed milk and lime juice until blended. Stir in 1 Tbsp. lime zest and vanilla paste; pour over cooled crust. Alternately arrange strawberries and peaches in closely spaced rows over filling. Combine the cinnamon and remaining 2 Tbsp. sugar; sprinkle over fruit.

3. Bake until custard looks set, 20-25 minutes. Cool completely on a wire rack. Cover and refrigerate at least 2 hours or overnight. Sprinkle with remaining 1 Tbsp. lime zest; cut into bars.

1 BAR: 226 cal., 11g fat (6g sat. fat), 64mg chol., 123mg sod., 30g carb. (20g sugars, 1g fiber), 4g pro.

FUDGY LAYERED IRISH MOCHA BROWNIES

My husband and I are fans of Irish cream, and I decided to try incorporating
it into a brownie. I started with my mom's yummy from-scratch recipe,
then spread on a "tipsy" frosting and ganache for good measure.
—*Sue Gronholz, Beaver Dam, WI*

PREP: 35 MIN. • **BAKE:** 25 MIN. + CHILLING • **MAKES:** 16 SERVINGS

⅔ cup all-purpose flour
½ tsp. baking powder
¼ tsp. salt
⅓ cup butter
6 Tbsp. baking cocoa
2 Tbsp. canola oil
½ tsp. instant coffee granules
1 cup sugar
2 large eggs, room temperature, beaten
1 tsp. vanilla extract

FROSTING
2 cups confectioners' sugar
¼ cup butter, softened
3 Tbsp. Irish cream liqueur

GANACHE TOPPING
1 cup semisweet chocolate chips
3 Tbsp. Irish cream liqueur
2 Tbsp. heavy whipping cream
½ tsp. instant coffee granules

1. Preheat oven to 350°. Sift together flour, baking powder and salt; set aside. In a small saucepan over low heat, melt butter. Remove from heat; stir in cocoa, oil and instant coffee granules. Cool slightly; stir in sugar and beaten eggs. Gradually add flour mixture and vanilla; mix well. Spread batter into a greased 8-in. square pan; bake until the center is set (do not overbake), about 25 minutes. Cool in pan on wire rack.

2. For frosting, whisk together confectioners' sugar and butter (the mixture will be lumpy). Gradually whisk in the Irish cream liqueur; beat until smooth. Spread over slightly warm brownies. Refrigerate until frosting is set, about 1 hour.

3. Meanwhile, prepare ganache: Combine all ingredients and microwave on high for 1 minute; stir. Microwave 30 seconds longer; stir until smooth. Cool slightly until ganache reaches a spreadable consistency. Spread over frosting. Refrigerate until set, 45-60 minutes.

1 BROWNIE: 295 cal., 14g fat (7g sat. fat), 43mg chol., 116mg sod., 41g carb. (34g sugars, 1g fiber), 2g pro.

"These brownies are amazing! They are so decadent. I will definitely be making them again."
—HKAROW9713, TASTEOFHOME.COM

CHOCOLATE
CHIP-CHERRY
CHUNK COOKIES

CHOCOLATE CHIP-CHERRY CHUNK COOKIES

My grandmas and mom came up with this dough by combining their favorite recipes, then tossing in semisweet chocolate chips, white chips and dried cherries. Dad churned the homemade ice cream to turn the cookies into ice cream sandwiches. We'd eat them on sunny summer afternoons to cool ourselves down in the heat. Pure bliss!
—Wade Rouse, Fennville, MI

PREP: 30 MIN. • BAKE: 10 MIN./BATCH + COOLING • MAKES: ABOUT 4 DOZEN

½ cup plus 1 Tbsp. butter, softened
½ cup sugar
¼ cup packed dark brown sugar
1 large egg, room temperature
1 tsp. vanilla extract
1 tsp. maple flavoring
1½ cups all-purpose flour
5 tsp. baking cocoa
½ tsp. baking soda
¼ tsp. salt
1 cup semisweet chocolate chips
1 cup white baking chips
½ cup dried cherries or dried cranberries
¼ cup sweetened shredded coconut

1. Preheat oven to 350°. Cream the butter, gradually adding the sugars, until light and fluffy, 5-7 minutes. Slowly beat in the egg, vanilla and maple flavoring.

2. In another bowl, sift together the flour, baking cocoa, baking soda and salt. Gradually beat into creamed mixture just until moistened (do not overbeat). Stir in semisweet chocolate and white baking chips, dried cherries and coconut.

3. Drop the cookie dough by tablespoonfuls 2 in. apart onto ungreased baking sheets. Flatten slightly. Bake until golden brown, 10-12 minutes. Cool on pans 5 minutes. Remove to wire racks to cool completely.

1 COOKIE: 92 cal., 5g fat (3g sat. fat), 10mg chol., 49mg sod., 12g carb. (9g sugars, 0 fiber), 1g pro.

COCONUT RUM BALLS

For as long as I can remember, my mother has made rum balls. I swapped in coconut rum for the traditional variety and added shredded coconut. The little no-bake bites look so pretty arranged on a tray or packaged in a decorative tin.
—Jana Walker, Macomb, MI

PREP: 25 MIN. + STANDING • MAKES: ABOUT 4½ DOZEN

1 pkg. (12 oz.) vanilla wafers, finely crushed
1 cup confectioners' sugar
2 Tbsp. baking cocoa
1 cup sweetened shredded coconut
1 cup chopped pecans
½ cup light corn syrup
¼ cup coconut rum
Additional confectioners' sugar

1. Whisk the crushed wafers, confectioners' sugar and baking cocoa. Stir in coconut and pecans. In a separate bowl, whisk corn syrup and rum; stir into the wafer mixture. Shape into 1-in. balls; let stand 1 hour.

2. Roll the balls in additional confectioners' sugar. Store in an airtight container.

1 COOKIE: 73 cal., 3g fat (1g sat. fat), 1mg chol., 31mg sod., 10g carb. (8g sugars, 1g fiber), 0 pro.

CARAMEL-PECAN COOKIE BUTTER BARS
PICTURED ON PAGE 202

I love cookie butter spread on toast, vanilla wafers and graham crackers.
One day when I was thinking about other ways to use that ingredient,
I tried mixing it into a pan of caramel-pecan bars. They were
an instant hit in my house and disappeared in a flash.
—*Sheryl Little, Cabot, AR*

PREP: 15 MIN. • BAKE: 15 MIN. + COOLING • MAKES: 2 DOZEN

½ cup butter, softened
½ cup sugar
½ cup packed brown sugar
½ cup Biscoff creamy
cookie spread
1 large egg, room
temperature
1¼ cups self-rising flour
2 cups pecan halves,
coarsely chopped
1 pkg. (11 oz.) caramels
3 Tbsp. half-and-half
cream
1 tsp. vanilla extract
1 cup (6 oz.) dark chocolate
chips
1 Tbsp. shortening

1. Preheat oven to 375°. In a large bowl, cream the butter, sugars and cookie butter until light and fluffy, 5-7 minutes. Beat in egg. Gradually beat in flour. Spread onto bottom of greased 13x9-in. baking pan. Sprinkle with pecans; press lightly into dough. Bake until edges are lightly browned, 15-20 minutes.

2. Meanwhile, in a large saucepan, combine caramels and cream. Cook and stir over medium-low heat until caramels are melted. Remove from heat; stir in vanilla. Pour over crust. Cool completely in pan on a wire rack.

3. In a microwave, melt chocolate chips and shortening; stir until smooth. Drizzle over bars; let stand until set. Cut into bars.

1 BAR: 285 cal., 17g fat (6g sat. fat), 20mg chol., 149mg sod., 34g carb. (25g sugars, 2g fiber), 3g pro.

ICEBOX HONEY COOKIES

These old-fashioned goodies have a twist of citrus and honey. My Grandma Wruble always seemed to have a batch fresh from the oven to serve—plus a roll of dough in the refrigerator ready to slice and bake.
—*Kristi Gleason, Flower Mound, TX*

PREP: 20 MIN. + CHILLING • BAKE: 15 MIN./BATCH • MAKES: 8 DOZEN

1½ cups shortening
2 cups packed brown sugar
2 large eggs, room
temperature
½ cup honey
1 tsp. lemon extract
4½ cups all-purpose flour
2 tsp. baking soda
2 tsp. baking powder
1 tsp. salt
1 tsp. ground cinnamon

1. In a large bowl, cream shortening and brown sugar until light and fluffy, 5-7 minutes. Add eggs, 1 at a time, beating well after each addition. Beat in honey and extract. Combine the remaining ingredients; gradually add to creamed mixture and mix well.

2. Shape into two 12-in. rolls; wrap each in plastic. Refrigerate 2 hours or until firm.

3. Preheat oven to 325°. Unwrap and cut into ¼-in. slices. Place 1 in. apart on ungreased baking sheets. Bake until golden brown, 12-14 minutes. Remove to wire racks to cool.

2 COOKIES: 147 cal., 6g fat (2g sat. fat), 9mg chol., 125mg sod., 21g carb. (12g sugars, 0 fiber), 1g pro.

ORANGE GINGERBREAD TASSIES

I make big platters of Christmas cookies every year, and it's fun to include different shapes. These miniature filled cups look so cute next to the cutouts, crescents and other varieties. The tassies blend gingerbread flavor with orange zest, but you could substitute lemon if you prefer.
—*Elisabeth Larsen, Pleasant Grove, UT*

PREP: 20 MIN. + CHILLING • BAKE: 15 MIN. + COOLING • MAKES: 2 DOZEN

½ cup butter, softened
4 oz. cream cheese, softened
¼ cup molasses
1 tsp. ground ginger
½ tsp. ground cinnamon
½ tsp. ground allspice
¼ tsp. ground cloves

1 cup all-purpose flour
½ cup white baking chips
¼ cup heavy whipping cream
2 Tbsp. butter
4 tsp. grated orange zest
Candied orange peel, optional

1. Beat the first 7 ingredients until light and fluffy, 5-7 minutes. Gradually beat in flour. Refrigerate, covered, until firm enough to shape, about 1 hour.

2. Preheat oven to 350°. Shape dough into twenty-four 1-in. balls; press evenly onto bottoms and up sides of ungreased mini-muffin cups. Bake until golden brown, 15-18 minutes. Press the centers with the handle of a wooden spoon to reshape as necessary. Cool completely in pan before removing to wire rack.

3. In a microwave-safe bowl, heat white baking chips, cream and butter until blended, stirring occasionally. Stir in orange zest; cool completely. Spoon into crusts. Refrigerate until filling is soft-set. If desired, garnish with orange peel.

1 COOKIE: 91 cal., 6g fat (4g sat. fat), 13mg chol., 43mg sod., 9g carb. (5g sugars, 0 fiber), 1g pro.

FROM GRANDMA'S KITCHEN: Always store gingerbread cookies separately from other cookies and sweets. The molasses and distinct spices in gingerbread can affect the flavor of other treats.

LEMONY LAYER BARS

One of my favorite desserts is a white chocolate cake with coconut lemon filling, dark chocolate frosting and almonds. This version of a seven-layer bar boasts all of those flavors. If you prefer a more traditional crust, simply replace the crushed saltines with graham crackers.
—*Arlene Erlbach, Morton Grove, IL*

PREP: 20 MIN. • BAKE: 25 MIN. + COOLING • MAKES: 2 DOZEN

2 cups crushed unsalted top saltines
½ cup butter, melted
1 cup white baking chips
1 cup sweetened shredded coconut
1 cup coarsely chopped almonds
1 cup (6 oz.) semisweet chocolate chips
1 can (14 oz.) sweetened condensed milk
¼ cup lemon curd
2 Tbsp. grated lemon zest, divided

1. Preheat oven to 375°. Line a 13x9-in. baking pan with parchment, letting ends extend up sides. In a large bowl, mix cracker crumbs and butter. Press onto the bottom of prepared pan. Sprinkle with white chips, coconut, almonds and chocolate chips.

2. In a small bowl, combine milk, lemon curd and 1 Tbsp. zest. Pour over chips. Sprinkle with remaining 1 Tbsp. zest. Bake until edges are golden brown, 25-30 minutes. Cool completely in pan on a wire rack. Lifting with parchment, remove from pan. Cut into bars. Store in an airtight container.

1 BAR: 245 cal., 14g fat (8g sat. fat), 20mg chol., 98mg sod., 27g carb. (21g sugars, 1g fiber), 4g pro.

CRISP ROSETTES

Shaped like delicate snowflakes and sprinkled with confectioners' sugar, fried rosettes make lovely winter treats. We have them at Christmastime and on other special occasions.
—*Rita Christianson, Glenburn, ND*

PREP: 5 MIN. • COOK: 1 HOUR + COOLING • MAKES: ABOUT 2½ DOZEN

2 eggs, room temperature
1 cup 2% milk
1 tsp. sugar
¼ tsp. salt
1 cup all-purpose flour
Oil for deep-fat frying
Confectioners' sugar

1. In a small bowl, beat the eggs, milk, sugar and salt. Gradually add flour; beat until smooth.

2. In a deep-fat fryer or electric skillet, heat 2½ in. of oil to 375°. Place rosette iron in hot oil for 30 seconds. Blot iron on paper towels, then dip iron in batter to three-fourths the way up the sides (do not let batter run over top of iron). Immediately place in hot oil; loosen rosette with fork and remove iron.

3. Fry for 1-2 minutes on each side or until golden brown. Remove to a wire rack covered with paper towels. Repeat with remaining batter. Sprinkle with confectioners' sugar before serving.

1 ROSETTE: 38 cal., 2g fat (0 sat. fat), 13mg chol., 28mg sod., 4g carb. (1g sugars, 0 fiber), 1g pro.

LEMONY
LAYER BARS

OREO RICE KRISPIES TREATS

Indulge in two treats—Oreos and Rice Krispies bars—at the same time! Chewy on the inside, these irresistible squares have a crispy, crunchy topping of crushed cookies for an eye-catching presentation.
—Taste of Home *Test Kitchen*

PREP: 20 MIN. + CHILLING • MAKES: 2 DOZEN

1 pkg. (10 oz.) miniature marshmallows
3 Tbsp. canola oil
5 cups Rice Krispies
20 Oreo cookies, coarsely crushed (2 cups)
1 pkg. (10 oz.) white baking chips, melted

In a microwave or a large saucepan over low heat, melt the marshmallows and oil; stir until smooth. Remove from heat; stir in the cereal and 1 cup chopped Oreos. Press the mixture into a lightly greased 13x9-in. baking pan, using waxed paper or a lightly greased spatula. Cool to room temperature. Spread melted white baking chips on top; sprinkle with remaining 1 cup chopped Oreos. Cut into bars.

1 BAR: 204 cal., 8g fat (3g sat. fat), 2mg chol., 122mg sod., 31g carb. (19g sugars, 1g fiber), 2g pro.

GRANDMA'S FAVORITE SUGAR COOKIES

Whenever we had company at our house, my mother would bring out a batch of her special cutouts. Our whole family cherishes her recipe.
—Ann DeHass, Wilmot, OH

PREP: 25 MIN. + CHILLING • BAKE: 10 MIN. • MAKES: ABOUT 2 DOZEN

½ cup butter, softened
1 cup plus 2 tsp. sugar, divided
1 egg, room temperature
1 tsp. vanilla extract
2⅔ cups all-purpose flour
1 tsp. baking powder
½ tsp. baking soda
½ tsp. salt
¼ tsp. ground nutmeg
½ cup sour cream
27 to 30 raisins

1. In a large bowl, cream butter and 1 cup sugar until light and fluffy, 5-7 minutes. Beat in the egg and vanilla. In another bowl, combine the flour, baking powder, baking soda, salt and nutmeg; add to creamed mixture alternately with the sour cream, beating well after each addition. Cover and refrigerate for 1-2 hours or until easy to handle.

2. On a lightly floured surface, roll the dough to ¼-in. thickness. Cut with a floured 2½-in. round cookie cutter. Place 2 in. apart on lightly greased baking sheets. Sprinkle with remaining sugar. Place a raisin in the center of each cookie.

3. Bake at 375° for 10-12 minutes or until set and the bottoms are lightly browned. Cool for 1 minute before removing to wire racks.

1 COOKIE: 121 cal., 5g fat (3g sat. fat), 19mg chol., 116mg sod., 18g carb. (9g sugars, 0 fiber), 2g pro.

CHERRY-FILLED CUTOUTS

Mom started baking these goodies in the 1950s. The golden sandwich rounds feature a ruby-red filling of cherry preserves and chopped almonds.
—*Beth Neels, Ontario, NY*

PREP: 40 MIN. + CHILLING • BAKE: 15 MIN./BATCH • MAKES: ABOUT 2 DOZEN

1 cup butter, softened
1 cup sugar
½ cup packed brown sugar
2 large eggs, room temperature
1 tsp. vanilla extract
4 cups all-purpose flour
1 tsp. baking soda
½ tsp. salt
1 cup cherry preserves
¼ cup chopped slivered almonds

1. Cream the butter and sugars until light and fluffy, 5-7 minutes. Beat in the eggs and vanilla. In another bowl, whisk together flour, baking soda and salt; gradually beat into the creamed mixture. Divide the dough in half. Shape each into a disk; wrap and refrigerate 4 hours or until firm enough to roll.

2. Preheat the oven to 375°. On a lightly floured surface, roll each portion of dough to ⅛-in. thickness. Using floured 2¾-in. and 3-in. cookie cutters, cut an equal number of circles in each size. Using a floured 1-in. cookie cutter, cut out centers from larger circles.

3. For filling, mix cherry preserves and almonds. Place the solid circles 1½ in. apart on parchment-lined baking sheets. Spoon 2 tsp. filling on center of each. Top with cutout circles.

4. Bake until golden brown, 12-15 minutes. Cool on the pans 5 minutes. Remove to wire racks to cool.

1 SANDWICH COOKIE: 240 cal., 9g fat (5g sat. fat), 36mg chol., 170mg sod., 38g carb. (21g sugars, 1g fiber), 3g pro.

FROM GRANDMA'S KITCHEN: Using a smaller dough circle on the bottom helps the top dough self-seal over the bottom. If you don't have a 2¾-in. cookie cutter, cut all of the circles with a 3-in. cutter, taking care not to spread the filling too close to the edge.

NO-BAKE
TRIPLE-CHOCOLATE
CRISPY BARS

NO-BAKE TRIPLE-CHOCOLATE CRISPY BARS

These bars are crowd pleasers! I've made them with chocolate hazelnut peanut butter spread and also with Biscoff cookie spread. The secret to making them soft and chewy is bringing the sugar mixture just to a boil and then cooking for only one minute. If it boils too long, they tend to be firmer and can become crumbly.

—*Dawn Lowenstein, Huntingdon Valley, PA*

PREP: 20 MIN. + COOLING • MAKES: 4 DOZEN

½ cup butter, cubed
¾ cup sugar
¾ cup packed brown sugar
½ cup baking cocoa
½ cup 2% milk or
   half-and-half cream
½ tsp. salt
1 jar (13 oz.) Nutella
1 jar (7 oz.) marshmallow
   creme
½ tsp. almond extract
3 cups Rice Krispies
1 cup milk chocolate
   English toffee bits

1. In a large saucepan, melt butter over low heat. Add sugars, baking cocoa, milk and salt; bring to a boil. Cook and stir over medium heat for 1 minute. Remove from the heat. Stir in Nutella, marshmallow creme and extract until melted. Stir in Rice Krispies.

2. Press into a greased 15x10x1-in. pan; cool slightly. Sprinkle with toffee bits; refrigerate until set. Cut into squares; store in an airtight container.

1 BAR: 132 cal., 6g fat (2g sat. fat), 7mg chol., 74mg sod., 19g carb. (17g sugars, 0 fiber), 1g pro.

OLD-FASHIONED GINGERBREAD

Dad told me his mother made gingerbread with hot water and that it was dense and rich with molasses. I didn't know how to re-create that treat until one day, an elderly woman gave me a special cookbook of childhood favorites—and there was the recipe! I tweaked it a bit by substituting shortening for the lard. Enjoy a piece at room temperature or warm and dripping with butter.

— *Cjwkat, tasteofhome.com*

PREP: 25 MIN. • BAKE: 35 MIN. + COOLING • MAKES: 9 PIECES

½ cup butter, cubed
¼ cup shortening, cubed
1 cup boiling water
2 large eggs,
   room temperature
1½ cups molasses
2 cups all-purpose flour
1 Tbsp. ground ginger
2 tsp. baking powder
1 tsp. ground cinnamon
½ tsp. salt
¼ tsp. baking soda
   Confectioners' sugar,
   optional

1. Preheat oven to 350°. Grease a 9-in. square baking pan; set aside. In a large bowl, mix butter, shortening and boiling water until smooth; cool slightly. Beat in eggs and molasses until well blended. In another bowl, whisk flour, ginger, baking powder, cinnamon, salt and baking soda; gradually beat into molasses mixture. Transfer to prepared pan.

2. Bake until a toothpick inserted in the center comes out clean, 35-40 minutes. Cool completely on wire rack. If desired, sprinkle with confectioners' sugar before serving.

1 PIECE: 414 cal., 17g fat (8g sat. fat), 68mg chol., 390mg sod., 62g carb. (40g sugars, 1g fiber), 4g pro.

GIMLET BARS

I love sipping a gimlet cocktail in hot weather. These lime squares are just the thing when my craving hits but summer is far away. If you want them a bit tangier, just add more zest.
—*Trisha Kruse, Eagle, ID*

PREP: 20 MIN. + STANDING • BAKE: 35 MIN. + COOLING • MAKES: 4 DOZEN

2 cups all-purpose flour
½ cup confectioners' sugar
½ tsp. salt
1 cup butter

FILLING
4 large eggs
2 cups sugar
⅓ cup all-purpose flour
¼ cup lime juice
¼ cup gin
1 Tbsp. grated lime zest
½ tsp. baking powder

GLAZE
1½ cups confectioners' sugar
2 Tbsp. lime juice
2 Tbsp. gin
1 tsp. grated lime zest

1. Preheat oven to 350°. Whisk the flour, confectioners' sugar and salt; cut in the butter until crumbly. Press onto the bottom of a greased 15x10x1-in. baking pan. Bake until golden brown, about 10 minutes. Cool on a wire rack.

2. For filling, whisk together all ingredients; spread over crust. Bake until filling is set, about 25 minutes. Cool completely in pan on a wire rack.

3. For glaze, whisk all ingredients until smooth; spread evenly over cooled bars. Let glaze set before serving.

1 BAR: 117 cal., 4g fat (3g sat. fat), 26mg chol., 66mg sod., 18g carb. (13g sugars, 0 fiber), 1g pro.

"Whoa! These are amazing! I skipped the gin and just used more lime juice, and my family is begging for them again. These are going into my permanent recipe collection."
—JUSTINE JOHNSON, TASTEOFHOME.COM

GINGER-DOODLES

Both of my grandmothers taught me how to bake when I was a child, and I've been doing it ever since. My brothers like snickerdoodles and I like gingersnaps. Mixing the two makes all of us happy!
—*Becky Toth, Havre, MT*

PREP: 25 MIN. • BAKE: 10 MIN./BATCH • MAKES: ABOUT 5 DOZEN

¾ cup butter, softened
1½ cups sugar, divided
½ cup packed brown sugar
1 large egg, room temperature
½ cup maple syrup
3¼ cups all-purpose flour
1 tsp. baking soda
¾ tsp. ground cinnamon, divided
½ tsp. ground ginger
¼ tsp. salt
¼ tsp. cream of tartar
¼ tsp. ground nutmeg

1. Preheat oven to 350°. In a large bowl, cream the butter, ½ cup sugar and brown sugar until light and fluffy, 5-7 minutes. Beat in egg and syrup. In another bowl, whisk flour, baking soda, ½ tsp. cinnamon, ginger, salt, cream of tartar and nutmeg; gradually beat into the creamed mixture.

2. In a small bowl, combine the remaining sugar and cinnamon. Shape the dough into 1-in. balls; roll in sugar mixture. Place 3 in. apart on ungreased baking sheets. Bake 10-12 minutes or until light brown. Remove to wire racks to cool.

FREEZE OPTION: Freeze cookies in freezer containers. To use, thaw before serving.

1 COOKIE: 80 cal., 2g fat (2g sat. fat), 9mg chol., 51mg sod., 14g carb. (8g sugars, 0 fiber), 1g pro.

TWO-TONE CARAMEL BROWNIES

These goodies are a mashup of some of my favorite sweets. A woman I worked with gave me her recipe for chocolate caramel brownies, and I wondered what they would taste like combined with my yellow cake mix bars. So I tried it, and was thrilled with the results!
—*Staci Perry Mergenthal, Verdi, MN*

PREP: 40 MIN. • BAKE: 20 MIN. + COOLING • MAKES: 40 SERVINGS

1 pkg. chocolate cake mix (regular size)
¾ cup butter, melted
1 can (5 oz.) evaporated milk, divided
1 pkg. (11 oz.) Kraft caramel bits
1 cup semisweet chocolate chips
1 pkg. yellow cake mix (regular size)

1 large egg, room temperature
½ cup plus 1 Tbsp. butter, softened, divided
1 can (14 oz.) sweetened condensed milk
1 pkg. (11½ oz.) milk chocolate chips

1. Preheat oven to 350°. Line a 13x9-in. baking pan with parchment; grease paper. In a large bowl, beat chocolate cake mix, melted butter and ⅓ cup evaporated milk until blended; batter will be thick. Reserve ¼ cup batter for topping. Spread remaining batter into prepared pan. Bake 6 minutes.

2. Meanwhile, in a microwave, melt caramel bits and remaining ⅓ cup evaporated milk; stir until smooth. Sprinkle hot chocolate crust with semisweet chips; pour caramel mixture over top.

3. In another large bowl, beat the yellow cake mix, egg and ½ cup softened butter until combined; batter will be thick. Reserve half for topping. Crumble the remaining mixture over caramel layer. Bake 6 minutes.

4. In a microwave, melt the sweetened condensed milk, milk chocolate chips and remaining 1 Tbsp. softened butter; stir until smooth. Pour over yellow cake layer. Sprinkle with the reserved yellow and chocolate cake batters. Bake until the top is golden brown, 20-25 minutes. Cool completely on a wire rack. Store in an airtight container.

1 BROWNIE: 272 cal., 13g fat (8g sat. fat), 27mg chol., 260mg sod., 38g carb. (28g sugars, 1g fiber), 3g pro.

BUTTER PECAN BARS WITH PENUCHE DRIZZLE

I've baked countless pans of these over the years. With a sprinkling of chopped pecans and extra molasses flavor from dark brown sugar, the bars are rich, chewy, nutty and buttery—all the good stuff! A drizzle of old-fashioned penuche icing takes them over the top. You could eat them without the penuche, but why?

—Kallee Krong-McCreery, Escondido, CA

PREP: 30 MIN. • BAKE: 25 MIN. + COOLING • MAKES: 2 DOZEN

2 cups packed
  dark brown sugar
½ cup butter, melted
2 large eggs, room
  temperature
1 Tbsp. vanilla extract
2 cups all-purpose flour
½ tsp. salt
1 cup chopped pecans,
  divided

ICING

3 Tbsp. butter
¼ cup packed
  dark brown sugar
1 Tbsp. 2% milk
½ cup confectioners' sugar

1. Preheat oven to 350°. In a large bowl, beat brown sugar and butter until blended. Beat in eggs, then vanilla. In another bowl, whisk flour and salt; gradually beat into sugar mixture. Stir in ¾ cup pecans. Pour into a greased 13x9-in. baking pan; sprinkle with remaining ¼ cup pecans.

2. Bake until a toothpick inserted in the center comes out clean (do not overbake). Cool completely in pan on a wire rack.

3. For the icing, in a small saucepan, melt butter over low heat. Stir in brown sugar; cook and stir 30 seconds. Add milk; cook and stir 30 seconds. Remove from heat; whisk in confectioners' sugar until smooth. Immediately drizzle over bars; let stand until set. Cut into bars.

1 BAR: 212 cal., 9g fat (4g sat. fat), 30mg chol., 103mg sod., 32g carb. (23g sugars, 1g fiber), 2g pro.

CHERRY BONBON COOKIES

Here's a very old recipe from my grandma that always brings back sweet memories. The maraschino cherry filling surprises everyone who tries one.

—Pat Habiger, Spearville, KS

PREP: 15 MIN. • BAKE: 20 MIN. + COOLING • MAKES: 2 DOZEN

½ cup butter, softened
¾ cup confectioners' sugar
2 Tbsp. milk
1 tsp. vanilla extract
1½ cups all-purpose flour
⅛ tsp. salt
24 maraschino cherries

GLAZE

1 cup confectioners' sugar
1 Tbsp. butter, melted
2 Tbsp. maraschino cherry
  juice
  Additional confectioners'
  sugar

1. Preheat oven to 350°. In a large bowl, cream butter and sugar until light and fluffy, 5-7 minutes. Add milk and vanilla. Combine flour and salt; gradually add to the creamed mixture.

2. Divide the dough into 24 portions; shape each portion around a maraschino cherry, forming a ball. Place on ungreased baking sheets. Bake 18-20 minutes or until lightly browned. Remove to wire racks to cool.

3. For glaze, combine sugar, butter and cherry juice until smooth. Drizzle over cookies. Dust with confectioners' sugar.

1 COOKIE: 113 cal., 4g fat (3g sat. fat), 12mg chol., 48mg sod., 18g carb. (12g sugars, 0 fiber), 1g pro.

BUTTER PECAN BARS
WITH PENUCHE DRIZZLE

COOKIE JAR GINGERSNAPS

My grandmother kept two cookie jars in her pantry. One of them, which I now have, always held a batch of these crisp and chewy gingersnaps. When my daughter made them for 4-H and entered them at the fair, she won a blue ribbon.

—*Deb Handy, Pomona, KS*

PREP: 20 MIN. • BAKE: 15 MIN./BATCH • MAKES: 3 DOZEN

¾ cup shortening
1 cup plus 2 Tbsp. sugar, divided
1 large egg, room temperature
¼ cup molasses

2 cups all-purpose flour
2 tsp. baking soda
1½ tsp. ground ginger
1 tsp. ground cinnamon
½ tsp. salt

1. Preheat oven to 350°. Cream shortening and 1 cup sugar until light and fluffy, 5-7 minutes. Beat in egg and molasses. In another bowl, combine next 5 ingredients; gradually add to the creamed mixture and mix well.

2. Shape level Tbsp. of cookie dough into balls. Dip 1 side of each ball into the remaining sugar; place 2 in. apart, sugary side up, on greased baking sheets. Bake until lightly browned and crinkly, 12-15 minutes. Remove to wire racks to cool.

1 COOKIE: 92 cal., 4g fat (1g sat. fat), 5mg chol., 106mg sod., 13g carb. (7g sugars, 0 fiber), 1g pro.

FROM GRANDMA'S KITCHEN: Because shortening melts at a higher temperature than butter, it's useful for baking cookies that you want to have a nice uniform shape.

AUDREY'S LEMON MERINGUE BARS

We have a prolific lemon tree in our backyard, and we're forever trying to find new ways to incorporate the beautiful yellow fruits into our cooking so that none go to waste. My teen daughter, Audrey, who knows my love of all things sweet, decided to test her baking skills by combining two of my favorites: lemon bars and lemon meringue pie. After a few intense hours in the kitchen (warding off her brothers), these scrumptious treats were born.

—*Monica Fearnside, Rancho Palos Verdes, CA*

PREP: 35 MIN. + COOLING • BAKE: 40 MIN. + CHILLING • **MAKES:** 2 DOZEN

2   **cups all-purpose flour**
½   **cup sugar**
¼   **tsp. salt**
1   **cup cold butter**

FILLING
1⅓   **cups sugar**
½   **cup lemon juice**
4   **large eggs, room temperature**
¼   **cup all-purpose flour**
2   **Tbsp. grated lemon zest**

MERINGUE
3   **large egg whites, room temperature**
1   **tsp. grated lemon zest**
¼   **tsp. cream of tartar**
7   **Tbsp. sugar**

1. Preheat oven to 350°. Line a 13x9-in. baking pan with parchment, letting ends extend up sides.

2. In a large bowl, combine flour, sugar and salt; cut in butter until the mixture resembles coarse crumbs. Press into bottom of prepared pan. Bake until light golden brown, 20-25 minutes. Cool completely on a wire rack.

3. For filling, in another large bowl, mix sugar, lemon juice, eggs, flour and zest until combined. Pour over crust. Bake until set and top is dry, 22-27 minutes.

4. Meanwhile, for meringue, in a large bowl, beat the egg whites with the lemon zest and cream of tartar on medium speed until foamy. Gradually add the sugar, 1 Tbsp. at a time, beating on high after each addition until the sugar is dissolved. Continue beating until stiff glossy peaks form. Spread or pipe over hot filling.

5. Bake until the meringue is golden brown, 15-18 minutes. Cool 1 hour on a wire rack. Refrigerate at least 4 hours before serving. Lifting with parchment, remove from pan. Cut into bars.

1 BAR: 200 cal., 9g fat (5g sat. fat), 51mg chol., 105mg sod., 29g carb. (19g sugars, 0 fiber), 3g pro.

COCONUT NUTELLA
BROWNIES

COCONUT NUTELLA BROWNIES

When my parents were coming over for dinner, I wanted to serve homemade brownies.
My mom loves coconut, so this recipe was perfect. I even lightened it up a bit
for those of us who were watching what we eat. Win-win!
—*Danielle Lee, West Palm Beach, FL*

PREP: 15 MIN. • BAKE: 25 MIN. + COOLING • MAKES: 2 DOZEN

½ cup butter, softened
1⅓ cups sugar
½ cup Nutella
4 large eggs, room
temperature
1 tsp. vanilla extract
1 cup all-purpose flour
½ cup whole wheat flour
⅔ cup Dutch-processed
cocoa
½ cup flaked coconut
½ cup old-fashioned oats

1. Preheat oven to 350°. In a large bowl, beat butter, sugar and Nutella until blended. Add eggs, 1 at a time, beating well after each addition. Beat in vanilla. In another bowl, whisk flours and cocoa; gradually beat into the butter mixture, mixing well. Fold in coconut and oats. Spread into a greased 13x9-in. baking pan.

2. Bake brownies until a toothpick comes out with moist crumbs, 22-25 minutes (do not overbake). Cool completely in pan on a wire rack. Cut into bars.

1 BROWNIE: 186 cal., 9g fat (5g sat. fat), 41mg chol., 50mg sod., 26g carb. (16g sugars, 4g fiber), 4g pro.

DATE SWIRL COOKIES

My granddaughter nicknamed my mother Cookie Grandma because she baked the most
wonderful cookies. Her crisp-chewy date swirls were a tradition every Christmas.
—*Donna Grace, Clancy, MT*

PREP: 30 MIN. + CHILLING • BAKE: 10 MIN./BATCH • MAKES: 4 DOZEN

FILLING
2 cups chopped dates
1 cup water
1 cup sugar
1 cup chopped nuts
2 tsp. lemon juice

DOUGH
1 cup butter, softened
1 cup packed brown sugar
1 cup sugar
3 large eggs, room
temperature
1 tsp. lemon extract
4 cups all-purpose flour
1 tsp. salt
¾ tsp. baking soda

1. In a saucepan, combine the filling ingredients. Cook over medium-low heat, stirring constantly, until mixture becomes stiff, 15-20 minutes. Chill.

2. For dough, cream the butter and sugars in a bowl. Add eggs, 1 at a time, beating well after each addition. Add extract. Combine flour, salt and baking soda; gradually add to creamed mixture and mix well. Chill for at least 1 hour.

3. On a lightly floured surface, roll out half of the cookie dough to a 12x9-in. rectangle, about ¼ in. thick. Spread with half of the filling. Roll up, starting with the long end. Repeat with remaining dough and filling. Wrap securely in waxed paper; chill overnight.

4. Cut rolls into ¼-in. slices. Place 2 in. apart on greased baking sheets. Bake at 375° for 8-10 minutes or until lightly browned. Cool on wire racks.

1 COOKIE: 160 cal., 6g fat (3g sat. fat), 22mg chol., 105mg sod., 26g carb. (17g sugars, 1g fiber), 2g pro.

KEY LIME BLONDIE BARS

Here's my tropical twist on traditional blondies. I gave them the flavor of classic Key lime pie and added cream cheese frosting as the decadent finishing touch.
—*Kristin LaBoon, Austin, TX*

PREP: 35 MIN. + CHILLING • BAKE: 25 MIN. + COOLING • MAKES: 16 SERVINGS

1⅓ cups graham cracker crumbs, divided
⅓ cup plus 2 Tbsp. melted butter, divided
3 Tbsp. plus ¼ cup packed brown sugar, divided
⅔ cup butter, softened
1 cup plus 1 Tbsp. sugar, divided
2 large eggs, room temperature
1 large egg white, room temperature
3 Tbsp. Key lime juice
4½ tsp. grated Key lime zest
1 cup all-purpose flour
½ tsp. plus ⅛ tsp. salt, divided
1 tsp. vanilla extract
⅛ tsp. ground cinnamon

FROSTING
¼ cup butter, softened
¼ cup cream cheese, softened
4 cups confectioners' sugar
2 Tbsp. 2% milk
1 tsp. vanilla extract
Key lime slices, optional

1. Preheat oven to 350°. Line a 9-in. square baking pan with parchment, letting the ends extend up the sides. Combine 1 cup cracker crumbs, ⅓ cup melted butter and 3 Tbsp. brown sugar; press onto the bottom of prepared pan. Bake 10 minutes. Cool on a wire rack.

2. For blondie layer, in a large bowl, cream softened butter and 1 cup sugar until light and fluffy, 5-7 minutes. Beat in eggs, egg white, and lime juice and zest. In a small bowl, mix flour and ½ tsp. salt; gradually add to creamed mixture, mixing well.

3. Spread over the crust. Bake until a toothpick inserted in the center comes out clean, 25-30 minutes (do not overbake). Cool completely in pan on a wire rack.

4. For streusel, combine the remaining ⅓ cup cracker crumbs, 2 Tbsp. melted butter, ¼ cup brown sugar, 1 Tbsp. sugar and ⅛ tsp. salt, along with the vanilla and cinnamon, until crumbly. Reserve ½ cup for topping.

5. In a large bowl, combine the 5 frosting ingredients; beat until smooth. Stir in the remaining ½ cup streusel. Spread over bars. Sprinkle with the reserved topping. Refrigerate at least 4 hours before cutting. Lifting with the parchment, remove from the pan. Cut into bars. Store in an airtight container in the refrigerator. If desired, garnish with sliced Key limes.

1 BLONDIE: 422 cal., 19g fat (11g sat. fat), 69mg chol., 283mg sod., 62g carb. (51g sugars, 1g fiber), 3g pro.

"I made these today and they are absolutely delicious! Thanks for the wonderful recipe."
—TAMMY2225, TASTEOFHOME.COM

CHOCOLATE PEANUT BUTTER DREAM BARS

Just about everyone likes the pairing of chocolate and peanut butter. If you prefer, change up the topping for these dreamy bars by sprinkling on your favorite combination of candies.
—*Cindi DeClue, Anchorage, AK*

PREP: 15 MIN. + COOLING • **BAKE:** 10 MIN. + CHILLING • **MAKES:** 12 SERVINGS

1 pkg. (16 oz.) Nutter Butter cookies, divided	½ cup confectioners' sugar
¼ cup butter, melted	⅓ cup crunchy peanut butter
1 pkg. (3.90 oz.) instant chocolate pudding mix	1 carton (8 oz.) frozen whipped topping, thawed
1½ cups 2% milk	¼ cup milk chocolate chips
4 oz. cream cheese, softened	¼ cup peanut butter chips

1. Preheat oven to 350°. In a large bowl, finely crush 24 of the cookies; stir in the melted butter. Press onto the bottom of an ungreased 9-in. square baking pan. Bake until lightly browned, about 10 minutes. Cool completely.

2. In a small bowl, whisk pudding mix and milk until smooth; spread over cooled crust. In another small bowl, beat cream cheese, confectioners' sugar and peanut butter. Fold in 1 cup whipped topping. Spoon cream cheese mixture over pudding; gently spread to cover pudding. Spread remaining whipped topping over cream cheese layer. Cover and refrigerate for at least 2 hours.

3. Coarsely crush the remaining 8 cookies. Sprinkle crushed cookies and chips over whipped topping before serving.

1 PIECE: 448 cal., 25g fat (12g sat. fat), 23mg chol., 300mg sod., 50g carb. (32g sugars, 2g fiber), 8g pro.

ITALIAN CREAM-FILLED CAKE BARS

These scrumptious bars use simple ingredients but are fancy enough to replace the cake at a birthday party. For a flavor twist, swap out the lemon zest in the crust for orange or lime. You could also add another layer before the filling—try raspberry jam, marmalade or even Nutella.

—Maria Morelli, West Kelowna, BC

PREP: 30 MIN. + CHILLING • BAKE: 30 MIN. + COOLING • MAKES: 2 DOZEN

¾ cup butter, softened
½ cup sugar
4 large egg yolks, room temperature
1½ tsp. grated lemon zest
2 tsp. vanilla extract
2 cups all-purpose flour
1 tsp. baking powder
Dash salt

FILLING
2⅓ cups plain whole milk yogurt
1⅔ cups sour cream
⅓ cup all-purpose flour
2 tsp. vanilla extract
4 large egg whites, room temperature
¾ cup sugar
Confectioners' sugar, optional

1. In a large bowl, cream butter and sugar until light and fluffy, 5-7 minutes. Add egg yolks, 1 at a time, beating well after each addition. Beat in zest and vanilla. In another bowl, whisk flour, baking powder and salt; gradually beat into creamed mixture.

2. Divide dough in half. Shape each into a disk; wrap. Refrigerate 1 portion and freeze 1 portion for 30 minutes.

3. Preheat oven to 350°. On a lightly floured surface, roll the refrigerated portion of dough to fit a greased 15x10x1-in. baking pan. Refrigerate while making filling.

4. Meanwhile, for filling, in a large bowl, combine the yogurt, sour cream, flour and vanilla. With clean beaters, beat the egg whites on medium speed until soft peaks form. Gradually add granulated sugar, 1 Tbsp. at a time, beating on high after each addition until sugar is dissolved. Continue beating until stiff glossy peaks form. Fold into yogurt mixture. Spread evenly over crust.

5. Using a box grater, grate the frozen dough portion over filling. Press lightly into filling. Bake until puffed and the edges are light brown, 30-35 minutes. Cool completely on a wire rack. Cut into bars; if desired, sprinkle with confectioners' sugar. Refrigerate leftovers.

1 PIECE: 198 cal., 11g fat (6g sat. fat), 53mg chol., 99mg sod., 22g carb. (12g sugars, 0 fiber), 4g pro.

ICED ORANGE COOKIES

I love making these citrusy bite-sized goodies at Christmastime, when oranges in Florida are plentiful. Every time the baking cookies fill my house with their wonderful aroma, I think of my grandmother, who shared the recipe.
—*Lori DiPietro, New Port Richey, FL*

PREP: 25 MIN. • **BAKE:** 10 MIN./BATCH + COOLING • **MAKES:** 4 DOZEN

½ **cup shortening**
1 **cup sugar**
2 **large eggs,**
   room temperature
½ **cup orange juice**
1 **Tbsp. grated orange zest**
2½ **cups all-purpose flour**
1½ **tsp. baking powder**
½ **tsp. salt**

ICING
2 **cups confectioners' sugar**
¼ **cup orange juice**
2 **Tbsp. butter, melted**
   Orange paste food
   coloring, optional

1. Preheat oven to 350°. In a large bowl, cream shortening and sugar until light and fluffy, 5-7 minutes. Add the eggs, 1 at a time, beating well after each addition. Beat in orange juice and orange zest. Combine the flour, baking powder and salt; gradually add to the creamed mixture.

2. Drop by tablespoonfuls 2 in. apart onto ungreased baking sheets. Bake until edges begin to brown, 10-12 minutes. Remove to wire racks to cool. In a small bowl, combine icing ingredients until smooth; drizzle over cooled cookies.

1 COOKIE: 87 cal., 3g fat (1g sat. fat), 9mg chol., 47mg sod., 15g carb. (9g sugars, 0 fiber), 1g pro.

FROM GRANDMA'S KITCHEN: Feel free to use your preferred citrus (lemon, lime, etc.) in place of orange and proceed as this recipe directs. However, keep in mind that using baking substitutions may change the flavor and texture of your cookies.

STRAWBERRY RHUBARB CHEESECAKE BARS

What a way to use up your rhubarb! These bars layer a buttery pecan shortbread
crust with a rich cheesecake filling and sweet-tart jam. For a more
substantial dessert, cut nine large squares instead of 16.
—*Amanda Scarlati, Sandy, UT*

PREP: 30 MIN. + CHILLING • BAKE: 15 MIN. + COOLING • MAKES: 16 SERVINGS

1 cup all-purpose flour
⅓ cup packed brown sugar
   Dash kosher salt
½ cup cold butter, cubed
⅓ cup finely chopped
   pecans

FILLING

1 pkg. (8 oz.) cream cheese,
   softened
¼ cup sugar
2 Tbsp. 2% milk
1 Tbsp. lemon juice
½ tsp. vanilla extract
   Dash kosher salt
1 large egg, room
   temperature,
   lightly beaten

JAM

½ cup sugar
2 Tbsp. cornstarch
1⅓ cups chopped fresh
   strawberries
1⅓ cups sliced fresh
   or frozen rhubarb
1 Tbsp. lemon juice

1. Preheat oven to 350°. Line an 8-in. square baking pan with
parchment, letting the ends extend up the sides. In a small bowl,
mix the flour, brown sugar and salt; cut in butter until crumbly.
Stir in pecans.

2. Press into bottom of prepared pan. Bake until edges just begin
to brown, 12-15 minutes. Cool completely on a wire rack.

3. In a large bowl, beat the cream cheese and sugar until smooth.
Beat in milk, lemon juice, vanilla and salt. Add egg; beat on low
speed just until blended. Pour over crust.

4. Bake until the filling is set, 15-20 minutes. Cool on a wire rack
for 1 hour.

5. For jam, in a small saucepan, mix the sugar and cornstarch.
Add the strawberries, rhubarb and lemon juice. Bring to a boil.
Reduce heat; simmer, uncovered, until mixture begins to thicken,
6-8 minutes. Cool completely. Spread over filling. Refrigerate until
set, 8 hours or overnight.

6. Using parchment, carefully remove cheesecake from baking
pan. Cut into bars for serving.

1 BAR: 215 cal., 13g fat (7g sat. fat), 41mg chol., 113mg sod.,
24g carb. (15g sugars, 1g fiber), 3g pro.

HUMBLE BUMBLE
CRUMBLE BARS

HUMBLE BUMBLE CRUMBLE BARS

When I was trying to think of a new treat for my bingo group, I asked my husband for ideas. He suggested a fruity bar. These berry-topped squares are lightly sweet, pretty and so easy.
—*Nancy Phillips, Portland, ME*

PREP: 30 MIN. • BAKE: 45 MIN. + COOLING • MAKES: 15 SERVINGS

½ cup butter, softened
¾ cup sugar
1 large egg, room temperature
2½ cups all-purpose flour
½ tsp. baking powder
¼ tsp. salt
¼ cup packed brown sugar
1 tsp. ground cinnamon

FILLING
2 cups chunky applesauce
½ tsp. ground cinnamon
⅛ tsp. ground nutmeg
2 cups fresh blackberries
2 cups fresh raspberries

1. Preheat oven to 350°. In a large bowl, cream butter and sugar until light and fluffy, 5-7 minutes. Beat in egg. In another bowl, whisk flour, baking powder and salt; gradually beat into creamed mixture. Reserve ½ cup crumb mixture for the topping. Press the remaining mixture onto bottom of a greased 13x9-in. baking pan. Bake until lightly browned, 12-15 minutes. Cool on a wire rack.

2. Stir the brown sugar and cinnamon into the reserved topping; set aside. In a large bowl, combine applesauce, cinnamon and nutmeg until blended. Spread over the crust; top with the berries and reserved topping. Bake until golden brown, 30-35 minutes. Cool in pan on a wire rack. Cut into bars.

1 BAR: 228 cal., 7g fat (4g sat. fat), 29mg chol., 109mg sod., 39g carb. (20g sugars, 3g fiber), 3g pro.

CHAMPAGNE BLONDIES

I was looking for a fun champagne dessert to take to a friend's bridal shower, but I couldn't find the right one. That's when I came up with bubbly blondies! I usually make them with white baking chips, but I've also used butterscotch and chocolate.
—*Heather Karow, Burnett, WI*

PREP: 25 MIN. • BAKE: 25 MIN. + COOLING • MAKES: 16 SERVINGS

½ cup butter, softened
1 cup packed light brown sugar
1 large egg, room temperature
¼ cup champagne
1¼ cups all-purpose flour
1 tsp. baking powder
¼ tsp. salt
½ cup white baking chips
½ cup chopped hazelnuts, optional

GLAZE
1 cup confectioners' sugar
2 Tbsp. champagne

1. Preheat oven to 350°. Line an 8-in. square baking pan with parchment, letting the ends extend up the sides. In a large bowl, beat the butter and brown sugar until crumbly, about 2 minutes. Beat in the egg and champagne (batter may appear curdled). In another bowl, whisk flour, baking powder and salt; gradually add to butter mixture. Fold in baking chips and, if desired, nuts.

2. Spread into the prepared pan. Bake until edges are brown and center is set (do not overbake), 25-30 minutes. Cool completely in pan on a wire rack.

3. Combine the glaze ingredients; drizzle over blondies. Lifting with parchment, remove blondies from pan. Cut into bars. Store in an airtight container.

1 BLONDIE: 203 cal., 8g fat (5g sat. fat), 28mg chol., 126mg sod., 32g carb. (24g sugars, 0 fiber), 2g pro.

RHUBARB CHERRY
PIE, PAGE 257

GRANDMA'S FAVORITE

CAKES & PIES

From luscious layers and dreamy frostings to golden
crusts and fabulous fillings, these cakes and pies
have it all. Of course they do—they're Grandma's!

FROSTED CHOCOLATE CAKE

Here is my mother's oldest and most popular chocolate cake recipe. I always thought such an amazing dessert should have a fancier name, but this is what she called it. Mom would say a different name wouldn't change the taste!

—Beth Bristow, West Plains, MO

PREP: 40 MIN. • **BAKE:** 25 MIN. + COOLING • **MAKES:** 16 SERVINGS

4 **large eggs, separated**
½ **cup baking cocoa**
½ **cup boiling water**
½ **cup butter, softened**
1 **cup packed brown sugar**
1 **cup sugar, divided**
1 **tsp. vanilla extract**
2½ **cups all-purpose flour**
1 **tsp. baking soda**
1 **tsp. cream of tartar**
¼ **tsp. salt**
1 **cup buttermilk**

FROSTING

¾ **cup butter, melted**
¾ **tsp. vanilla extract**
6 **cups confectioners' sugar**
3 **Tbsp. whole milk**
   Dark or additional regular baking cocoa, optional

1. Place egg whites in a large bowl; let stand at room temperature 30 minutes. In a small bowl, mix the cocoa and boiling water until smooth; cool slightly. Line the bottoms of 2 greased 9-in. round baking pans with parchment; grease parchment.

2. Preheat oven to 375°. Cream butter, brown sugar and ¾ cup sugar until light and fluffy, 5-7 minutes. Beat in the vanilla and 1 egg yolk at a time. In another bowl, whisk together the flour, baking soda, cream of tartar and salt. Add to the creamed mixture alternately with buttermilk, beating after each addition. Stir in cocoa mixture.

3. With clean beaters, beat the egg whites on medium speed until soft peaks form. Gradually add remaining ¼ cup sugar, 1 Tbsp. at a time, beating on high after each addition until sugar is dissolved. Continue beating until stiff peaks form. Fold into batter. Transfer to prepared pans. Bake until a toothpick inserted in center comes out clean, 23-28 minutes.

4. Cool in pans 10 minutes before removing to wire racks; remove parchment. Cool completely.

5. Beat together the first 4 frosting ingredients. Spread between layers and over top and sides of cake. If desired, dust top lightly with cocoa.

1 PIECE: 510 cal., 16g fat (10g sat. fat), 86mg chol., 283mg sod., 89g carb. (71g sugars, 1g fiber), 5g pro.

"What an outstanding recipe! I made this for our grandson's birthday and it was amazing. Our grandson, and everyone else at the party, thought it was great. The cake sliced like a dream and tasted absolutely delicious."
—SGRONHOLZ, TASTEOFHOME.COM

APRICOT UPSIDE-DOWN CAKE

When I first sampled this golden upside-down cake from my Aunt Anne, I couldn't believe how good it was. Apricots give it a unique and attractive twist.
—*Ruth Ann Stelfox, Raymond, AB*

PREP: 30 MIN. • **BAKE:** 35 MIN. + COOLING • **MAKES:** 9 SERVINGS

- 2 **large eggs, separated**
- 2 **cans (15 oz. each) apricot halves**
- ¼ **cup butter, cubed**
- ½ **cup packed brown sugar**
- ⅔ **cup cake flour**
- ¾ **tsp. baking powder**
- ¼ **tsp. salt**
- ⅔ **cup sugar**

1. Place the egg whites in a small bowl; let stand at room temperature 30 minutes. Preheat oven to 350°. Drain apricots, reserving 3 Tbsp. syrup (discard remaining syrup); set aside.

2. Place the butter in a 9-in. square baking dish. Place in oven 3-4 minutes or until the butter is melted; swirl carefully to coat evenly. Sprinkle with brown sugar. Arrange the apricot halves in a single layer over brown sugar, cut side up.

3. In a small bowl, whisk the cake flour, baking powder and salt. In a large bowl, beat egg yolks until slightly thickened. Gradually add sugar, beating on high speed until thick and lemon-colored. Beat in reserved apricot syrup. Fold in flour mixture.

4. With clean beaters, beat egg whites on medium speed until stiff peaks form. Fold into the batter. Spoon over apricots. Bake 35-40 minutes or until a toothpick inserted in the center comes out clean. Cool 10 minutes before inverting onto a serving plate. Serve warm.

1 PIECE: 272 cal., 6g fat (4g sat. fat), 55mg chol., 162mg sod., 53g carb. (44g sugars, 1g fiber), 3g pro.

MERINGUE TORTE

My grandmother, who came here from Sweden when she was 21, would treat us to this luscious torte on our birthdays. It's still a family favorite.
—*Ruth Grover, Portland, CT*

CAKES & PIES

PREP: 40 MIN. • BAKE: 30 MIN. + COOLING • MAKES: 16-18 SERVINGS

¾ cup butter, softened
¾ cup sugar
6 large egg yolks,
  room temperature
1 tsp. vanilla extract
1½ cups all-purpose flour
1½ tsp. baking powder
6 Tbsp. 2% milk

MERINGUE
6 large egg whites,
  room temperature
1½ cups sugar
½ tsp. vanilla extract
½ cup plus 3 Tbsp. finely
  chopped walnuts, divided

FILLING
2 cups heavy
  whipping cream
¼ cup confectioners' sugar
2 cups fresh raspberries

1. In a large bowl, cream butter and sugar until light and fluffy, 5-7 minutes. Add egg yolks, 1 at a time, beating well after each addition. Beat in vanilla. Combine flour and baking powder; add to the creamed mixture alternately with milk, beating well after each addition. Pour into 3 parchment-lined 9-in. round baking pans; set aside.

2. In a large bowl, beat egg whites on medium speed until foamy. Gradually beat in sugar, 1 Tbsp. at a time, on high until stiff glossy peaks form and the sugar is dissolved. Add vanilla. Fold in ½ cup walnuts. Spread meringue evenly over cake batter; sprinkle with remaining walnuts.

3. Bake at 325° for 30-35 minutes or until the meringue is lightly browned. Cool on wire racks for 10 minutes (meringue will crack). Loosen the edges of cakes from pans with a knife. Using 2 large spatulas, carefully remove 1 cake to a serving plate, meringue side up. Carefully remove remaining cakes, meringue side up, to wire racks.

4. In a large bowl, beat cream until it begins to thicken. Gradually add confectioners' sugar; beat until stiff peaks form. Carefully spread half filling over cake on serving plate; top with half the raspberries. Repeat layers. Top with remaining cake. Store in the refrigerator.

1 PIECE: 364 cal., 22g fat (12g sat. fat), 128mg chol., 144mg sod., 38g carb. (28g sugars, 1g fiber), 5g pro.

OLD-FASHIONED
RHUBARB CAKE

**GRANDMA'S
SECRET**
When selecting fresh rhubarb,
look for firm stalks that are
unbent and free of bruises.
Stalks should also have a
slight sheen to them.

OLD-FASHIONED RHUBARB CAKE

Shared by my great-aunt, this homey cake is especially yummy during rhubarb season
and tastes extra special with the old-fashioned milk topping. But people love
this even with frozen rhubarb and modern-day whipped topping.
—Marilyn Homola, Hazel, SD

PREP: 20 MIN. • **BAKE:** 35 MIN. • **MAKES:** 12 SERVINGS

½   cup butter, softened
1¼ cups sugar, divided
1   large egg, room
    temperature
1   cup buttermilk
1   tsp. vanilla extract
2   cups all-purpose flour
1   tsp. baking soda
½   tsp. salt
2   cups chopped rhubarb
½   tsp. ground cinnamon

MILK TOPPING
1½ cups whole milk
⅓   cup sugar
1   tsp. vanilla extract

1. Preheat oven to 350°. In a bowl, cream butter and 1 cup sugar. Add egg; beat well. Combine buttermilk and vanilla; set aside.

2. Combine the flour, baking soda and salt; add alternately with buttermilk and vanilla to the creamed mixture. Stir in rhubarb. Spread in a greased 13x9-in. baking pan.

3. Combine the remaining sugar with cinnamon; sprinkle over batter. Bake until a toothpick inserted in center comes out clean, about 35 minutes.

4. For the topping, combine all ingredients; pour over individual squares.

1 PIECE: 286 cal., 9g fat (6g sat. fat), 40mg chol., 323mg sod., 46g carb. (29g sugars, 1g fiber), 5g pro.

MOM'S MAPLE-APPLE PIE

Mom's apple pie may be a cliché, but others have tried and failed to rival my mother's recipe.
At holiday time, my siblings and I always make sure she's the one doing dessert!
—Rebecca Little, Park Ridge, IL

PREP: 30 MIN. • **BAKE:** 40 MIN. + COOLING • **MAKES:** 8 SERVINGS

1   cup sugar
2   Tbsp. all-purpose flour
1½ tsp. ground cinnamon
½   tsp. ground nutmeg
¼   tsp. salt
6   medium tart apples
    (about 2¼ lbs.), peeled
    and thinly sliced
1   Tbsp. lemon juice
1   (14.1 oz.) refrigerated
    pie pastry
2   Tbsp. butter
3   Tbsp. maple syrup,
    divided
    Warm maple syrup,
    optional

1. In a small bowl, combine the first 5 ingredients. In a large bowl, toss apples with lemon juice. Add sugar mixture; toss to coat.

2. Unroll 1 pastry sheet into a 9-in. pie plate; trim even with the rim. Add filling. Dot with butter; drizzle with 2 Tbsp. maple syrup. Unroll the remaining pastry; place over filling. Trim, seal and flute edge. Cut slits in top. Brush pastry with 1 Tbsp. maple syrup.

3. Bake at 425° for 40-45 minutes or until crust is golden brown and filling is bubbly. Cover the pie loosely with foil during the last 20 minutes if needed to prevent overbrowning. Remove foil. Cool on a wire rack. If desired, serve with warm maple syrup.

1 PIECE: 438 cal., 17g fat (8g sat. fat), 18mg chol., 295mg sod., 70g carb. (42g sugars, 2g fiber), 2g pro.

RICOTTA PIE (PIZZA DOLCE) WITH CHOCOLATE & RASPBERRY

When my grandmother was a young girl, ricotta pie always made an appearance on Easter. It still does, but now we have it at Christmas, Thanksgiving and even birthday parties, too. Each generation has perfected a new little twist on the recipe. My mother upped the chocolate factor, and I added the thin layer of raspberry.

—Stephen DeBenedictis, Wakefield, MA

PREP: 1 HOUR • **BAKE:** 30 MIN. + COOLING • **MAKES:** 6 SERVINGS

3 cups all-purpose flour
1 cup plus 2 Tbsp. butter
3 egg yolks
3 Tbsp. cold water

RASPBERRY LAYER
1½ cups fresh or frozen
  raspberries, thawed
¼ cup sugar
2 Tbsp. cornstarch
1 cup semisweet
  chocolate chips

FILLING
1½ cups ricotta cheese
2 Tbsp. all-purpose flour
1½ tsp. vanilla extract
2 eggs
½ cup sugar

FINISHING
1 egg white
2 Tbsp. coarse sugar

1. Place the flour in a large bowl; cut in the butter until crumbly. In a small bowl, whisk egg yolks and water; gradually add to the flour mixture, tossing with a fork until dough forms a ball. Divide dough in half so that 1 portion is slightly larger than the other. Wrap smaller portion in plastic wrap and refrigerate.

2. Divide remaining dough into 6 portions. Roll out each portion to fit a 5-in. pie plate; transfer pastry to pie plates. Set aside.

3. Press the raspberries through a sieve; discard the seeds. In a small saucepan, combine sugar and cornstarch. Stir in the raspberry puree. Bring to a boil; cook and stir for 2 minutes or until thickened. Remove from heat. Spread over the bottom of each crust. Sprinkle with chocolate chips.

4. In a large bowl, beat the ricotta cheese, flour and vanilla until blended. In a small bowl, beat eggs on high speed for 3 minutes. Gradually add the sugar, beating until the mixture becomes thick and lemon-colored. Fold into the ricotta mixture. Spread into the pastry shells.

5. Roll out remaining pastry; make lattice crusts. Trim, seal and flute edges. Whisk egg white; brush over lattice tops. Sprinkle with coarse sugar.

6. Transfer pies to a baking sheet. Bake at 350° for 30-35 minutes or until the crust is golden and the filling is set. Cool on a wire rack. Refrigerate until serving.

1 MINI PIE: 964 cal., 54g fat (32g sat. fat), 271mg chol., 391mg sod., 107g carb. (49g sugars, 5g fiber), 20g pro.

PECAN CAKE WITH COOKIE BUTTER FROSTING

Mom and I bought a jar of cookie butter to try it out, and we fell in love with it. I knew the flavor would go well with maple syrup and pecans, so I came up with this easy cake. If you like, dress it up with more pecan halves arranged on top.
—*Natalie Larsen, Grand Prairie, TX*

PREP: 20 MIN. • BAKE: 25 MIN. + COOLING • MAKES: 20 SERVINGS

½ cup pecan halves
½ cup sugar
½ cup packed brown sugar
1 cup butter, softened
4 large eggs, room temperature
¼ cup maple syrup
2 Tbsp. 2% milk
1⅔ cups all-purpose flour
3 tsp. baking powder
½ tsp. salt

FROSTING
½ cup butter, softened
2 cups confectioners' sugar
1 cup Biscoff creamy cookie spread
¼ cup 2% milk

1. Preheat oven to 350°. Grease a 13x9-in. baking pan.

2. Place pecans and sugars in a food processor; process until ground. In a large bowl, cream butter and pecan mixture until blended. Add eggs, 1 at a time, beating well after each addition. Beat in maple syrup and milk. In another bowl, whisk flour, baking powder and salt; gradually add to creamed mixture, beating well.

3. Transfer to prepared pan. Bake until a toothpick inserted in the center comes out clean, 25-30 minutes. Cool completely in pan on a wire rack.

4. In a large bowl, combine all frosting ingredients; beat until smooth. Spread over cake. Refrigerate leftovers.

1 PIECE: 363 cal., 21g fat (10g sat. fat), 74mg chol., 259mg sod., 41g carb. (29g sugars, 1g fiber), 3g pro.

FROM GRANDMA'S KITCHEN: This recipe calls for reduced-fat milk in both the cake and frosting. If you don't have reduced-fat milk on hand, simply substitute fat-free or whole milk.

GRANDMA PRUIT'S VINEGAR PIE

Made in a cast-iron skillet, this recipe has been in our family for generations.
No get-together of ours would be complete without this rustic pie.
—*Suzette Pruit, Houston, TX*

PREP: 40 MIN. • **BAKE:** 1 HOUR + COOLING • **MAKES:** 8 SERVINGS

2 cups sugar
3 Tbsp. all-purpose flour
¼ to ½ tsp. ground nutmeg
Pastry for double-crust pie
½ cup butter, cubed
⅔ cup white vinegar
1 qt. hot water

1. Preheat oven to 450°. Whisk together sugar, flour and nutmeg; set aside. On a lightly floured surface, roll one-third of pie dough to a ⅛-in.-thick circle; cut into 2x1-in. strips. Layer a deep 12-in. enamel-coated cast-iron skillet or ovenproof casserole with half the strips; sprinkle with half the sugar mixture. Dot with half the butter. Repeat sugar and butter layers.

2. Roll remaining two-thirds of pie dough to a ⅛-in.-thick circle. Place over filling, pressing against sides of skillet or casserole. Cut a slit in top. Add the vinegar to hot water; slowly pour vinegar mixture through slit. Liquid may bubble up through the crust; this is normal. To catch spills, line an oven rack with foil.

3. Bake until crust is golden brown, about 1 hour. Cover the edge loosely with foil during the last 15-20 minutes if needed to prevent overbrowning. Remove foil. Cool on a wire rack.

1 PIECE: 545 cal., 25g fat (13g sat. fat), 41mg chol., 316mg sod., 78g carb. (50g sugars, 0 fiber), 2g pro.

PASTRY FOR DOUBLE-CRUST PIE (9 IN.): Combine 2½ cups all-purpose flour and ½ tsp. salt; cut in 1 cup cold butter until crumbly. Gradually add ⅓-⅔ cup ice water, tossing with a fork until dough holds together when pressed. Divide dough in thirds. Shape each into a disk; wrap in plastic. Refrigerate at least 1 hour.

"I love this recipe! It brings back memories of my childhood days and my mother cooking over an old cook stove in our tiny kitchen."
—SUE598, TASTEOFHOME.COM

MAMAW EMILY'S STRAWBERRY CAKE

My husband loved his mamaw's strawberry cake and thought no one could duplicate it. After I tried making it, I was thrilled when he said it was just as scrumptious as he remembered.
—*Jennifer Bruce, Manitou, KY*

PREP: 15 MIN. • **BAKE:** 25 MIN. + COOLING • **MAKES:** 12 SERVINGS

- 1 pkg. white cake mix (regular size)
- 1 pkg. (3 oz.) strawberry gelatin
- 3 Tbsp. sugar
- 3 Tbsp. all-purpose flour
- 1 cup water
- ½ cup canola oil
- 2 large eggs, room temperature
- 1 cup finely chopped strawberries

FROSTING
- ½ cup butter, softened
- ½ cup crushed strawberries
- 4½ to 5 cups confectioners' sugar

1. Preheat oven to 350°. Line the bottoms of 2 greased 8-in. round baking pans with parchment; grease parchment.

2. In a large bowl, combine the cake mix, gelatin, sugar and flour. Add the water, oil and eggs; beat on low speed 30 seconds. Beat on medium 2 minutes. Fold in chopped strawberries. Transfer to prepared pans.

3. Bake until a toothpick inserted in the center comes out clean, 25-30 minutes. Cool in pans 10 minutes before removing to wire racks; remove paper. Cool completely.

4. For the frosting, in a small bowl, beat butter until creamy. Beat in crushed strawberries. Gradually beat in enough confectioners' sugar to reach the desired consistency. Spread frosting between layers and over top and sides of cake.

1 PIECE: 532 cal., 21g fat (7g sat. fat), 51mg chol., 340mg sod., 85g carb. (69g sugars, 1g fiber), 4g pro.

FROM GRANDMA'S KITCHEN: You'll be smitten with the nostalgic charm of this rich pink buttercream frosting, but when you want a change of pace, try icing the cake with whipped cream or whipped topping and serve it with fresh berries.

GERMAN BLACK FOREST CAKE

This Old World dessert recipe goes back to my German great-grandma.
My mother gave me a copy when I got married, and I hope to pass it down to my own children.
—*Stephanie Travis, Fallon, NV*

PREP: 45 MIN. + COOLING • BAKE: 30 MIN. + COOLING • MAKES: 12 SERVINGS

1 cup whole milk
3 large eggs, room
  temperature
½ cup canola oil
3 tsp. vanilla extract
2 cups plus 2 Tbsp.
  all-purpose flour
2 cups sugar
¾ cup baking cocoa
1½ tsp. baking powder
¾ tsp. baking soda
¾ tsp. salt

FILLING
2 cans (14½ oz. each)
  pitted tart cherries
1 cup sugar
¼ cup cornstarch
3 Tbsp. cherry brandy
  or 2 tsp. vanilla extract

WHIPPED CREAM
3 cups heavy
  whipping cream
⅓ cup confectioners' sugar

1. Preheat oven to 350°. Line bottoms of 2 greased 9-in. round baking pans; grease paper.

2. In a large bowl, beat the milk, eggs, oil and vanilla until well blended. In another bowl, whisk the flour, sugar, cocoa, baking powder, baking soda and salt; gradually beat into milk mixture.

3. Transfer to the prepared pans. Bake 30-35 minutes or until a toothpick inserted in the center comes out clean. Cool in pans 10 minutes before removing to wire racks; remove paper. Cool cake layers completely.

4. Meanwhile, for the filling, drain cherries, reserving ½ cup juice. In a small saucepan, whisk sugar, cornstarch and reserved juice; add cherries. Cook and stir over low heat 10-12 minutes or until thickened and bubbly. Remove from heat; stir in cherry brandy. Cool completely.

5. In a large bowl, beat whipping cream until it begins to thicken. Add confectioners' sugar; beat until stiff peaks form.

6. Using a long serrated knife, cut each cake horizontally in half. Place 1 cake layer on a serving plate. Top with 1½ cups whipped cream. Spread ¾ cup filling to within 1 in. of the edge. Repeat twice. Top with remaining cake layer. Frost top and sides of cake with remaining whipped cream, reserving some to pipe decorations, if desired. Spoon remaining filling onto top of cake. Refrigerate until serving.

1 PIECE: 659 cal., 34g fat (15g sat. fat), 136mg chol., 329mg sod., 84g carb. (59g sugars, 2g fiber), 7g pro.

MOCHA BUTTERCREAM YULE LOG

This coffee-infused yule log is a tradition at our Christmas gatherings.
The filling recipe came from an aunt, and the buttercream frosting was my creation.
—*Rosie Flanagan, Buchanan, MI*

PREP: 30 MIN. • BAKE: 15 MIN. + COOLING • MAKES: 12 SERVINGS

5 large eggs, separated,
  room temperature
⅔ cup sugar
2 Tbsp. all-purpose flour
3 Tbsp. baking cocoa

FILLING
2 Tbsp. plus 1½ tsp.
  all-purpose flour
½ cup whole milk
½ cup sugar
½ cup butter, softened
½ tsp. vanilla extract
½ cup chopped walnuts,
  optional

MOCHA BUTTERCREAM
   FROSTING
1 cup butter, softened
½ cup confectioners' sugar
1 Tbsp. baking cocoa
1 tsp. strong brewed coffee
  Confectioners' sugar,
  optional
  Chopped walnuts,
  optional

1. Preheat oven to 350°. In a large bowl, beat the egg yolks at high speed until light and fluffy, 4-6 minutes. Gradually add the sugar, beating until the mixture is thick and light-colored. Add the flour and cocoa, beating on low speed. In another bowl, beat the egg whites until soft peaks form; fold into batter. Mix until no streaks of white remain.

2. Grease a 15x10x1-in. baking pan; line with waxed paper, and grease and flour the paper. Spread the batter evenly in pan. Bake until cake springs back when touched lightly, 12-15 minutes. Cool 5 minutes. Invert onto a tea towel dusted with cocoa. Gently peel off paper. Roll up cake in the towel jelly-roll style, starting with a short side. Cool completely on a wire rack.

3. For filling, combine the flour and milk in a saucepan. Cook over low heat; stirring until thick. Cool. In a bowl, cream sugar, butter and vanilla. Add the flour mixture; beat until fluffy. Fold in walnuts if desired. Unroll cake; spread the filling over cake to within ½ in. of the edges. Roll up again, without towel; trim the ends. Place on a platter, seam side down.

4. For frosting, in a small bowl, beat the butter until fluffy. Beat in the sugar, cocoa and coffee. Spread over the cake. Sprinkle with confectioners' sugar and walnuts if desired.

1 PIECE: 351 cal., 26g fat (15g sat. fat), 140mg chol., 217mg sod., 29g carb. (25g sugars, 0 fiber), 4g pro.

MOM-MOM'S WHITE POTATO PIE

My Mom-Mom Beatrice taught me how to make a white potato pie when I was 12 years old. I always remembered, and now I bake it for holiday parties. The staff where I work has fallen in love with it—so much so that I actually get orders for pies at Christmastime!
—*Loretta Hooks, Dover, DE*

PREP: 35 MIN. • **BAKE:** 50 MIN. + COOLING • **MAKES:** 2 PIES (8 SERVINGS EACH)

¾ **cup plus 1 Tbsp. sugar, divided**

3½ **tsp. ground cinnamon, divided**

2 **frozen deep-dish pie crusts (9 in.)**

3 **lbs. potatoes, peeled and cubed**

½ **cup butter, softened**

3 **large eggs, room temperature**

½ **cup sweetened condensed milk**

⅛ **tsp. vanilla extract**

¾ **cup evaporated milk**

1½ **tsp. ground nutmeg**
  Confectioners' sugar, optional

1. Preheat oven to 350°. In a small bowl, combine 1 Tbsp. sugar and ½ tsp. cinnamon. Sprinkle half the mixture in the bottoms of both pie crusts; bake until lightly browned, 7-10 minutes.

2. Meanwhile, place the potatoes in a large saucepan; add water to cover. Bring to a boil. Reduce the heat; cook, uncovered, until tender, about 10-15 minutes, stirring occasionally. Drain.

3. In a large bowl, mash the potatoes with butter; beat until fluffy. Add eggs, sweetened condensed milk and vanilla; mix well. Stirring continuously, slowly add the evaporated milk; mix until smooth. Add remaining sugar, cinnamon and nutmeg; mix well. Pour the potato mixture into prepared crusts; do not over-fill. Sprinkle with remaining cinnamon sugar mixture.

4. Bake until pie is set or until a knife inserted in the center comes out clean, about 45 minutes. Cool on a wire rack 1 hour before serving. If desired, sprinkle with confectioner's sugar.

NOTE: Using a food mill or potato ricer to mash the potatoes will produce a very smooth filling.

1 PIECE: 308 cal., 13g fat (6g sat. fat), 57mg chol., 168mg sod., 43g carb. (17g sugars, 2g fiber), 6g pro.

GINGERBREAD CAKE
Dolloped with whipped topping and sprinkled with sugar,
this dark, moist cake is such a treat. A dear aunt shared the recipe.
—*Ila Mae Alderman, Galax, VA*

PREP: 10 MIN. • BAKE: 30 MIN. • MAKES: 9 SERVINGS

⅓ cup shortening
½ cup sugar
1 large egg, room
   temperature
¾ cup water
½ cup molasses

1½ cups all-purpose flour
1 tsp. ground ginger
½ tsp. baking soda
¼ tsp. salt
   Whipped topping and
   confectioners' sugar

1. Preheat oven to 350°. In a large bowl, cream the shortening
and sugar until light and fluffy, 5-7 minutes. Beat in the egg.
Combine the water and molasses. Combine the flour, ginger,
baking soda and salt; add to creamed mixture alternately with
molasses mixture, beating well after each addition. Pour into
a greased 8-in. square baking pan.

2. Bake until a toothpick inserted in the center comes out clean,
28-32 minutes. Dust with confectioners' sugar and serve warm
with whipped topping.

1 PIECE: 241 cal., 8g fat (2g sat. fat), 24mg chol., 150mg sod.,
40g carb. (22g sugars, 1g fiber), 3g pro.

FROM GRANDMA'S KITCHEN: Save time by making this cake
up to 2 days early. Simply wait until you're ready to serve
before adding the whipped topping and confectioners' sugar.

CAKES & PIES

GOLDEN HARVEST APPLE PIE

When the occasion calls for a time-honored pie just like Grandma used to make, look no further.
This recipe features a from-scratch crust and lends a hint of orange to a classic filling.
—*Drew Menne, Vineyard Haven, MA*

PREP: 30 MIN. • BAKE: 55 MIN. + COOLING • MAKES: 8 SERVINGS

2 cups all-purpose flour
1 tsp. salt
¾ cup shortening
5 Tbsp. cold water

FILLING
2 Tbsp. all-purpose flour
½ cup sugar
1 tsp. ground cinnamon
1 tsp. ground nutmeg
6 cups thinly sliced
   peeled tart apples
3 Tbsp. orange marmalade
2 Tbsp. butter
1 Tbsp. milk

1. In a large bowl, combine the flour and salt; cut in the shortening until crumbly. Gradually add water, tossing with a fork until dough forms a ball. Divide dough in half so 1 portion is slightly larger than the other. Roll out larger portion to fit a 9-in. pie plate. Transfer pastry to pie plate. Trim pastry even with edge.

2. Sprinkle flour over the pastry. Combine the sugar, cinnamon and nutmeg; layer into pastry alternately with apples. Dot with marmalade and butter.

3. Roll out the remaining pastry to fit top of pie. Place over filling. Trim, seal and flute edges. Cut slits in pastry. Brush with milk.

4. Bake at 425° for 15 minutes. Reduce the heat to 375°; bake 40-50 minutes longer or until crust is golden brown and filling is bubbly. Cool completely on a wire rack.

1 PIECE: 413 cal., 21g fat (6g sat. fat), 8mg chol., 320mg sod., 52g carb. (25g sugars, 2g fiber), 4g pro.

CHOCOLATE ESPRESSO LAVA CAKE

Perked up with espresso powder, this slow-cooker dessert will satisfy even the strongest
chocolate craving. Warm servings are gooey and saucy but not super sweet—just perfect!
—*Lisa Renshaw, Kansas City, MO*

PREP: 15 MIN. • COOK: 3 HOURS + STANDING • MAKES: 16 SERVINGS

1 pkg. chocolate fudge
   cake mix (regular size)
1 Tbsp. instant
   espresso powder
3 cups 2% milk
1 pkg. (3.9 oz.) instant
   chocolate pudding mix
1 cup semisweet
   chocolate chips
1 cup white baking chips

1. Prepare the cake mix batter according to package directions, adding espresso powder before mixing. Transfer to a greased 4-qt. slow cooker.

2. In a small bowl, whisk the milk and pudding mix 2 minutes. Let stand until soft-set, about 2 minutes. Pour over batter. Cook, covered, on low 3-3½ hours or until a toothpick inserted in the cake portion comes out with moist crumbs.

3. Sprinkle the top with chocolate chips and baking chips. Turn off slow cooker; remove insert. Let stand, uncovered, until chips are softened, 15-30 minutes. Serve warm.

⅔ CUP: 327 cal., 15g fat (6g sat. fat), 41mg chol., 317mg sod., 45g carb. (29g sugars, 2g fiber), 5g pro.

GOLDEN HARVEST
APPLE PIE

GRANDMA'S STRAWBERRY SHORTCAKE

Piles of juicy strawberries and huge layers of fresh whipped cream made Grandma's shortcake an extra-special treat. Dad added even more indulgence by buttering the biscuits!
—*Shirley Joan Helfenbein, Lapeer, MI*

PREP: 30 MIN. • **BAKE:** 20 MIN. + COOLING • **MAKES:** 8 SERVINGS

- 2 **cups all-purpose flour**
- 2 **Tbsp. sugar**
- 3 **tsp. baking powder**
- ½ **tsp. salt**
- ½ **cup cold butter, cubed**
- 1 **large egg, room temperature, beaten**
- ⅔ **cup half-and-half cream**
- 1 **cup heavy whipping cream**
- 2 **Tbsp. confectioners' sugar**
- ⅛ **tsp. vanilla extract**
  Additional butter
- 1½ **cups fresh strawberries, sliced**

1. Preheat oven to 450°. Combine the flour, sugar, baking powder and salt. Cut in butter until the mixture resembles coarse crumbs. In another bowl, whisk the egg and half-and-half. Add all at once to crumb mixture; stir just until moistened.

2. Spread batter into a greased 8-in. round baking pan, slightly building up the edges. Bake until golden brown, 16-18 minutes. Remove from pan; cool on a wire rack.

3. Beat heavy cream until it begins to thicken. Add confectioners' sugar and vanilla; beat until stiff peaks form. Split the cake in half crosswise; butter bottom layer. Spoon half the strawberries over bottom layer. Spread with some whipped cream. Cover with top cake layer. Top with the remaining berries and whipped cream. Cut into wedges.

1 PIECE: 381 cal., 25g fat (16g sat. fat), 98mg chol., 447mg sod., 32g carb. (8g sugars, 1g fiber), 6g pro.

CHOCOLATE-AMARETTO MOUSSE PIE

You really need only a sliver of this rich, silky pie to feel satisfied. My father's favorite dessert, it boasts a fluffy chocolate-almond filling and a thin chocolate shell.
—*Jamie Burkhart, Windsor, MO*

PREP: 15 MIN. + FREEZING • **COOK:** 20 MIN. + CHILLING • **MAKES:** 8 SERVINGS

1 tsp. plus ½ cup butter, divided
2 cups semisweet chocolate chips, divided
1 can (14 oz.) sweetened condensed milk
¼ tsp. salt
¼ cup water
½ cup amaretto
2 cups heavy whipping cream, whipped
¼ cup slivered almonds, toasted

1. Line a 9-in. pie plate with foil and grease the foil with 1 tsp. butter; set aside.

2. In a small saucepan over low heat, melt 1 cup chocolate chips with ¼ cup butter; quickly spread in an even layer over bottom and sides of prepared pan. Freeze for 30 minutes.

3. In a small saucepan over low heat, heat the condensed milk, salt and remaining butter and chips until melted; stir until well blended. Gradually stir in the water; cook over medium heat for 5 minutes. Add amaretto; cook for 5 minutes or until thickened, stirring constantly. Cool to room temperature.

4. Fold half of the whipped cream into chocolate mixture. Using the foil, lift the chocolate shell out of the pan; gently peel off foil. Return shell to the pie plate; spoon filling into shell. Garnish with the remaining whipped cream; sprinkle with almonds. Chill for 3 hours or until set.

1 PIECE: 742 cal., 52g fat (31g sat. fat), 128mg chol., 246mg sod., 62g carb. (56g sugars, 3g fiber), 8g pro.

"I love this pie, which I topped off with a few raspberries. It was so delicious, my husband couldn't wait to have it again. It's also easy and pretty to serve."
—BONITO15, TASTEOFHOME.COM

HARVEY
WALLBANGER
CAKE

HARVEY WALLBANGER CAKE

My Aunt Martha, who lived to the ripe old age of 94, could find a way to incorporate vodka or rum into almost any cake. This recipe was taped to her kitchen cabinet!
—*Lynda Szczepanik, Highland Park, IL*

PREP: 20 MIN. • **BAKE:** 45 MIN. + COOLING • **MAKES:** 12 SERVINGS

1 pkg. orange cake mix (regular size)
1 pkg. (3.4 oz.) instant vanilla pudding mix
4 large eggs, room temperature
½ cup canola oil
¾ cup orange juice
¼ cup vodka
¼ cup Galliano liqueur

GLAZE
2½ cups confectioners' sugar
4 Tbsp. orange juice
2 Tbsp. butter, melted
¼ tsp. vanilla extract
Optional: Assorted white sprinkles and citrus fruit segments

1. Preheat oven to 350°. Grease and flour a 10-in. tube pan.

2. In a large bowl, combine the first 7 ingredients; beat on low speed 30 seconds. Beat on medium 2 minutes. Transfer batter to prepared pan.

3. Bake until the top of cake springs back when lightly touched, 45-50 minutes. Cool in pan 10 minutes before removing to a wire rack to cool completely.

4. In a small bowl, mix the glaze ingredients until smooth. Pour over the cake. If desired, top with white sprinkles and serve with segmented citrus fruit.

1 PIECE: 447 cal., 16g fat (3g sat. fat), 67mg chol., 370mg sod., 71g carb. (53g sugars, 0 fiber), 4g pro.

RHUBARB CHERRY PIE

PICTURED ON PAGE 234

As a young girl, I dreamed of making desserts just like my mother. I inherited her well-used rolling pin—one that's 2 feet long and 8 inches wide! I use it to prepare her rhubarb pie, which I put my own spin on by replacing the strawberries with tart cherries.
—*Eunice Hurt, Murfreesboro, TN*

PREP: 10 MIN. + STANDING • **BAKE:** 40 MIN. • **MAKES:** 8 SERVINGS

3 cups sliced fresh or frozen rhubarb (½-in. pieces)
1 can (16 oz.) pitted tart red cherries, drained
1¼ cups sugar
¼ cup quick-cooking tapioca
4 to 5 drops red food coloring, optional
Pastry for double-crust pie (9 in.)

1. In a large bowl, combine the first 5 ingredients; let stand for 15 minutes. Line a 9-in. pie plate with crust. Trim to ½ in. beyond the rim of plate. Add filling. Top with a lattice or other decorative crust. Trim and seal strips to edge of bottom crust; flute edge.

2. Bake at 400° until the crust is golden and the filling is bubbling, 40-50 minutes.

1 PIECE: 433 cal., 14g fat (6g sat. fat), 10mg chol., 206mg sod., 75g carb. (44g sugars, 1g fiber), 3g pro.

RED VELVET MARBLE CAKE

I watched my grandma prepare her red velvet showstopper for gatherings many times. The fluffy butter frosting perfectly complements the decadent marble cake.
—*Jodi Anderson, Overbrook, KS*

PREP: 20 MIN. • **BAKE:** 30 MIN. + COOLING • **MAKES:** 16 SERVINGS

¾ **cup butter, softened**
2¼ **cups sugar**
3 **large eggs, room temperature**
4½ **tsp. white vinegar**
1½ **tsp. vanilla extract**
3¾ **cups cake flour**
1½ **tsp. baking soda**
1½ **cups buttermilk**
3 **Tbsp. baking cocoa**
4½ **tsp. red food coloring**

FROSTING

1 **cup butter, softened**
9 **cups confectioners' sugar**
3 **tsp. vanilla extract**
⅔ **to ¾ cup 2% milk**

1. Preheat oven to 350°. Line bottoms of 2 greased 9-in. round baking pans with parchment; grease paper.

2. In a large bowl, cream the butter and sugar until light and fluffy, 5-7 minutes. Add eggs, 1 at a time, beating well after each addition. Beat in the vinegar and vanilla. In another bowl, whisk flour and baking soda; add to creamed mixture alternately with buttermilk, beating well after each addition.

3. Transfer half the batter to another bowl; stir in the cocoa and food coloring until blended. Alternately drop plain and chocolate batters by ¼ cupfuls into prepared pans, dividing batter evenly between pans. To make batter level in pans, bang pans several times on counter.

4. Bake 30-35 minutes or until a toothpick inserted in the center comes out clean. Cool 10 minutes before removing from pans to wire racks to cool completely.

5. In a large bowl, beat butter, confectioners' sugar, vanilla and enough milk to reach a spreading consistency. Spread frosting between layers and over top and sides of cake.

1 PIECE: 701 cal., 22g fat (13g sat. fat), 90mg chol., 342mg sod., 123g carb. (96g sugars, 1g fiber), 5g pro.

NANA'S CHOCOLATE CUPCAKES
WITH MINT FROSTING

These mint-chocolate cupcakes are special to our family because my Nana used to bake them for Christmas every year. Now I carry on the tradition. For a more indulgent version, double the frosting and pile it high before adding the candies.
—*Chekota Hunter, Cassville, MO*

PREP: 25 MIN. • **BAKE:** 15 MIN. + COOLING • **MAKES:** 1 DOZEN

½ cup baking cocoa
1 cup boiling water
¼ cup butter, softened
1 cup sugar
2 large eggs, room temperature
1⅓ cups all-purpose flour
2 tsp. baking powder
¼ tsp. salt
¼ cup unsweetened applesauce

FROSTING

1 cup confectioners' sugar
3 Tbsp. butter, softened
4 tsp. heavy whipping cream
Dash peppermint extract
1 drop green food coloring, optional
2 Tbsp. miniature semisweet chocolate chips
Mint Andes candies, optional

1. Preheat oven to 375°. Line 12 muffin cups with paper or foil liners. Mix cocoa and boiling water until smooth; cool completely.

2. Beat butter and sugar until blended. Beat in eggs, 1 at a time. In another bowl, whisk together the flour, baking powder and salt; add to butter mixture alternately with applesauce, beating well after each addition. Beat in cocoa mixture.

3. Fill prepared muffin cups three-fourths full. Bake until a toothpick inserted in center comes out clean, 15-18 minutes. Cool 10 minutes before removing to a wire rack to cool completely.

4. For frosting, beat the confectioners' sugar, butter, cream and extract until smooth. If desired, tint the frosting green with food coloring. Stir in chocolate chips. Spread over cupcakes. If desired, top with candies.

1 CUPCAKE: 253 cal., 9g fat (5g sat. fat), 51mg chol., 196mg sod., 41g carb. (28g sugars, 1g fiber), 3g pro.

STRAWBERRY BUTTERMILK SKILLET SHORTCAKE

I vividly remember my grandmother preparing this from-scratch skillet shortcake,
a family recipe that's more than 100 years old. We still make it every summer
and enjoy big pieces warm from the oven with whipped cream.

—*Claudia Lamascolo, Melbourne, FL*

PREP: 25 MIN. • **BAKE:** 50 MIN. • **MAKES:** 10 SERVINGS

10 Tbsp. shortening
¼ cup butter, softened
1 cup sugar
2 large eggs, room temperature
2½ cups all-purpose flour
3 tsp. baking powder
½ tsp. salt
⅔ cup buttermilk

STREUSEL TOPPING

⅔ cup all-purpose flour
½ cup sugar
1 tsp. ground cinnamon
¼ tsp. ground allspice
½ cup butter, softened
2 cups sliced fresh strawberries
Whipped cream

1. Preheat oven to 350°. In a large bowl, cream shortening, butter and sugar until light and fluffy, 5-7 minutes. Add eggs, 1 at a time, beating well after each addition. In another bowl, whisk the flour, baking powder and salt; add to the creamed mixture alternately with the buttermilk, beating well after each addition. Transfer to a 10-12-in. cast-iron or other ovenproof skillet.

2. For the streusel topping, in a small bowl, mix the flour, sugar, cinnamon and allspice; cut in the butter until crumbly. Sprinkle over batter. Top with strawberries. Bake until the center is puffed and the edges are golden brown, 50-60 minutes. Serve warm with whipped cream.

1 PIECE: 526 cal., 27g fat (12g sat. fat), 74mg chol., 418mg sod., 64g carb. (33g sugars, 2g fiber), 6g pro.

MARSHMALLOW PUMPKIN PIE

Mom was a fantastic cook and always willing to reveal the secrets to her specialties.
This was one of her all-time favorite pies. It calls for a graham cracker crust,
but feel free to use a baked pastry crust or gingersnap crust instead.

—*Ruth Ferris, Billings, MT*

PREP: 20 MIN. + CHILLING • **MAKES:** 8 SERVINGS

1 pkg. (10 oz.) large marshmallows
1 cup canned pumpkin
1 tsp. ground cinnamon
½ tsp. salt
½ tsp. ground ginger
½ tsp. ground nutmeg
2 cups whipped topping
1 graham cracker crust (9 in.)
Additional whipped topping, optional

1. In a large saucepan, combine the first 6 ingredients; cook and stir over medium heat 8-10 minutes or until marshmallows are melted. Remove from heat; cool to room temperature.

2. Fold in whipped topping. Spoon into crust. Refrigerate 3 hours or until set. If desired, serve with additional whipped topping.

1 PIECE: 280 cal., 9g fat (4g sat. fat), 0 chol., 287mg sod., 49g carb. (33g sugars, 2g fiber), 2g pro.

STRAWBERRY BUTTERMILK
SKILLET SHORTCAKE

**GRANDMA'S
SECRET**
Skip the streusel and save
a bit a time. Simply sprinkle
cinnamon and sugar on top
for a glistening treat.

CHOCOLATE POUND CAKE

Wonderful with ice cream, this sugar-dusted cake is also delicate enough to serve in small pieces for an afternoon tea.
—*Ann Perry, Sierra Vista, AZ*

PREP: 20 MIN. • **BAKE:** 1½ HOURS + COOLING • **MAKES:** 12 SERVINGS

- 8 **milk chocolate bars (1.55 oz. each)**
- 2 **Tbsp. water**
- ½ **cup butter, softened**
- 2 **cups sugar**
- 4 **large eggs, room temperature**
- 2 **tsp. vanilla extract**
- 2½ **cups cake flour, sifted**
- ½ **tsp. salt**
- ¼ **tsp. baking soda**
- 1 **cup buttermilk**
- ½ **cup chopped pecans, optional**
- **Confectioners' sugar, optional**

1. Preheat oven to 325°. In a saucepan, melt chocolate with water over low heat. Mixture will begin to harden.

2. In a large bowl, cream butter and sugar until light and fluffy, 5-7 minutes. Add the eggs, 1 at a time, beating well after each addition. Beat in the vanilla and chocolate mixture. Combine the flour, salt and baking soda; add to creamed mixture alternately with buttermilk. Fold in nuts if desired.

3. Pour into a greased and floured 10-in. tube pan or fluted tube pan. Bake for 1½ hours or until a toothpick inserted in the center comes out clean. Let stand for 10 minutes before removing from the pan to a wire rack to cool. Sprinkle with confectioners' sugar if desired.

1 PIECE: 353 cal., 11g fat (6g sat. fat), 93mg chol., 248mg sod., 59g carb. (36g sugars, 1g fiber), 5g pro.

"Everyone loved this cake—even all the kids. Pair it with some vanilla ice cream or whipped cream."
—KSUPEY, TASTEOFHOME.COM

GRANDMA PIETZ'S CRANBERRY CAKE PUDDING

Warm cranberry cake draped in a sweet vanilla sauce is such a treat for Christmas or anytime.
Simple and unusual, the recipe has been an heirloom in our family for generations.
—*Lisa Potter, Camp Douglas, WI*

PREP: 30 MIN. • BAKE: 20 MIN. • MAKES: 15 SERVINGS (2 CUPS SAUCE)

- 3 Tbsp. butter, softened
- 1 cup sugar
- 1 large egg, room temperature
- 2 cups all-purpose flour
- 2 tsp. baking powder
  Dash salt
- 1 cup 2% milk
- 2 cups fresh or frozen cranberries, thawed

SAUCE
- 2 cups packed brown sugar
- 1 cup water
- ½ cup sugar
- 3 Tbsp. butter
- ¼ tsp. vanilla extract

1. Preheat oven to 350°. Grease a 13x9-in. baking pan.

2. In a large bowl, beat the butter and sugar until crumbly. Beat in the egg. In another bowl, whisk the flour, baking powder and salt; add to the butter mixture alternately with the milk, beating well after each addition. If desired, coarsely chop cranberries. Fold cranberries into batter.

3. Transfer to the prepared pan. Bake until a toothpick inserted in center comes out clean, 20-25 minutes.

4. In a large saucepan, combine the brown sugar, water, sugar and butter; bring to a boil over medium heat, stirring constantly to dissolve the sugar. Cook and stir until slightly thickened; stir in vanilla. Serve warm with cake.

1 PIECE WITH 2 TBSP. SAUCE: 311 cal., 5g fat (3g sat. fat), 26mg chol., 125mg sod., 64g carb. (50g sugars, 1g fiber), 3g pro.

MOM'S LEMON CUSTARD PIE

Growing up, we were always thrilled when Mom brought this custard pie to the table for dessert
after dinner. The beaten egg whites lend a delicate texture to the scrumptious lemon filling.
—*Jeannie Fritson, Kearney, NE*

PREP: 20 MIN. • BAKE: 1 HOUR + COOLING • MAKES: 8 SERVINGS

- Dough for single-crust pie
- 1 cup sugar
- 1 Tbsp. butter, softened
- 2 large eggs, room temperature, separated
- 1 cup whole milk
- 3 Tbsp. all-purpose flour
- ⅛ tsp. salt
- ¼ cup lemon juice
- 2 tsp. grated lemon zest
  Optional: Whipped cream, lemon slices and fresh mint

1. Preheat oven to 325°. On a lightly floured surface, roll dough to a ⅛-in.-thick circle; transfer to a 9-in. pie plate. Trim crust to ½ in. beyond rim of plate; flute edge. Refrigerate while preparing filling.

2. In a large bowl, beat the sugar and butter until well blended. Add the egg yolks, 1 at a time, beating well after each addition. Add the milk, flour and salt; mix well. Stir in lemon juice and zest; set aside. In a small bowl, beat egg whites until stiff peaks form; gently fold into lemon mixture.

3. Pour into crust. Bake until lightly browned and a knife inserted in the center comes out clean, about 1 hour. Cool on a wire rack. If desired, garnish with whipped cream, lemon and mint. Store in the refrigerator.

1 PIECE: 315 cal., 14g fat (9g sat. fat), 37mg chol., 217mg sod., 45g carb. (27g sugars, 1g fiber), 4g pro.

BANANA
POUND CAKE

BANANA POUND CAKE

A basic pound cake recipe from my great-aunt became a new treat when I added bananas.
It pops out of the pan perfectly and has a drizzle of vanilla glaze.
—Nancy Zimmerman, Cape May Court House, NJ

PREP: 20 MIN. • BAKE: 1¼ HOURS + COOLING • MAKES: 12 SERVINGS

3 tsp. plus 3 cups sugar,
divided
1 cup butter, softened
6 large eggs, room
temperature
1 cup mashed ripe bananas
(about 2 medium)
1½ tsp. vanilla extract
½ tsp. lemon extract
3 cups all-purpose flour
¼ tsp. baking soda
1 cup sour cream

GLAZE
1½ cups confectioners' sugar
½ tsp. vanilla extract
3 to 4 tsp. 2% milk

1. Grease a 10-in. fluted tube pan. Sprinkle with 3 tsp. sugar; set aside.

2. In a large bowl, cream butter and the remaining 3 cups sugar until light and fluffy, 5-7 minutes. Add eggs, 1 at a time, beating well after each addition. Stir in bananas and extracts. Combine flour and baking soda; add to the creamed mixture alternately with sour cream, beating just until combined.

3. Pour into the prepared pan (pan will be full). Bake at 325° until a toothpick inserted near center comes out clean, 75-85 minutes. Cool for 10 minutes before removing from pan to a wire rack to cool completely.

4. In a small bowl, whisk the glaze ingredients until smooth; drizzle over cake. Store in the refrigerator. May be frozen for up to 1 month.

1 PIECE: 600 cal., 22g fat (13g sat. fat), 138mg chol., 192mg sod., 96g carb. (69g sugars, 1g fiber), 7g pro.

SPICED BUTTERNUT SQUASH PIE

Mom's homegrown squash was the main ingredient in her nicely spiced pie. When she had
a bumper crop, we got excited. We knew we had a lot of yummy desserts to look forward to!
—Johnna Poulson, Celebration, FL

PREP: 20 MIN. • BAKE: 40 MIN. + COOLING • MAKES: 8 SERVINGS

1 refrigerated pie crust
3 large eggs
1½ cups mashed cooked
butternut squash
1 cup fat-free milk
⅔ cup fat-free
evaporated milk
¾ cup sugar
½ tsp. salt
1 tsp. ground cinnamon
½ tsp. ground ginger
¼ tsp. ground nutmeg
¼ tsp. ground cloves
Sweetened whipped
cream, optional

1. Preheat oven to 450°. Unroll the pie crust into a 9-in. pie plate; flute the edge. Place eggs, squash, milks, sugar, salt and spices in a food processor; process until smooth. Pour into crust. Bake on a lower oven rack 10 minutes.

2. Reduce the oven setting to 350°. Bake 30-40 minutes longer or until a knife inserted in center comes out clean. Cool on a wire rack; serve or refrigerate within 2 hours. If desired, serve with whipped cream.

1 PIECE: 266 cal., 9g fat (4g sat. fat), 76mg chol., 313mg sod., 41g carb. (24g sugars, 2g fiber), 7g pro.

VERTICAL CARROT CAKE
PICTURED ON COVER

This topsy-turvy update of a cherished classic is guaranteed to impress guests.
The browned butter cream cheese frosting takes the cake to new heights!
—*Mark Neufang, Milwaukee, WI*

PREP: 1½ HOURS + CHILLING • BAKE: 20 MIN. + COOLING • MAKES: 16 SERVINGS

CARROT CAKE
- ½ **cup plus 1 Tbsp. all-purpose flour**
- ½ **tsp. ground ginger**
- ½ **tsp. ground cinnamon**
- ¼ **tsp. ground nutmeg**
- ¼ **tsp. salt**
- ⅛ **tsp. ground cloves**
- 1 **cup pecan halves, toasted**
- ½ **lb. carrots, peeled and finely grated**
- 1 **Tbsp. minced fresh gingerroot**
- ½ **tsp. grated orange zest**
- 8 **large eggs, separated, room temperature**
- ⅔ **cup plus 2 Tbsp. sugar, divided**

BROWNED BUTTER CREAM CHEESE FROSTING
- 1½ **cups unsalted butter, cubed and divided**
- 4 **large egg whites**
- 1 **cup sugar**
  Dash salt
- 1 **tsp. vanilla extract**
- 2 **pkg. (8 oz. each) cream cheese, softened**

1. Preheat oven to 350°. Line 2 greased 15x10x1-in. baking pans with parchment; grease paper. Set aside. Sift flour, ground ginger, cinnamon, nutmeg, salt and cloves together twice. Place pecans in a food processor; pulse until finely ground. Transfer to a bowl; toss with carrots, fresh ginger and zest.

2. In a large bowl, beat the egg yolks until slightly thickened. Gradually add ⅔ cup sugar, beating on high speed until thick and lemon-colored. Fold in flour mixture, then carrot mixture.

3. Place egg whites in another large bowl. With clean beaters, beat egg whites on medium until soft peaks form. Gradually add the remaining sugar, 1 Tbsp. at a time, beating on high after each addition until sugar is dissolved. Continue beating until stiff glossy peaks form. Fold a fourth of the whites into batter, then fold in the remaining whites. Transfer to prepared pans, spreading evenly.

4. Bake until golden brown and the tops spring back when lightly touched, 18-22 minutes. Cool 5 minutes. Invert the cakes onto tea towels dusted with confectioners' sugar. Gently peel off the paper; trim the ends. Roll up cakes in towels jelly-roll style, starting with a short side. Cool completely on a wire rack.

5. For the frosting, place 1 cup butter in a small heavy saucepan; melt over medium heat. Heat until golden brown, 5-7 minutes, stirring constantly. Remove from the heat. Cool until thick and creamy, but not hard, stirring occasionally.

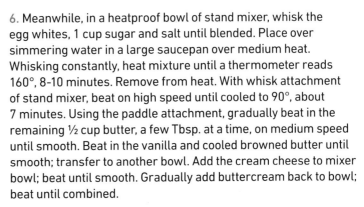

6. Meanwhile, in a heatproof bowl of stand mixer, whisk the egg whites, 1 cup sugar and salt until blended. Place over simmering water in a large saucepan over medium heat. Whisking constantly, heat mixture until a thermometer reads 160°, 8-10 minutes. Remove from heat. With whisk attachment of stand mixer, beat on high speed until cooled to 90°, about 7 minutes. Using the paddle attachment, gradually beat in the remaining ½ cup butter, a few Tbsp. at a time, on medium speed until smooth. Beat in the vanilla and cooled browned butter until smooth; transfer to another bowl. Add the cream cheese to mixer bowl; beat until smooth. Gradually add buttercream back to bowl; beat until combined.

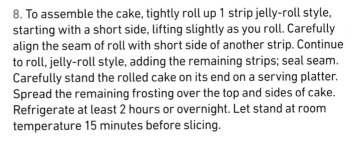

7. Unroll cakes; cut each into two 15x5-in. strips. Spread 1 cup frosting on each strip to within ½ in. of edges. Refrigerate until frosting is firm, at least 20 minutes.

8. To assemble the cake, tightly roll up 1 strip jelly-roll style, starting with a short side, lifting slightly as you roll. Carefully align the seam of roll with short side of another strip. Continue to roll, jelly-roll style, adding the remaining strips; seal seam. Carefully stand the rolled cake on its end on a serving platter. Spread the remaining frosting over the top and sides of cake. Refrigerate at least 2 hours or overnight. Let stand at room temperature 15 minutes before slicing.

1 PIECE: 445 cal., 34g fat (18g sat. fat), 167mg chol., 193mg sod., 30g carb. (25g sugars, 1g fiber), 7g pro.

FROM GRANDMA'S KITCHEN: Once the vertical cake has been assembled and frosted, it can be stored in the refrigerator, covered, for up to 3 days. When storing leftover cut slices, press a piece of parchment or waxed paper against the cut side to keep each cake slice from drying out.

DIRT DESSERT,
PAGE 293

GRANDMA'S FAVORITE

DESSERTS

At Grandma's meals, saving room for dessert can
be hard to do. But her legendary cheesecakes, trifles,
tarts, puddings and other treats are always worth it!

MOM'S FRIED APPLES

My mom made these cinnamon-sugar apples when I was growing up. When I prepare them now, it's a trip down memory lane. They're so good warm from the skillet with a scoop of vanilla ice cream.
—*Margie Tappe, Prague, OK*

PREP: 15 MIN. • **COOK:** 30 MIN. • **MAKES:** 8 SERVINGS

½ **cup butter, cubed**
6 **medium unpeeled tart red apples, sliced**
¾ **cup sugar, divided**
¾ **tsp. ground cinnamon Vanilla ice cream, optional**

1. Melt butter in a large cast-iron or other ovenproof skillet. Add apples and ½ cup sugar; stir to mix well. Cover and cook over low heat for 20 minutes or until apples are tender, stirring frequently.

2. Add the cinnamon and remaining sugar. Cook and stir over medium-high heat 5-10 minutes longer. If desired, serve with ice cream.

1 SERVING: 235 cal., 12g fat (7g sat. fat), 31mg chol., 116mg sod., 35g carb. (31g sugars, 3g fiber), 0 pro.

CHOCOLATE CANNOLI

Indulge in double the delight—two Italian classics in one! We piped a rich, chocolaty cannoli filling into beautiful pizzelle cookies.
—Taste of Home *Test Kitchen*

PREP: 45 MIN. + COOLING • **COOK:** 5 MIN./BATCH • **MAKES:** 12 FILLED PIZZELLE

1 **large egg, room temperature**
¼ **cup sugar**
¼ **cup butter, melted**
½ **tsp. vanilla extract**
¼ **tsp. grated lemon zest**
⅛ **tsp. almond extract**
½ **cup all-purpose flour**
¼ **tsp. baking powder**

FILLING
¾ **cup sugar**
3 **Tbsp. cornstarch**
1 **cup whole milk**
1⅛ **tsp. vanilla extract**
1 **drop cinnamon oil, optional**
1¾ **cups ricotta cheese**
1 **milk chocolate candy bar with almonds (4¼ oz.), chopped**
½ **cup chopped pistachios**

1. In a large bowl, beat the egg, sugar, butter, vanilla, lemon zest and almond extract until blended. Combine the flour and baking powder; stir into egg mixture and mix well.

2. Bake in a preheated pizzelle iron according to manufacturer's directions until golden brown. Remove cookies and immediately shape into tubes. Place on wire racks to cool.

3. In a small saucepan, combine the sugar and cornstarch. Stir in milk until smooth. Bring to a boil; cook and stir for 2 minutes or until thickened. Stir in the vanilla and cinnamon oil if desired. Cool completely.

4. In a large bowl, beat ricotta cheese until smooth. Gradually beat in the custard mixture. Fold in the chocolate. Spoon or pipe into the shells. Dip each side in pistachios. Serve immediately. Refrigerate leftovers.

1 SERVING: 289 cal., 15g fat (8g sat. fat), 47mg chol., 124mg sod., 33g carb. (25g sugars, 1g fiber), 8g pro.

GRANDMA'S SECRET
Granny Smith, Golden Delicious, Empire, Braeburn and Cortland apples are the best apples for cooking. They're firm, hold their shape when cooked and are readily available.

MOM'S
FRIED APPLES

BING CHERRY-AMARETTI FOOL

When Bing cherries are in season, I make this custard-style fool.
The sweet fruit and whipped cream balance perfectly with
the sour cream, and crushed cookies add a little crunch.
—*Mary Ann Lee, Clifton Park, NY*

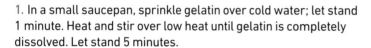

PREP: 30 MIN. + CHILLING • MAKES: 8 SERVINGS

- 1 envelope unflavored gelatin
- ⅓ cup cold water
- 1 cup sour cream
- ½ cup sugar
- 1 Tbsp. lemon juice
- ½ tsp. almond extract
- ½ tsp. vanilla extract
- 2 cups coarsely chopped fresh Bing or other dark sweet cherries, divided
- 1 cup heavy whipping cream
- 1 cup coarsely crushed amaretti cookies (about 16 cookies)
- Optional toppings: Fresh mint leaves, Bing cherries and additional crushed amaretti cookies

1. In a small saucepan, sprinkle gelatin over cold water; let stand 1 minute. Heat and stir over low heat until gelatin is completely dissolved. Let stand 5 minutes.

2. Place sour cream, sugar, lemon juice, extracts, 1 cup cherries and gelatin mixture in a blender; cover and process until cherries are pureed. Transfer to a large bowl.

3. In a small bowl, beat the cream until soft peaks form. Remove ½ cup whipped cream; reserve for topping. Gently fold remaining whipped cream into cherry mixture. Fold in crushed cookies and remaining chopped cherries. Divide the mixture among 8 dessert dishes. Refrigerate at least 2 hours.

4. Serve with the reserved whipped cream and optional toppings as desired.

1 SERVING: 323 cal., 19g fat (10g sat. fat), 41mg chol., 26mg sod., 36g carb. (32g sugars, 1g fiber), 4g pro.

PEANUT BUTTER BROWNIE TRIFLE

Feed the crowd at your next get-together with a luscious brownie trifle. The ever-popular combination of chocolate and peanut butter is guaranteed to please.

—*Nancy Foust, Stoneboro, PA*

PREP: 1 HOUR + CHILLING • **MAKES:** 20 SERVINGS (1 CUP EACH)

1 **fudge brownie mix (13x9-in. pan size)**
1 **pkg. (10 oz.) peanut butter chips**
2 **pkg. (13 oz. each) miniature peanut butter cups**
4 **cups cold 2% milk**
2 **pkg. (5.1 oz. each) instant vanilla pudding mix**
1 **cup creamy peanut butter**
4 **tsp. vanilla extract**
3 **cartons (8 oz. each) frozen whipped topping, thawed**

1. Preheat oven to 350°. Prepare brownie batter according to package directions; stir in peanut butter chips. Bake in a greased 13x9-in. baking pan 20-25 minutes or until a toothpick inserted in center comes out with moist crumbs (do not overbake). Cool on a wire rack; cut into ¾-in. pieces.

2. Cut the peanut butter cups in half; set aside ⅓ cup for garnish. In a large bowl, whisk the milk and pudding mixes for 2 minutes (mixture will be thick). Add peanut butter and vanilla; mix well. Fold in 1½ cartons whipped topping.

3. Place a third of the brownies in a 5-qt. glass bowl; top with a third of the remaining peanut butter cups. Spoon a third of the pudding mixture over the top. Repeat layers twice. Cover with remaining whipped topping; garnish with reserved peanut butter cups. Refrigerate until chilled.

1 CUP: 680 cal., 38g fat (15g sat. fat), 28mg chol., 547mg sod., 73g carb. (54g sugars, 3g fiber), 13g pro.

"I made this for a potluck at work. It was hugely popular. I got so many compliments and was told by my boss that I have to bring it every year from now on. Job security for the win! The trifle is so simple to make—I never imagined that it would be such a hit, but everyone loved it."
—CHRISTINE, TASTEOFHOME.COM

BLUEBERRY TURNOVERS

Golden-brown turnovers drizzled with a confectioners' sugar glaze—what a treat!
Best served the day they're made, these berry-filled pastries are perfect for both breakfast and dessert.
—Taste of Home *Test Kitchen*

PREP: 45 MIN. • BAKE: 15 MIN. • MAKES: 8 SERVINGS

2 cups fresh or frozen
    blueberries, divided
2 Tbsp. sugar
1 Tbsp. cornstarch
2 tsp. grated lemon zest
2 Tbsp. butter
1 pkg. (17.3 oz.) frozen puff
    pastry, thawed
1 large egg
1 Tbsp. water
½ cup confectioners' sugar
1 Tbsp. 2% milk

1. Preheat oven to 450°. In a large saucepan, combine ½ cup blueberries, sugar, cornstarch and lemon zest. Mash well with a fork. Bring to a boil over low heat; cook and stir until thickened, 1-2 minutes. Remove from the heat. Stir in butter and remaining 1½ cups blueberries.

2. Unfold puff pastry. On a lightly floured surface, roll out each pastry sheet into a 12-in. square. Cut each into 4 squares. Spoon 3 Tbsp. of filling into the center of each square; fold diagonally in half and press edges to seal. Place on an ungreased baking sheet. Beat egg and water; brush over pastry.

3. Bake until golden brown, 12-15 minutes. Combine the confectioners' sugar and milk; drizzle over turnovers. Serve warm or at room temperature.

1 TURNOVER: 400 cal., 20g fat (6g sat. fat), 31mg chol., 235mg sod., 51g carb. (14g sugars, 5g fiber), 6g pro.

FROM GRANDMA'S KITCHEN: Take care not to overfill the turnovers. While it may be tempting to heap on the sweet filling, spooning in more than 3 Tbsp. makes it much more likely your turnovers will leak. Be sure to seal each turnover well.

LAMINGTON ROULADE

Born in Australia, I came to the United States via a teacher exchange program and now have an American husband and two children. In my mother country, this cake roll is a popular dessert for special occasions. It disappears fast when I serve it here in the U.S., too!
—Susan Fagan, Lexington, SC

PREP: 45 MIN. • **BAKE:** 10 MIN. + CHILLING • **MAKES:** 12 SERVINGS

DESSERTS

3 **large eggs**
½ **cup superfine sugar**
¾ **cup all-purpose flour**
1 **tsp. baking powder**
¼ **tsp. salt**
2 **Tbsp. plus ½ cup unsweetened finely shredded coconut, divided**
¾ **cup plus 2 Tbsp. heavy whipping cream, divided**
½ **cup red raspberry preserves**
4 **oz. bittersweet chocolate, coarsely chopped**
2 **Tbsp. butter, cubed**

1. Preheat oven to 400°. Line the bottom of a greased 15x10x1-in. baking pan with waxed paper and grease the paper.

2. In a large bowl, beat eggs on high speed 5 minutes. Gradually add sugar, beating until thick and lemon-colored. In another bowl, whisk the flour, baking powder and salt; fold into the egg mixture. Transfer to prepared pan, spreading evenly.

3. Bake 7-9 minutes or until the top springs back when lightly touched. Cool 5 minutes. Invert onto a kitchen towel sprinkled with 2 Tbsp. coconut. Gently peel off paper. Roll up cake in the towel jelly-roll style, starting with a short side. Cool completely on a wire rack.

4. In a small bowl, beat ¾ cup heavy cream until stiff peaks form. Unroll cake; spread preserves over cake to within ½ in. of edges. Spread whipped cream over preserves. Roll up again, without the towel. Place on a platter, seam side down. Refrigerate, covered, at least 1 hour.

5. In a microwave, melt the chocolate and butter with remaining cream; stir until smooth. Spread over the top and sides of cake. Sprinkle with remaining coconut; let stand until set.

1 PIECE: 261 cal., 16g fat (10g sat. fat), 82mg chol., 122mg sod., 29g carb. (20g sugars, 2g fiber), 4g pro.

CHEESECAKE ROLLS

Craving cheesecake but don't have time to make a traditional one?
Bake up a pan of sweet stuffed rolls using refrigerated dough,
whipped cream cheese and frozen blueberries.
—*Jennifer Stalcup, Vancouver, WA*

PREP: 20 MIN. • BAKE: 20 MIN. + COOLING • MAKES: 8 SERVINGS

1 **tube (16.3 oz.) large refrigerated flaky biscuits, such as Pillsbury Grands!**
1 **cup whipped cream cheese**
2 **Tbsp. honey**

¾ **cup frozen wild unsweetened blueberries**
1 **Tbsp. butter, melted**
1 **tsp. sugar**
⅓ **cup confectioners' sugar**
2 **Tbsp. 2% milk**
½ **tsp. lemon juice**

1. Preheat oven to 350°. On a lightly floured surface, separate the biscuits and flatten each to a 5-in. circle. In a small bowl, combine cream cheese and honey; gently fold in blueberries. Place 2 Tbsp. mixture in the center of each circle. Bring edges of dough together above filling; twist and pinch to seal.

2. Place on parchment-lined baking sheets, seam side down. Brush with butter; sprinkle with granulated sugar.

3. Bake until golden brown, 18-21 minutes. Remove from pans to wire racks to cool for 10 minutes. Meanwhile, whisk together the confectioners' sugar, milk and lemon juice; brush over rolls. Cool completely. Refrigerate until chilled, if desired. Sprinkle with additional confectioners' sugar. Refrigerate leftovers.

1 ROLL: 299 cal., 14g fat (8g sat. fat), 24mg chol., 535mg sod., 38g carb. (16g sugars, 1g fiber), 4g pro.

PECAN DATE PUDDING

My great-grandmother and grandmother always added big dollops of whipped cream to servings of their warm, nutty pudding. We never had a holiday without it.
—*Patricia Rutherford, Winchester, IL*

PREP: 20 MIN. • **BAKE:** 50 MIN. • **MAKES:** 8 SERVINGS

1 cup all-purpose flour
2 cups packed brown
  sugar, divided
1½ tsp. baking powder
¼ tsp. salt
2 Tbsp. butter, divided
¾ cup whole milk
1 cup chopped dates
1 cup chopped pecans
2 cups water
  Whipped cream, optional

1. Preheat oven to 350°. In a bowl, combine the flour, 1 cup brown sugar, baking powder and salt. Melt 1 Tbsp. butter; combine with the milk. Stir into the flour mixture until smooth. Fold in dates and pecans. Transfer to a greased 8-in. square baking dish.

2. In a large saucepan, bring remaining 1 cup brown sugar and water to a boil. Cook and stir until the sugar is dissolved. Remove from the heat; stir in remaining 1 Tbsp. butter until melted. Pour over batter.

3. Bake until a toothpick inserted near the center of cake comes out clean, 50-60 minutes. Serve warm. If desired, top with whipped cream.

1 SERVING: 452 cal., 14g fat (3g sat. fat), 10mg chol., 213mg sod., 83g carb. (67g sugars, 3g fiber), 4g pro.

PEACH MELBA TRIFLE

Transform a purchased angel food cake into a dream of a dessert with just fruit and a few other ingredients. If you don't have fresh peaches handy, substitute canned ones.
—*Christina Moore, Casar, NC*

PREP: 20 MIN. + CHILLING • **MAKES:** 12 SERVINGS

2 pkg. (12 oz. each)
  frozen unsweetened
  raspberries, thawed
1 Tbsp. cornstarch
1½ cups fat-free
  peach yogurt
⅛ tsp. almond extract
1 carton (8 oz.) frozen
  reduced-fat whipped
  topping, thawed
2 prepared angel food
  cakes (8 to 10 oz. each),
  cut into 1-in. cubes
  (about 8 cups)
4 small peaches, peeled
  and sliced (about 2 cups)

1. In a large saucepan, mix berries and cornstarch until blended. Bring to a boil; cook and stir 1-2 minutes or until thickened. Strain seeds; cover and refrigerate.

2. In a large bowl, mix yogurt and extract; fold in whipped topping. In a 4-qt. bowl, layer half each of the cake cubes, yogurt mixture and peaches. Repeat layers. Refrigerate, covered, at least 3 hours before serving. Serve with raspberry sauce.

⅔ CUP: 201 cal., 3g fat (2g sat. fat), 1mg chol., 298mg sod., 41g carb. (10g sugars, 3g fiber), 4g pro.

PECAN DATE
PUDDING

STRAWBERRY PRETZEL DESSERT MINIS

Guests at your next potluck or picnic will line up for these individual Mason jars filled with luscious layers. Feel free to make the treats in advance and refrigerate them until serving.

—Aldene Belch, Flint, MI

PREP: 30 MIN. • **BAKE:** 15 MIN. + CHILLING • **MAKES:** 32 SERVINGS

2 cups crushed pretzels (about 8 oz.)
¾ cup butter, melted
3 Tbsp. sugar

FILLING
2 cups whipped topping
1 pkg. (8 oz.) cream cheese, softened
1 cup sugar

TOPPING
2 pkg. (3 oz. each) strawberry gelatin
2 cups boiling water
2 pkg. (16 oz. each) frozen sweetened sliced strawberries, thawed

1. Preheat oven to 350°. In a small bowl, combine pretzels, butter and sugar; spread onto a baking sheet. Bake until crisp and lightly browned, 12-15 minutes. Cool completely on a wire rack; break into small pieces.

2. For filling, in a small bowl, beat whipped topping, cream cheese and sugar until smooth. Refrigerate until chilled.

3. For topping, in a large bowl, dissolve gelatin in boiling water. Stir in sweetened strawberries; chill until partially set, about 1 hour. Carefully layer pretzel mixture, filling and topping into 4-oz. glass jars. Chill until firm, at least 2 hours. If desired, serve with additional whipped topping and pretzels.

1 JAR: 172 cal., 8g fat (5g sat. fat), 19mg chol., 151mg sod., 25g carb. (20g sugars, 1g fiber), 2g pro.

HONEY NUT & CREAM CHEESE BAKLAVA

Here's a traditional recipe that looks and tastes as though it took hours to create
but is actually easy to prepare. What cook doesn't love that?
—*Cheryl Snavely, Hagerstown, MD*

PREP: 30 MIN. • BAKE: 35 MIN. + COOLING • MAKES: 3 DOZEN

**Butter-flavored
cooking spray**
½ **cup spreadable honey nut
cream cheese**
1¼ **cups sugar, divided**
3 **cups chopped walnuts**
1 **pkg. (16 oz., 14x9-in.
sheets) frozen phyllo
dough, thawed**
1 **cup water**
½ **cup honey**

1. Preheat oven to 350°. Coat a 13x9-in. baking pan with cooking spray. In a large bowl, mix cream cheese and ¼ cup sugar until blended. Stir in walnuts.

2. Unroll the phyllo dough; trim to fit into the pan. Layer 20 sheets of phyllo in prepared pan, spritzing each with cooking spray. Keep the remaining phyllo covered with a damp towel to prevent it from drying out.

3. Spread with half of the walnut mixture. Layer with 5 more phyllo sheets, spritzing each with cooking spray. Spread the remaining walnut mixture over phyllo. Top with the remaining phyllo sheets, spritzing each with cooking spray.

4. Cut into 1½-in. diamonds. Bake 35-40 minutes or until golden brown. Meanwhile, in a saucepan, combine the water, honey and remaining sugar; bring to a boil, stirring to dissolve sugar. Reduce heat; simmer, uncovered, 10 minutes. Pour over warm baklava.

5. Cool completely in pan on a wire rack. Refrigerate, covered, until serving.

1 PIECE: 156 cal., 8g fat (1g sat. fat), 1mg chol., 64mg sod., 20g carb. (12g sugars, 1g fiber), 3g pro.

GRANDMA'S SECRET
To pour batter easily into hot oil, simply use a liquid measuring cup or a turkey baster.

TRADITIONAL FUNNEL CAKES

TRADITIONAL FUNNEL CAKES

When I was in high school, I treated my family to these funnel cakes every Sunday after church. They're crisp and tender, just like the kind we ate at the state fair.
—*Susan Tingley, Portland, OR*

PREP: 15 MIN. • **COOK:** 5 MIN./BATCH • **MAKES:** 8 SERVINGS

2 cups 2% milk
3 large eggs, room temperature
¼ cup sugar
2 cups all-purpose flour
2 tsp. baking powder
Oil for deep-fat frying
Confectioners' sugar
Lingonberry jam or red currant jelly

1. In a large bowl, combine the milk, eggs and sugar. Combine flour and baking powder; beat into egg mixture until smooth.

2. In a cast-iron or electric skillet, heat 2 in. oil to 375°. Cover the bottom of a funnel spout with your finger; ladle ½ cup batter into funnel. Holding the funnel several inches above the skillet, release your finger and move funnel in a spiral motion until all the batter is released. Scrape funnel with a rubber spatula if needed.

3. Fry until golden brown, 1 minute on each side. Drain on paper towels. Repeat with remaining batter. Dust with confectioners' sugar. Serve warm with jam.

1 FUNNEL CAKE: 300 cal., 15g fat (2g sat. fat), 84mg chol., 157mg sod., 33g carb. (10g sugars, 1g fiber), 8g pro.

APPLE DUMPLINGS

It's impossible to resist these crispy golden dumplings filled with apples and topped with a sweet caramel sauce. Just add a scoop of vanilla ice cream and dig in!
—*Jody Fisher, Stewartstown, PA*

PREP: 20 MIN. • **BAKE:** 55 MIN. • **MAKES:** 6 SERVINGS

2 cups all-purpose flour
1 tsp. salt
⅔ cup shortening
4 to 5 Tbsp. cold water
2 cups chopped peeled tart apples (about 5 medium)
2 cups packed brown sugar
1 cup water
¼ cup butter, cubed
Vanilla ice cream

1. In a large bowl, combine the flour and salt; cut in shortening until crumbly. Gradually add cold water, tossing with a fork until dough forms a ball. On a lightly floured surface, roll out dough into a 12x18-in. rectangle. Cut into 6 squares.

2. Place ⅓ cup chopped apples in center of each square. Brush edges of dough with water; fold up corners to center and pinch to seal. Place in a greased 13x9-in. baking dish. Bake, uncovered, at 350° for 30 minutes.

3. In a small saucepan, combine brown sugar, water and butter; bring to a boil, stirring constantly. Remove from the heat. Pour over dumplings. Bake 25-30 minutes longer or until apples are tender. Serve warm with ice cream.

1 SERVING: 711 cal., 29g fat (10g sat. fat), 20mg chol., 500mg sod., 109g carb. (77g sugars, 2g fiber), 4g pro.

FROZEN CHOCOLATE MINT DESSERT

When fixing my great-aunt's grasshopper pie, I accidentally put in too much mint. To cut that taste, I added something gooey and chocolaty. I flipped the whole pie upside-down on top of a brownie crust!

—Sarah Newman, Mahtomedi, MN

PREP: 40 MIN. + FREEZING • **MAKES:** 24 SERVINGS

- 1 **pkg. fudge brownie mix (13x9-in. pan size)**
- 2 **large egg whites, room temperature**
- ¼ **cup unsweetened applesauce**
- 2 **tsp. vanilla extract**
- ½ **cup baking cocoa**
- 1½ **cups fat-free milk**
- 2 **pkg. (16 oz. each) large marshmallows**
- ½ **tsp. mint extract**
- 1 **carton (16 oz.) frozen reduced-fat whipped topping, thawed**
- 7 **Oreo cookies, crushed (about ⅔ cup)**

1. In a large bowl, combine the fudge brownie mix, egg whites, applesauce and vanilla. Spread into a 13x9-in. baking dish coated with cooking spray. Bake at 350° for 18-22 minutes or until a toothpick inserted in center comes out clean. Cool on a wire rack.

2. In a Dutch oven, combine baking cocoa and milk. Cook and stir over medium heat until the cocoa is dissolved. Stir in the marshmallows until melted. Remove from heat; stir in mint extract. Cool completely.

3. Fold in whipped topping. Spread over brownies. Sprinkle with cookie crumbs. Cover and freeze for at least 8 hours. Remove from the freezer 10 minutes before serving.

1 PIECE: 293 cal., 6g fat (3g sat. fat), 1mg chol., 141mg sod., 60g carb. (38g sugars, 1g fiber), 3g pro.

OLD-FASHIONED RICE PUDDING

As a girl, I always waited eagerly at the dinner table when I knew we were having rice pudding. Now I prepare it for my husband, and he enjoys it as much as I do.

—Sandra Melnychenko, Grandview, MB

PREP: 10 MIN. • **BAKE:** 1 HOUR • **MAKES:** 6 SERVINGS

- 3½ **cups 2% milk**
- ½ **cup uncooked long grain rice**
- ⅓ **cup sugar**
- ½ **tsp. salt**
- ½ **cup raisins**
- 1 **tsp. vanilla extract** **Ground cinnamon, optional**

1. Preheat oven to 325°. Place the first 4 ingredients in a large saucepan; bring to a boil over medium heat, stirring constantly. Transfer to a greased 1½-qt. baking dish.

2. Bake, covered, 45 minutes, stirring every 15 minutes. Stir in raisins and vanilla; bake, covered, until the rice is tender, about 15 minutes. If desired, sprinkle with cinnamon. Serve warm or refrigerate and serve cold.

¾ CUP: 214 cal., 3g fat (2g sat. fat), 11mg chol., 266mg sod., 41g carb. (25g sugars, 1g fiber), 6g pro.

FROM GRANDMA'S KITCHEN: For extra creamy rice pudding, add an egg yolk. Avoid scrambling the egg by removing a small amount of the hot mixture and whisking it into the yolk, then add all of it back into the dish. A thermometer inserted into the baked pudding should read 160° to ensure the yolk has cooked through.

GRILLED FRUIT PHYLLO TART

Mom used to serve a fruit salad that included whipped topping and cream cheese. This dessert reminds me of her recipe. When I made the tart for a bridal shower, everyone loved the flaky phyllo crust and unexpected grilled flavor.
—*Laura McAllister, Morganton, NC*

PREP: 30 MIN. • GRILL: 10 MIN. • MAKES: 12 SERVINGS

3 Tbsp. butter, melted
4 tsp. canola oil
8 sheets phyllo dough (14x9-in. size)
1 large lemon
3 medium peaches, peeled and halved
2 cups large fresh strawberries, stems removed
4 slices fresh pineapple (½ in. thick)
⅓ cup packed brown sugar
½ tsp. salt
½ cup heavy whipping cream
1 pkg. (8 oz.) cream cheese, softened
⅓ cup confectioners' sugar
2 Tbsp. chopped fresh mint

1. Preheat oven to 400°. In a small bowl, mix the butter and oil. Brush a 15x10x1-in. baking pan with some of the butter mixture. Place 1 sheet of phyllo dough into the prepared pan; brush with butter mixture. Layer with 7 additional phyllo sheets, brushing each layer. (Keep remaining phyllo covered with a damp towel to prevent it from drying out.) Bake 5-7 minutes or until golden brown (phyllo will puff up during baking). Cool completely.

2. Finely grate 1 Tbsp. lemon zest. Cut lemon crosswise in half; squeeze the juice into a bowl. In a large bowl, toss the peaches, strawberries, pineapple, brown sugar, salt, and lemon zest and juice. Remove strawberries; thread fruit onto 3 metal or soaked wooden skewers.

3. Place fruit on oiled grill rack. Grill, covered, over medium heat until fruit is tender, turning once, 8-10 minutes for the pineapple slices and peaches, 4-5 minutes for the strawberries. Remove and set aside.

4. In a small bowl, beat cream until soft peaks form. In another bowl, beat cream cheese and confectioners' sugar until smooth. Fold in whipped cream. Spread over phyllo crust. Slice grilled fruit; arrange over filling. Sprinkle with mint; cut into pieces.

1 PIECE: 233 cal., 15g fat (8g sat. fat), 38mg chol., 216mg sod., 24g carb. (18g sugars, 2g fiber), 3g pro.

SNICKERDOODLE CHEESECAKE

My maternal grandmother always preferred sewing and quilting to cooking and baking,
but she was the only person I knew who made snickerdoodles. I couldn't resist
combining those yummy cookies with cheesecake, my favorite dessert.
Sometimes I'll drizzle the pieces with a little maple syrup.

—Lisa Varner, El Paso, TX

PREP: 25 MIN. • **BAKE:** 70 MIN. + CHILLING • **MAKES:** 16 SERVINGS

2 cups cinnamon graham cracker crumbs (about 14 whole crackers)
½ cup butter, melted
3 pkg. (8 oz. each) cream cheese, softened
1 cup sugar, divided
1 tsp. ground cinnamon
1 tsp. vanilla extract
4 large eggs, room temperature, lightly beaten
1½ cups cinnamon baking chips
2 cups sour cream

1. Preheat oven to 325°. Place a greased 9-in. springform pan on a double thickness of heavy-duty foil (about 18 in. square). Wrap foil securely around pan.

2. Mix the cracker crumbs and melted butter. Press onto bottom and 1½ in. up sides of prepared pan.

3. Beat the cream cheese and ¾ cup sugar until smooth. Beat in the cinnamon and vanilla. Add the eggs; beat on low speed just until blended. Fold in the cinnamon baking chips. Pour into crust. Place springform pan in a larger baking pan; add 1 in. of hot water to larger pan.

4. Bake until the center is just set and the top appears dull, 70-80 minutes. Remove the springform pan from the water bath. Cool cheesecake on a wire rack 10 minutes. Loosen the side from pan with a knife; remove the foil. Cool 1 hour longer. Refrigerate overnight, covering when completely cooled.

5. Remove rim from pan. Mix sour cream and remaining sugar; spread over cheesecake.

1 PIECE: 513 cal., 35g fat (19g sat. fat), 112mg chol., 343mg sod., 42g carb. (33g sugars, 1g fiber), 8g pro.

EASY APPLE STRUDEL

My family is always thrilled when I serve apple strudel. To cut down
on calories and prep, I made changes to the classic version.
We think my variation is just as good!

—*Joanie Fuson, Indianapolis, IN*

PREP: 30 MIN. • BAKE: 35 MIN. • MAKES: 6 SERVINGS

⅓ cup raisins
2 Tbsp. water
¼ tsp. almond extract
3 cups coarsely chopped
   peeled apples
⅓ cup plus 2 tsp. sugar,
   divided
3 Tbsp. all-purpose flour

¼ tsp. ground cinnamon
2 Tbsp. butter, melted
2 Tbsp. canola oil
8 sheets phyllo dough
   (14x9-in. size)
   Confectioners' sugar,
   optional

1. Preheat oven to 350°. Place raisins, water and almond extract
in a large microwave-safe bowl; microwave, uncovered, on high
for 1½ minutes. Let stand 5 minutes. Drain. Add apples, ⅓ cup
sugar, flour and cinnamon; toss to combine.

2. In a small bowl, mix the melted butter and oil; remove 2 tsp.
mixture for brushing top. Place 1 sheet of phyllo dough on a work
surface; brush lightly with some of the butter mixture. (Keep the
remaining phyllo covered with a damp towel to prevent it from
drying out.) Layer with 7 additional phyllo sheets, brushing each
layer with some of the butter mixture. Spread apple mixture over
phyllo to within 2 in. of 1 long side.

3. Fold the short edges over the filling. Roll up jelly-roll style,
starting from the side with a 2-in. border. Transfer to a baking
sheet coated with cooking spray. Brush with the reserved butter
mixture; sprinkle with remaining 2 tsp. sugar. With a sharp knife,
cut diagonal slits in top of strudel.

4. Bake until golden brown, 35-40 minutes. Cool on a wire rack.
If desired, dust with confectioners' sugar before serving.

1 PIECE: 229 cal., 9g fat (3g sat. fat), 10mg chol., 92mg sod., 37g carb.
(24g sugars, 2g fiber), 2g pro.

*"This yummy recipe comes close to my grandma's
authentic apple strudel—without all the hard work
and heaps of calories!"*
—ANNGODSELL, TASTEOFHOME.COM

GRANDMOTHER'S BREAD PUDDING

I was raised by my grandmother, and this bread pudding is one of her best recipes.
Besides looking after my siblings and me, she worked the farm, ran another
business on the side and cooked us amazing homemade food.
How she did all of that, I'll never know!
—*Sherrie Hill, St. Louis, MO*

PREP: 20 MIN. • **BAKE:** 50 MIN. • **MAKES:** 9 SERVINGS

PUDDING
- **1 cup sugar**
- **2 large eggs, beaten**
- **2 cups whole milk**
- **2 tsp. pumpkin pie spice**
- **2 tsp. vanilla extract**
- **4 cups day-old torn white or French bread**
- **1 cup raisins**

CUSTARD SAUCE
- **3 large egg yolks**
- **¾ cup sugar**
- **¼ cup cornstarch**
- **3 cups whole milk**
- **2 tsp. vanilla extract**

1. For pudding, combine the first 5 ingredients in a large bowl. Add bread and raisins; mix well. Turn into a greased 9-in. square baking pan. Bake at 350° for 50 minutes.

2. Meanwhile, for sauce, combine yolks, sugar and cornstarch in the top of a double boiler. Gradually add the milk, stirring until smooth. Cook over boiling water, stirring constantly, until mixture thickens and coats a metal spoon. Remove from the heat and stir in vanilla. Serve pudding and sauce warm or chilled.

1 SERVING: 379 cal., 8g fat (4g sat. fat), 137mg chol., 169mg sod., 69g carb. (55g sugars, 1g fiber), 9g pro.

ITALIAN PINEAPPLE TRIFLE

Our Christmas Eve celebration just wouldn't be the same without this Italian favorite.
The cool, no-bake trifle is a rich but refreshing finale for our holiday dinner.
—*Ann-Marie Milano, Milton, MA*

PREP: 30 MIN. + CHILLING • **MAKES:** 16 SERVINGS

- **1 carton (15 oz.) ricotta cheese**
- **11 oz. cream cheese, softened**
- **¾ cup sugar**
- **2 tsp. vanilla extract, divided**
- **2 cups heavy whipping cream**
- **2 cans (8 oz. each) unsweetened crushed pineapple, drained**
- **1 can (15¾ oz.) lemon pie filling**
- **3 pkg. (3 oz. each) ladyfingers, split**

1. In a small bowl, beat ricotta, cream cheese, sugar and 1 tsp. vanilla until fluffy. In a large bowl, whip heavy cream until stiff peaks form; fold into ricotta mixture.

2. In another bowl, combine pineapple, pie filling and remaining vanilla. In a 3-qt. trifle bowl or glass serving bowl, arrange 2 packages of ladyfingers over the bottom and up the sides.

3. Layer a third of the ricotta mixture, a third of the pineapple mixture and half of the remaining ladyfingers. Repeat layers once. Layer remaining ricotta and pineapple mixtures. Cover and refrigerate several hours or overnight.

1 CUP: 362 cal., 21g fat (13g sat. fat), 98mg chol., 256mg sod., 37g carb. (28g sugars, 0 fiber), 7g pro.

SPICED MANGO-ALMOND TART

The world is full of tart recipes—but this one just may be the most gorgeous!
For an extra-special finish, add confectioners' sugar, whipped cream and mint leaves.
—*Lisa Speer, Palm Beach, FL*

PREP: 35 MIN. + FREEZING • BAKE: 25 MIN./BATCH • MAKES: 2 TARTS (8 SERVINGS EACH)

1 pkg. (17.3 oz.) frozen puff pastry, thawed
⅔ cup almond paste, divided
2 large mangoes, peeled and thinly sliced
2 Tbsp. lemon juice
3 Tbsp. packed brown sugar
1½ tsp. ground cinnamon
½ tsp. ground ginger
Dash ground cloves

1. Preheat oven to 375°. Working with 1 puff pastry sheet at a time, unfold the pastry onto a large sheet of parchment dusted lightly with flour. Roll pastry into a 10-in. square. Transfer pastry and parchment to a baking sheet. Using a sharp knife, score a ½-in. border around edges of pastry.

2. On a second sheet of parchment, roll ⅓ cup almond paste to ⅛-in. thickness. Peel off almond paste in pieces and arrange on puff pastry, keeping within edges of cut border.

3. In a large bowl, toss the mangoes with the lemon juice; arrange half the mangoes over the almond paste. In a small bowl, mix the brown sugar and spices; sprinkle half the mixture over mangoes. Place tart in freezer to chill, about 10 minutes. Repeat with the remaining ingredients.

4. Bake 25-35 minutes or until the crust is golden brown. If baking 2 tarts at a time, switch position of pans halfway through baking. Serve warm.

1 PIECE: 232 cal., 11g fat (2g sat. fat), 0 chol., 103mg sod., 32g carb. (12g sugars, 4g fiber), 3g pro.

FROM GRANDMA'S KITCHEN: Select mangoes that give slightly when gently pressed. If you need to ripen mangoes quickly, set them in a brown paper bag. Roll up the bag tightly and let the bag sit out for a day or two.

PEACH CREAM PUFFS

On hot sunny days, we crave something light, airy and cool. Golden-brown cream puffs
stuffed with a peach filling and whipped cream are hard to beat!
—Angela Benedict, Dunbar, WV

PREP: 55 MIN. + COOLING • **BAKE:** 25 MIN. + COOLING • **MAKES:** 16 SERVINGS

1 cup water
½ cup butter, cubed
⅛ tsp. salt
1 cup all-purpose flour
4 large eggs, room temperature

FILLING
4 medium peaches, peeled and cubed (about 3 cups)
½ cup sugar
½ cup water
½ cup peach schnapps liqueur or peach nectar
½ tsp. ground cinnamon
¼ tsp. ground nutmeg

WHIPPED CREAM
2 cups heavy whipping cream
½ cup confectioners' sugar
3 Tbsp. peach schnapps liqueur, optional
Additional confectioners' sugar

1. Preheat oven to 400°. In a large saucepan, bring the water, butter and salt to a rolling boil. Add flour all at once and beat until blended. Cook over medium heat, stirring vigorously until mixture pulls away from the sides of pan and forms a ball. Transfer dough to a large bowl; let stand 5 minutes.

2. Add the eggs, 1 at a time, beating well after each addition until smooth. Continue beating until mixture is smooth and shiny.

3. Cut a ½-in. hole in the tip of a pastry bag. Transfer dough to the bag; pipe sixteen 2-in. mounds 3 in. apart onto parchment-lined baking sheets.

4. Bake on a lower oven rack 25-30 minutes or until puffed, very firm and golden brown. Pierce side of each puff with tip of a knife to allow steam to escape. Cool completely on wire racks.

5. Meanwhile, in a large saucepan, combine filling ingredients; bring to a boil, stirring occasionally. Reduce the heat; simmer, uncovered, 25-30 minutes or until mixture is slightly thickened and peaches are tender. Cool completely.

6. In a bowl, beat the cream until it begins to thicken. Add the confectioners' sugar and, if desired, peach schnapps; beat until soft peaks form.

7. Cut the top third off each cream puff. Pull out and discard soft dough from inside tops and bottoms.

8. To serve, spoon 2 Tbsp. whipped cream into each bottom; top with 2 Tbsp. filling and 2 Tbsp. additional whipped cream. Replace tops. Dust with additional confectioners' sugar.

1 CREAM PUFF WITH ¼ CUP WHIPPED CREAM AND 2 TBSP. FILLING: 256 cal., 18g fat (11g sat. fat), 103mg chol., 94mg sod., 21g carb. (14g sugars, 1g fiber), 3g pro.

STAR-SPANGLED PARFAITS

We think the best time to enjoy this dessert is midsummer, when the blueberries are thick in our northern woods. If you like raspberries, toss in some of those, too.
—*Anne Theriault, Wellesley, MA*

TAKES: 15 MIN. • **MAKES:** 4 SERVINGS

2 cups fresh strawberries, cut into ½-in. pieces
2 cups fresh blueberries
4 tsp. reduced-fat raspberry walnut vinaigrette
¾ cup fat-free vanilla or strawberry Greek yogurt
2 tsp. minced fresh mint
Unsweetened shredded coconut, optional

1. Place the strawberries and blueberries in separate bowls. Drizzle each with 2 tsp. vinaigrette; toss to coat. In a small bowl, mix yogurt and mint.

2. Spoon strawberries into 4 parfait glasses. Layer each with yogurt mixture and blueberries. If desired, top with coconut.

1 PARFAIT: 172 cal., 7g fat (5g sat. fat), 0 chol., 41mg sod., 24g carb. (17g sugars, 5g fiber), 5g pro. **DIABETIC EXCHANGES:** 1 fruit, 1 fat, ½ starch.

DIRT DESSERT

PICTURED ON PAGE 268

My mom used to make this yummy treat, and I just loved it. Arrange colorful gummy worms on top of the crushed cookie "dirt" for extra fun when you're serving kids.
—*Kristi Linton, Bay City, MI*

PREP: 30 MIN. + CHILLING • **MAKES:** 20 SERVINGS

1 pkg. (8 oz.) cream cheese, softened
¼ cup butter, softened
1 cup confectioners' sugar
3½ cups cold 2% milk
2 pkg. (3.4 oz. each) instant vanilla pudding mix
1 carton (12 oz.) frozen whipped topping, thawed
1 pkg. (15½ oz.) Oreo cookies, crushed
Shaved white chocolate, optional

1. In a large bowl, beat cream cheese, butter and confectioners' sugar until smooth. In a large bowl, whisk milk and pudding mixes for 2 minutes; let stand for 2 minutes or until soft-set. Gradually stir into cream cheese mixture. Fold in whipped topping.

2. Spread 1⅓ cups crushed cookies into an ungreased 13x9-in. dish. Layer with half the pudding mixture and half the remaining cookies. Repeat layers. Refrigerate for at least 1 hour before serving. Serve with shaved white chocolate if desired.

½ CUP: 278 cal., 13g fat (7g sat. fat), 16mg chol., 316mg sod., 38g carb. (26g sugars, 1g fiber), 3g pro.

CHOCOLATE RUGELACH

Many bakeries sell these traditional pastries, but I think they're best when made at home.
I added chocolate to the cinnamon-nut filling because everything's better with chocolate!
—*Fern Holody, Lavallette, NJ*

PREP: 30 MIN. + CHILLING • BAKE: 20 MIN./BATCH + COOLING • MAKES: 4 DOZEN

DESSERTS

1 cup unsalted butter,
  softened
4 oz. cream cheese,
  softened
½ cup sour cream
5 Tbsp. sugar, divided
1¾ cups all-purpose flour
8 oz. semisweet chocolate,
  chopped
1 cup chopped walnuts
⅓ cup dried currants
1½ tsp. ground cinnamon
½ cup seedless
  raspberry jam
2 Tbsp. plus 2 tsp. water,
  divided
1 large egg white
4 tsp. cinnamon sugar

1. In a large bowl, beat butter and cream cheese until smooth. Add sour cream and 2 Tbsp. sugar; mix until combined. Gradually beat in flour. Divide dough into 4 portions. Shape each into a disk; wrap and refrigerate 30 minutes or until easy to handle.

2. Preheat oven to 350°. Place the chocolate, nuts, currants, cinnamon and remaining 3 Tbsp. sugar in a food processor; cover and process until finely chopped. In a microwave-safe bowl, combine jam and 2 Tbsp. water. Microwave on high until thinned, 5-10 seconds; whisk.

3. Working with 1 portion of dough at a time, roll each into a 10-in. circle on a well floured surface. Brush with a fourth of the jam mixture. Sprinkle with a fourth of the chocolate mixture (about ½ cup), pressing lightly to adhere. Cut each into 12 wedges. Roll up wedges from the wide ends; place 2 in. apart on parchment-lined baking sheets, point side down. In a small bowl, whisk egg white and remaining 2 tsp. water; brush over pastries. Sprinkle with cinnamon sugar.

4. Bake until golden brown, 20-25 minutes. Remove from pans to wire racks to cool completely.

1 PASTRY: 125 cal., 8g fat (4g sat. fat), 13mg chol., 10mg sod., 10g carb. (5g sugars, 1g fiber), 2g pro.

GRANDMA'S SECRET

Store Chocolate Rugelach in an airtight container at room temperature for up to 3 days, or freeze for 2 to 3 months.

CHOCOLATE HAZELNUT PUDDING TORTE

Here's my busy-mom version of classic Italian tiramisu. The torte is so easy to prepare with convenience items and goes together hours in advance. The hardest thing is waiting for it to chill so you can eat it!
—*Cheryl Snavely, Hagerstown, MD*

PREP: 15 MIN. + CHILLING • **MAKES:** 8 SERVINGS

24 soft ladyfingers, divided
½ cup Nutella, divided
1½ cups half-and-half cream
1 pkg. (3.4 oz.) instant French vanilla pudding mix
1 carton (12 oz.) frozen whipped topping, thawed
Grated or shaved chocolate

1. Arrange 12 ladyfingers in an 11x7-in. dish. Spread with half the Nutella.

2. In a large bowl, whisk the cream and pudding mix for about 2 minutes. Stir in whipped topping. Spread half the mixture over Nutella. Top with remaining ladyfingers; spread with remaining Nutella and then remaining pudding mixture. Sprinkle with grated or shaved chocolate. Refrigerate, covered, 8 hours or overnight. Refrigerate leftovers.

1 PIECE: 390 cal., 18g fat (11g sat. fat), 67mg chol., 347mg sod., 46g carb. (37g sugars, 1g fiber), 5g pro.

BERRY, LEMON & DOUGHNUT HOLE TRIFLE

After my son called and said he was bringing home his college roommates, I improvised and whipped up a simple trifle in less than 30 minutes. It's been a family favorite ever since!
—*Ellen Riley, Murfreesboro, TN*

TAKES: 25 MIN. • **MAKES:** 10 SERVINGS

2 cups cold 2% milk
1 pkg. (3.4 oz.) instant lemon pudding mix
1 carton (8 oz.) frozen whipped topping, thawed and divided
16 to 32 plain doughnut holes
3 cups fresh strawberries, halved
2 cups fresh blueberries

1. Whisk the milk and lemon pudding mix for about 2 minutes. Let stand for 2 minutes or until soft-set. Fold in 2½ cups whipped topping; set aside.

2. Place half the doughnut holes in a 3-qt. trifle bowl; spread half the pudding mixture over the top. Top the pudding with half the strawberries and blueberries. Repeat layers. Top with remaining whipped topping. Chill until serving.

1 CUP: 250 cal., 11g fat (7g sat. fat), 6mg chol., 250mg sod., 33g carb. (24g sugars, 2g fiber), 3g pro.

GERMAN APPLE STRUDEL

This Old World recipe has just what you want when you're looking for authentic apple strudel, from the thin layers of flaky homemade pastry to the spiced apple-raisin filling.

—Darlene Brenden, Salem, OR

PREP: 1 HOUR + STANDING • **BAKE:** 45 MIN./BATCH • **MAKES:** 2 STRUDELS (8 PIECES EACH)

3 cups all-purpose flour
½ cup canola oil, divided
¾ cup warm water (120°)
1 large egg, room temperature, lightly beaten

FILLING
1½ cups fresh bread crumbs
6 cups chopped peeled apples (about 6 medium)
½ cup raisins
1 cup sugar
1½ tsp. ground cinnamon
⅓ cup butter, melted
3 Tbsp. sour cream

1. Place the flour in a mixer bowl; beat in ¼ cup oil (the mixture will be slightly crumbly). In a small bowl, slowly whisk the warm water into the beaten egg; add to flour mixture, mixing well. Beat in remaining oil until smooth. Transfer to a greased bowl, turning once to grease the top. Cover and let rest in a warm place about 30 minutes.

2. Preheat oven to 350°. Spread bread crumbs into an ungreased 15x10x1-in. baking pan. Bake 10-15 minutes or until golden brown, stirring occasionally. Cool completely.

3. Tape a 30x15-in. sheet of parchment onto a work surface; dust lightly with flour. Divide the dough in half; place 1 portion on parchment and roll to a very thin 24x15-in. rectangle. (Keep remaining dough covered.) Remove tape from parchment.

4. Sprinkle ¾ cup bread crumbs over the rectangle to within 1 in. of edges. Starting 3 in. from a short side, sprinkle 3 cups apples and ¼ cup raisins over a 3-in.-wide section of dough. Mix sugar and cinnamon; sprinkle half of the mixture over the fruit. Drizzle with half of the melted butter.

5. Roll up jelly-roll style, starting at fruit-covered end and lifting with parchment; fold in sides of dough as you roll to contain filling. Using parchment, transfer the strudel to a 15x10x1-in. baking pan; trim parchment to fit pan.

6. Bake on lowest oven rack 45-55 minutes or until golden brown, brushing top with sour cream 2 times while baking. Repeat with remaining ingredients.

7. Using parchment, transfer to a wire rack to cool. Serve warm or at room temperature.

NOTE: To make fresh bread crumbs, tear bread into pieces and place in a food processor; pulse until fine crumbs form. Two to 3 bread slices will yield 1½ cups crumbs.

1 PIECE: 285 cal., 12g fat (3g sat. fat), 24mg chol., 61mg sod., 42g carb. (20g sugars, 2g fiber), 4g pro.

LEMON &
BLUEBERRY
PIZZA

LEMON & BLUEBERRY PIZZA

Slices of this fruity dessert pizza are wonderful served after dinner, paired with afternoon tea or presented as a special breakfast treat. Feel free to use a 13x9-inch pan instead of a pizza pan—just pat the crust over the bottom and ½ inch up the sides of the pan.
—*JM Holt, Mendota Heights, MN*

PREP: 30 MIN. • BAKE: 25 MIN. + CHILLING • MAKES: 16 SERVINGS

1 **pkg. lemon cake mix (regular size)**
1¼ **cups quick-cooking oats, divided**
8 **Tbsp. butter, softened, divided**
1 **large egg, room temperature, lightly beaten**
¼ **cup sugar**
⅓ **cup sliced almonds**
1 **pkg. (8 oz.) cream cheese, softened**
½ **cup lemon curd**
1 **can (21 oz.) blueberry pie filling**

1. Preheat oven to 350°. In a large bowl, beat the cake mix, 1 cup oats and 6 Tbsp. butter on low speed until coarse crumbs form. Reserve 1 cup mixture for the topping. To remaining mixture, beat in egg. Press dough onto an ungreased 12-in. pizza pan; pinch the edges to form a rim. Bake for 12 minutes.

2. Meanwhile, to reserved topping, add sugar, remaining ¼ cup oats and 2 Tbsp. butter. Stir in almonds. In another bowl, beat cream cheese and lemon curd until smooth. Spread par-baked crust with cream cheese mixture. Gently spoon the pie filling over the top. Sprinkle with the almond mixture. Bake until the topping is lightly browned, 20-25 minutes. Cool completely on a wire rack. Refrigerate at least 4 hours before serving. Refrigerate leftovers.

1 PIECE: 363 cal., 14g fat (8g sat. fat), 49mg chol., 324mg sod., 57g carb. (37g sugars, 2g fiber), 3g pro.

MINIATURE PEANUT BUTTER CHEESECAKES

My mother gave me her recipe for mini candy-filled cheesecakes. With a peanut butter cup inside, they're fun for Christmas or any special occasion.
—*Mary Ann Dell, Phoenixville, PA*

PREP: 20 MIN. • BAKE: 15 MIN. + CHILLING • MAKES: 6 SERVINGS

⅓ **cup graham cracker crumbs**
1 **Tbsp. sugar**
5 **tsp. butter, melted**

FILLING
4 **oz. cream cheese, softened**
¼ **cup sugar**
2 **tsp. all-purpose flour**
2 **Tbsp. beaten egg**
¼ **tsp. vanilla extract**
6 **miniature peanut butter cups**

1. In a small bowl, combine the cracker crumbs, sugar and butter. Press onto the bottoms of 6 paper-lined muffin cups; set aside.

2. In a small bowl, beat the cream cheese, sugar and flour until smooth. Add the egg and vanilla; beat on low speed until just combined. Place a peanut butter cup in the center of each muffin cup; fill with cream cheese mixture.

3. Bake at 350° for 15-18 minutes or until the center is set. Cool on a wire rack for 10 minutes before removing from pan to a wire rack to cool completely. Refrigerate for at least 2 hours.

1 CHEESECAKE: 206 cal., 13g fat (7g sat. fat), 47mg chol., 143mg sod., 20g carb. (16g sugars, 0 fiber), 3g pro.

RECIPE INDEX